MORE PRAISE FOR
UNIT X

"Rouses more curiosity about what happens next than anything I might have binge-watched . . . [*Unit X*] offers a front-row seat to the battle before the war."
——**Reid Hoffman, cofounder of LinkedIn and Inflection AI and coauthor of the #1** *New York Times* **bestselling** *The Startup of You*

"Moves beyond what has been achieved to explore the prospects for more transformational innovation . . . The drama in the book, however, comes from what the authors call the 'antibodies' in the system, as a sclerotic Pentagon bureaucracy and congressional staffers bent on protecting their privileges threatened to block the innovation unit's progress."
——*Foreign Affairs*

"Essential reading for understanding how technology will change the future of warfare—and the risks America faces if China's military innovates faster than ours."
——**Chris Miller, author of the** *New York Times* **bestselling** *Chip War: The Fight for the World's Most Critical Technology*

"Fascinating . . . The authors' easy style recreates dialog at meetings and gives the reader a good feel for the ups and downs of navigating the personalities and dynamics of the Pentagon and Congress."
——*The Cipher Brief*

"Vivid storytelling . . . Raj Shah and Christopher Kirchhoff show how it's possible to coax creativity out of bureaucracies and fight for change in institutions designed to sustain the status quo."
——**Adam Grant, author of the #1** *New York Times* **bestselling** *Think Again* **and** *Hidden Potential,* **and host of the podcast** *Re:Thinking*

"Exceedingly important. *Unit X* shows why a partnership between the military services and the technology companies of Silicon Valley and other startup hubs is vital in the race to dramatically change the future of warfare."

—**General David Petraeus, US Army (Ret.), former CIA director, and coauthor of the *New York Times* bestselling *Conflict: The Evolution of Warfare from 1945 to Ukraine***

"An unnerving tour de force. *Unit X* always feels high-stakes, and the ongoing tug-of-war it chronicles is central to whether the nation prevails in the contests to come."

—**Admiral James Stavridis (US Navy, Ret.), 16th Supreme Allied Commander of NATO, and author of *2054: A Novel***

"Pulls no punches . . . [*Unit X*] shows what's possible once you get out of the old-think box. While this is the story of the Pentagon's epiphany, it can apply just as well to businesses mired in habit and in need of resuscitation. And it's a fun read, too."

—**Vint Cerf, winner of the A.M. Turing Award and a cofounder of the Internet**

"Intriguing. From backroom bureaucratic battles to venture capital pitches, *Unit X* recounts one of the most significant junctures in U.S. military history. It should be required reading."

—**Amy Zegart, Ph.D., senior fellow at the Hoover Institution; professor of political science, by courtesy, Stanford University; and author of *Spies, Lies, and Algorithms: The History and Future of American Intelligence***

"Compelling. Those who put themselves in harm's way to preserve freedom should consider Chris Kirchhoff and Raj Shah American heroes. The message of these pages is clear: credibly deterring conflict involves leveraging our innovation dominance, which means elevating the pivotal role of DIU."

—**Rear Admiral Hugh Wyman Howard III, former commander of DEVGRU (SEAL Team Six) and Naval Special Warfare**

"Engaging and important. This is the story of a trailblazing Pentagon unit designed to harness American intellect, spur innovation, and maximize entrepreneurship so that peace will be preserved and the free world defended."

—**Lt. General H. R. McMaster, U.S. Army (Ret.), former National Security Advisor, and** *New York Times* **bestselling author of** *Battlegrounds: The Fight to Defend the Free World*

"An extraordinary accomplishment . . . A gripping, firsthand account of the authors' role in building and leading the innovation unit within the Department of Defense that is helping to get America ready for the future of warfare."

—**Christian Brose, chief strategy officer of Anduril Industries, visiting fellow at the Hoover Institution, and author of** *The Kill Chain: Defending America in the Future of High-Tech Warfare*

UNIT X

HOW THE PENTAGON AND SILICON VALLEY ARE TRANSFORMING THE FUTURE OF WAR

RAJ M. SHAH AND **CHRISTOPHER KIRCHHOFF**

SCRIBNER

NEW YORK   AMSTERDAM/ANTWERP   LONDON
TORONTO   SYDNEY/MELBOURNE   NEW DELHI

Scribner
An Imprint of Simon & Schuster, LLC
1230 Avenue of the Americas
New York, NY 10020

For more than 100 years, Simon & Schuster has championed authors and the stories they create. By respecting the copyright of an author's intellectual property, you enable Simon & Schuster and the author to continue publishing exceptional books for years to come. We thank you for supporting the author's copyright by purchasing an authorized edition of this book.

No amount of this book may be reproduced or stored in any format, nor may it be uploaded to any website, database, language-learning model, or other repository, retrieval, or artificial intelligence system without express permission. All rights reserved. Inquiries may be directed to Simon & Schuster, 1230 Avenue of the Americas, New York, NY 10020 or permissions@simonandschuster.com.

Copyright © 2024 by Raj M. Shah and Christopher Kirchhoff

All rights reserved, including the right to reproduce this book or portions thereof in any form whatsoever. For information, address Scribner Subsidiary Rights Department, 1230 Avenue of the Americas, New York, NY 10020.

First Scribner trade paperback edition June 2025

Scribner and design are trademarks of Simon & Schuster, LLC

Simon & Schuster strongly believes in freedom of expression and stands against censorship in all its forms. For more information, visit BooksBelong.com.

For information about special discounts for bulk purchases, please contact Simon & Schuster Special Sales at 1-866-506-1949 or business@simonandschuster.com.

The Simon & Schuster Speakers Bureau can bring authors to your live event. For more information, or to book an event, contact the Simon & Schuster Speakers Bureau at 1-866-248-3049 or visit our website at www.simonspeakers.com.

Interior design by Hope Herr-Cardillo

Manufactured in the United States of America

10 9 8 7 6 5 4 3 2 1

Library of Congress Cataloging-in-Publication Data has been applied for.

ISBN 978-1-6680-3138-4
ISBN 978-1-6680-3139-1 (pbk)
ISBN 978-1-6680-3143-8 (ebook)

*To the memory of Ash Carter
and the innovators in the U.S. Armed Forces
he singularly unleashed.*

*And to Yuko, Manu, and John,
who put up with our shenanigans,
including occasional trips to conflict zones.*

If there are to be yet unimagined weapons affecting the balance of military power tomorrow, we want to have the men and the means to imagine them first.

—James Killian,
science advisor to Dwight Eisenhower

The second decade of the 21st Century was one of colossal missed opportunities for the U.S. military. The Pentagon missed the advent of modern software development, the move to cloud computing, the commercial space revolution, the centrality of data, and the rise of AI and machine learning. It's a story of the U.S. getting ambushed by the future.

—Christian Brose, staff director,
U.S. Senate Armed Services Committee

I think Henry Ford once said, "If I'd asked customers what they wanted, they would've told me a faster horse."

—Steve Jobs

CONTENTS

Introduction: Slow Burn 1

Chapter One: Unit X 11

Chapter Two: Zeroized 25

Chapter Three: The Gonkulator 45

Chapter Four: A New Kill Chain for North Korea 73

Chapter Five: Unit X Loses the X 99

Chapter Six: Washington and the Rise of the Machines 133

Chapter Seven: Venture Capital Goes to War 177

Chapter Eight: Ukraine and the Battlefield of the Future .. 199

Chapter Nine: From Steel to Silicon 219

Acknowledgments 247

Acronyms 253

Bibliography 255

Notes 267

Photo Credits 301

Index 303

CAST OF CHARACTERS

Madeleine Albright: Secretary of State under President Bill Clinton; early to sound the alarm about the threat artificial intelligence posed to democracies and the world order. (d. 2022)

Ylli Bajraktari: Chief of staff to the national security advisor; subsequently became executive director of the National Security Commission on Artificial Intelligence.

Payam Banazadeh: Iranian-born Stanford entrepreneur and former NASA engineer who founded Capella Space, breakthrough developer of synthetic aperture radar (SAR) technology.

Doug Beck: Apple vice president and navy combat veteran put in command of DIUx's Reserve Unit; later became DIUx's third director.

Philip Bilden: Cofounder, HarbourVest Partners and cofounder of Shield Capital.

JoeBen Bevirt: Raised in an off-the-grid commune by hippie parents, founded Joby Aviation, and invented a flying car that can carry four people while flying in near silence and landing like a helicopter.

Mike Brown: CEO of Symantec who became DIUx's second director and brought to light China's penetration of U.S. venture capital deals to transfer technology to the People's Liberation Army.

Steve "Bucky" Butow: Major General, Air National Guard; led DIUx Space Portfolio.

Ash Carter: Secretary of Defense under President Obama. (d. 2022)

Lauren Dailey: DIUx's acquisition lead who pioneered a way for the Pentagon to rapidly buy and scale $70 billion of hardware and software from startups and tech companies.

Jared Dunnmon: Technical lead, DIU Artificial Intelligence Portfolio.

David Goldfein: Twenty-first chief of staff, United States Air Force.

Jeff "Cobra" Harrigian: Combined force air component commander, CENTCOM, Southwest Asia. The CAOC fell under his command.

Richard Jenkins: British adventurer, entrepreneur, and founder of Saildrone, whose autonomous seagoing sailboats are revolutionizing marine science and U.S. naval strategy.

Palmer Luckey: Founder of two "unicorn" companies: Oculus, maker of virtual reality headsets, and Anduril Industries, developer of hardware and software for defense.

Jim Mattis: Secretary of Defense under President Trump; former general, U.S. Marine Corps.

John McCain: Senator from Arizona and chairman, Senate Armed Services Committee. (d. 2018)

H. R. McMaster: National security advisor to President Trump and architect of the bipartisan shift to competition with China.

Todd Park: U.S. chief technology officer under President Obama.

CAST OF CHARACTERS

Eric Schmidt: Former CEO of Google; subsequently, chair of the Defense Innovation Board and the National Security Commission on Artificial Intelligence.

Jack Shanahan: Lieutenant general, U.S. Air Force; director, Pentagon's Joint Artificial Intelligence Center.

Reuben Sorensen: Nuclear physicist; led the Joint Staff J-39's North Korean nuclear missile defeat mission.

Sandy Winnefeld: Admiral, U.S. Navy; vice chairman of the Joint Chiefs of Staff.

Bob Work: Deputy Secretary of Defense; former U.S. Marine colonel and naval strategist.

Note: A comprehensive list of acronyms appearing in the pages that follow can be found with their meanings on page 253.

INTRODUCTION: SLOW BURN

It was three in the morning, pitch black. Raj M. Shah, a twenty-seven-year-old U.S. Air Force captain, two weeks into his first tour of combat duty in 2006, was piloting an F-16 Viper along the border between Iraq and Iran when he suddenly realized he couldn't easily tell which side of the border he was on. This was a problem, because American pilots who flew into Iranian airspace ran the risk of causing an international incident—or worse, not flying back out. The F-16 was a remarkable machine—it could fly at twice the speed of sound and outmaneuver any fighter jet in the world—but, frustratingly, its outdated navigation system couldn't graphically pinpoint the plane's location on a moving map. Slip over the line at five hundred miles per hour and in less than a minute Raj could be eight miles into Iran, well within range of its anti-aircraft batteries.

There was no way to update the navigation software. So Raj figured out a hack. Back in the barracks, he had a Compaq iPAQ, a handheld device for checking email and playing Tetris. He loaded it with civilian navigation software and digital maps, snuck it into the cockpit, and kept it strapped to his knee as he flew. The software in that little $300 gadget did a better job of telling him where he was than the system in a $30 million jet.

That was the first time Raj realized how far Silicon Valley had leapt ahead of defense contractors like General Dynamics and Lockheed Martin when it came to developing new technology, especially software.

A decade later, in 2016, when Raj, now a civilian, visited the air force command center in Qatar that coordinated the combat missions he flew, he found that instead of catching up, the military had fallen even further behind.

The outside world had self-driving cars, virtual reality goggles, and smartphones that could summon an Uber, handle banking, and pay for groceries. You could ask Siri for directions and tell Alexa to play Miles Davis. But in the military control center where airmen handled the life-or-death business of routing jets, directing air strikes, and managing refueling tankers over an active battlefield, in the middle of the war against ISIS, U.S. service members were using outdated Windows PCs and running software programs older than the officers using them. The air force controllers in Qatar weren't the only ones forced to use antiquated technology. Legacy tech riddled the military's ranks. It was as if the military had resigned itself to becoming a display in the Museum of Computer History. You could visit an army, air force, or naval base to see what people used in the past, then go to Best Buy to see how far technology had evolved.

But this time in Qatar, Raj could do a lot more about it than attach a pocket computer to his knee. The Secretary of Defense had appointed us (Raj and Chris) to run Defense Innovation Unit Experimental (DIUx), or Unit X for short, the Pentagon's newly created outpost in Silicon Valley that was charged with bringing modern technology to the U.S. military. Before taking over DIUx, Raj had founded a cybersecurity startup, which he successfully sold, and he was looking for a chance to do it again. Chris, a Harvard educated Ph.D. political scientist, was the lead strategist for technology at the National Security Council. He'd spent over a decade working at the highest levels of government, attending meetings in the White House Situation Room and traveling with the chairman of the Joint Chiefs of Staff. We had complementary backgrounds. Raj was a tech guy who knew about national security. Chris was a national security guy who understood tech.

Our mission at DIUx wasn't just to find hardware and software so military units around the world could better perform their mission. It was to disrupt and transform the culture of the largest and possibly most bureaucratic organization in the world by infusing its clogged arteries with the nimble, agile DNA of Silicon Valley—in other words, to hack the Pentagon.

Imagine a stealthy electric flying car that lands like a helicopter, flies in near silence, and can autonomously navigate behind enemy lines to drop off, pick up, or resupply U.S. forces. Or tiny AI-powered quadcopters that can map the inside of a building and recognize faces of terrorists before Navy SEALs break down the door. Or a constellation of microsatellites that can see through clouds, enabling intelligence agencies to keep a constant eye on ISIS troop movements and North Korean missiles. Or a fleet of seagoing drones that can scan for threats for a fraction of the price of a single navy destroyer, for years at a time.

All these advanced technologies—and many more like them—were being developed in 2016 when Raj visited Qatar. They were designed not by brand-name defense companies but by plucky startups in Silicon Valley. And guess what? The U.S. military barely knew anything about them.

DIUx would drive a massive and long-overdue revamping of tools and capabilities that would mean the difference between victory and defeat, life and death. The U.S. had fallen dangerously behind its rivals when it came to technology. By the time we were recruited to DIUx, it was an open secret inside the Pentagon that if the U.S. went to war with China, we'd lose far more soldiers, sailors, marines, and airmen than our war plans anticipated. We might very well suffer an outright defeat, ending the era of American supremacy that began at the Second World War's end.

Modern warfare—whether against sophisticated militaries or crafty insurgents—is no longer just about multibillion-dollar battleships, aircraft carriers, and stealth bombers. Small bands of ISIS fighters have successfully foiled SEAL raids with hobby drones sold on Amazon. Ukrainians have similarly stymied the Russian Army by using quadcopters and citizen spot-reports, submitted by smartphone, to direct fire at advancing tank columns. Even illiterate farmers in Afghanistan can build improvised explosive devices powerful enough to blow apart our most heavily armored vehicles. And while our aircraft carriers project an image of supremacy, they can now be sunk in the opening minutes of a battle by an adversary's hypersonic missile.

For decades, the United States maintained superiority by deploying better technology than anyone we might face on the battlefield. But starting around the year 2000, our advantage began to erode. The world changed as commercial technology surged, but we didn't. The Pentagon spends three-quarters of a trillion dollars a year—roughly $5,000 from every taxpayer, more in total than the GDP of Saudi Arabia—but until recently we were buying the wrong things. Our shopping list contained the same old expensive, unwieldy, and even obsolete weapons systems—the F-16 with no moving map—while our rivals sought new technologies that cost a fraction of what we were spending, built with off-the-shelf components churned out in China and Taiwan.

A decade into the new millennium China especially was speeding past us in 5G telecommunications, investing heavily in autonomy, artificial intelligence, and surveillance. In a boom heard around the world, its military leapt ahead of ours in October 2021 by launching the world's first nuclear-capable hypersonic weapon—an arrowhead-shaped sheath of titanium that flies at ten times the speed of sound, can't be seen by early warning radars, and, unlike slower intercontinental ballistic missiles, can change direction in flight, evading all known defenses. With this weapon, the People's Liberation Army can strike anywhere in the world in under fifteen minutes. The chairman of the Joint Chiefs of Staff called it "China's Sputnik Moment," comparable to the surprise Soviet launch of the world's first satellite in 1957.

How had this happened? How did the country with the largest economy and most innovative technology companies fall so far behind?

Quite simply, sometime in the 1990s, Silicon Valley and the Pentagon stopped talking to each other. The two-decade explosion of consumer electronics that began in the 2000s somehow became invisible to the Pentagon.

Even as Apple, Google, Microsoft, and Amazon grew into technical and business behemoths, each bigger by market capitalization than the entire defense industry combined, the Department of Defense was content to keep dealing with a handful of giant defense contractors, like Lockheed Martin, Northrop Grumman, and Raytheon—known in Washington as the "primes." This arrangement suited members of Congress who controlled the budget, because they were keen to protect the job-creating mega-contracts that had brought prosperity to their districts. The Pentagon even relied on the primes to develop the military's IT and software, a folly akin to hiring Microsoft to build an aircraft carrier. Nobody bothered to talk to Google about AI or to Amazon about cloud services, even though those companies and others like them now harnessed the brainpower of the world's best engineers and technologists, and collectively wielded research and development budgets larger than the Pentagon's own. The Pentagon had even less of an idea how to work productively with hundreds of tiny startups building astonishing stuff that no one else had thought to invent. The disconnect was not just about hardware or software or how to buy both. It was also about the new way Silicon Valley worked, coupling concentrations of talent with incremental infusions of capital. Rather than becoming curious about how to build transformational technology with the speed and efficiency of a startup, the Pentagon stuck to its old labs full of old scientists who built things the old way. The two worlds drifted apart. For two decades, no Secretary of Defense even bothered to set foot in Silicon Valley—not when Google invented search or Apple the iPhone or Facebook social networks or Amazon cloud storage.

For its part, the Valley had soured on doing business with the Pentagon. Startups didn't need the headache of dealing with a customer that took years to close a sale and then even more years to start using the product and paying for it. Too often, promising products were abandoned in their journey to the battlefield. In a reference to Psalm 23, they died in what's called the Pentagon's "Valley of Death," a hellscape of unused products and the skeletons of entrepreneurs and companies that didn't make it to the other side. Tech companies had no idea how to navigate the corridors of power inside the Pentagon, while the primes had spent decades wining and dining generals and building massive lobbying machines. Moreover, many engineers and technologists in Silicon Valley had deep moral objections to creating products that might be used to kill people, and they demanded their companies refuse to sign contracts with the military or intelligence agencies. Young people working in the Valley grew up watching the botched invasion of Iraq. They might have seen *Saving Private Ryan*, but their formative memories of the military were of the abuses at Abu Ghraib, torture at Guantánamo, and drone strikes that killed civilians.

The final break came in 2013, when Google and others learned, via material leaked by Edward Snowden, that the National Security Agency was surreptitiously tapping their data interconnects to vacuum up intelligence about foreign threats. The rest of the world now looked at American tech firms as extensions of American intelligence agencies—as spies. Not only was their own government spying on them, Silicon Valley engineers learned, but no one could any longer trust the companies they worked for to secure their data—not Americans, not Europeans, not customers in international markets. To many in Silicon Valley, the U.S. government had become the enemy.

In ordinary times, the de facto divorce between technologists on the West Coast and policymakers on the East Coast wouldn't imperil the future of American power. In California, coders would continue to code and venture capitalists would continue to fund new companies. In Washington, policymakers would continue giving speeches and writing strategies. But the 2010s weren't ordinary times. Other militaries sensed the fragility of what held together the world order—the ability of the U.S. military to unquestionably win wars and keep the peace. Russia's Vladimir Putin, Chinese president Xi Jinping, the supreme leader of Iran, and North Korea's Kim Jong-un each saw new ways to defeat the U.S. technologically.

While most people on both coasts missed the significance of what was happening, a few of us saw the slow-motion car crash that had already begun, and we started doing all we could to stop it.

A turning point came in 2015 when President Barack Obama appointed Ash Carter to be Secretary of Defense. Carter, a Rhodes Scholar and physicist, had been in and out of various Pentagon roles since the 1990s. For most of that time he'd been pounding the table about the shift toward commercial technology and its implications for defense. The Pentagon was devoting too much of its budget to chasing legacy technology and not enough to the future, Carter said. In a prophetic 2001 paper, he wrote, "Tomorrow's defense innovations will largely be derivatives of technology developed and marketed by commercial companies for commercial motives." The military "must be the world's fastest adapter and adopter of commercial technology into defense systems." At first, nobody listened. But as soon as Carter was sworn in as secretary, he traveled to Silicon Valley, hoping to make amends by giving an address to the tech industry. He was *not* welcomed with open arms. Google, still furious about the Snowden revelations, refused to let him set foot on its campus. Carter instead went to Stanford, which had become a kind of Switzerland for visiting government officials—neutral ground. There he spoke to an audience of CEOs and influential venture capitalists, the kingmakers who'd helped build the world's most valuable companies. He began by acknowledging the damage that the NSA had caused by spying on tech companies. It wasn't quite an apology, but close enough.

Then he made his pitch: the military needed their help. Carter talked about defending our way of life at a time when democracies were coming under new threats. Whatever feelings those in the audience might have about warfare, he said, surely they agreed that if the U.S. did go to war, it would be better to win than to lose. But unless we could set aside our differences and work together, that might not happen. That's what was at stake. Did they want to live in a world where the U.S. became a second-rate power? Carter wasn't openly alarmist, but the digerati understood.

Carter also reminded his audience of influential executives that some of Silicon Valley's biggest companies had succeeded by building their products on research funded by the government. Google got its start with a grant by the National Science Foundation, and its self-driving cars grew out of a Grand Challenge by DARPA, the Defense Advanced Research Projects Agency. DARPA had invented the Internet as well as Siri, Apple's AI-powered voice assistant.

Now it was time for Silicon Valley to repay the favor.

"We need to drill holes in the wall that exists between the Department of Defense and the commercial and scientific sector," Carter implored.

He promised that the Pentagon would change its ways. He vowed to shake up the Department of Defense and adopt the nimble business practices of Silicon Valley. Most importantly, he wanted to start buying tech products. *Lots* of tech products. The skeptics in the audience might not have been moved by the stuff about defending the Western liberal order—but they did care about money. And the Pentagon spends more money than any organization in the world. Carter's message was loud and clear: the Pentagon was open for business and wanted to push a giant shopping cart down the aisles of Silicon Valley.

Since shopping on the West Coast is hard to do from the East Coast, Carter announced that the Pentagon would open an embassy-slash-venture-fund in Silicon Valley called the Defense Innovation Unit Experimental, or DIUx. A thirty-person team would be housed in an office building at Moffett Field, a decommissioned naval air station in Mountain View, across the fence from Google's campus.

The historical resonance wasn't lost on military innovators. Admiral Moffett—the station's namesake—had figured out in the 1920s that aircraft carriers, not battleships, would win the next war. The father of naval aviation died in a fiery 1933 crash on the dirigible USS *Akron*, then the world's largest blimp. Had he not reoriented naval doctrine, we might be speaking German or Japanese.

At the very place where military innovators figured out how to harness the power of carrier-launched aircraft, a group of technologists and uniformed officers from each military service would scour the Valley to find commercial products that could be adapted for military use. They'd be the military's on-site matchmaker. If a SEAL team needed a way to shoot down the commercial drones disrupting their raids, DIUx would find a startup to build a drone-killer, and the navy would deploy it. If a new company came to DIUx with a game-changing cybersecurity tool, DIUx would find a customer in the military that would buy the product. With the military as an early user, the startup could get up and running. And with the promise of future revenue the military could provide, venture capital firms would be more likely to invest. This was Carter's vision: to use military money not just to buy existing products but to help entrepreneurs develop new ones, and to harness the financial power of venture capital firms to back more businesses selling to the Defense Department. Thanks to DIUx, the Pentagon would be able to draw on the resources and brainpower of commercial tech companies in Silicon Valley for the first time in years. This infusion of new technology and new thinking, Carter hoped, would inspire the military to mimic those methods, bringing speed and efficiency to a culture of cost overruns and delays. DIUx would be the fulcrum on which Carter would pivot the entire U.S. military. If DIUx was successful, the military would spend the rest of the 2010s readying itself for the conflicts many saw coming in the 2020s.

But DIUx faced a daunting challenge—how to fix the parts of the Pentagon that would open the floodgates to commercial technology. Carter had vowed to speed things up and transform its risk-averse culture so that innovative products could zip from office parks in Palo Alto and Mountain View into the hands of service members without getting lost in the Valley of Death. That sounded great, but after thirty years of neglect, the Valley of Death was now Grand Canyon–sized. It was unclear how a scrappy little band of people in a makeshift office was going to ferry key technologies across it.

The Department of Defense is the largest organization in the world, with 3 million employees, a sprawling set of offices that oversee the army, air force, navy, and marines, more rules and regulations than the Byzantine Empire, and an ingrained resistance to change. This was the organization that fielded fighter jets with outdated navigation systems and operated command centers with decades-old mainframes running software so buggy that the bugs had bugs. Now they were going to start using artificial intelligence and iPhones?

Carter's plan envisioned Silicon Valley's founders and engineers eagerly answering his call. But, as Snowden had revealed, this was the same group the government had secretly manipulated to conduct espionage. The Iraq War, warrantless wiretapping, and drone strikes were things many in Silicon Valley opposed. How could a group of people so understandably alienated from the hard power of the military be enticed to help enhance its lethality? They'd come of age building technology that would make the world a better, not deadlier, place.

It was easy to give a speech about innovation and transformation and drilling holes in walls. But who in their right mind would sign up to do the drilling?

Well, that was us.

CHAPTER ONE
UNIT X

At first neither of us wanted the job.

Defense Innovation Unit Experimental was already six months old when Secretary of Defense Ash Carter asked us to lead it and become his personal emissaries to Silicon Valley. The original team at DIUx had started off so badly that Silicon Valley had already written off the group as a hollow embodiment of Carter's promise to rebuild ties. The office was "out of Schlitz," as the Milwaukee beer slogan went, better to be avoided than engaged.

To be fair, our predecessors had been dealt a bad hand and played it poorly. Initially announced as a department-wide priority, the launch of DIUx was overseen by Bob Work, the Deputy Secretary of Defense, a forceful advocate who'd coined DIUx's name and was one of the first officials to worry the U.S. could be defeated technologically. Work had led the review of the Pentagon's growing inadequacy in a top-secret effort known as the Advanced Capabilities and Deterrence Panel. He then handed the new unit to the Pentagon's fourth-highest official, the head of acquisition and technology, who—fatally—transferred responsibility three layers farther down. The office that came to oversee DIUx was located nowhere near the outer "E-ring" corridor of the Pentagon, the power center of the military where generals and admirals enjoy the building's only outside views through bullet- and bombproof windows.

It wasn't even near the office of the fourth-highest official. Instead, it was around the corner, down a narrow corridor, behind multiple doors, and through a windowless passageway, a route that resembled a dimly lit maze in the catacombs of the Pentagon. It was in the Pentagon's equivalent of Eastern Siberia.

Deep in this bureaucratic wilderness the acting official in charge of setting up Carter's advanced technology incubator shared the opinion of his boss four levels up, as good bureaucrats do, that DIUx was a cute idea but not the game-changing fulcrum Carter envisioned. Charged with turning Carter's idea into a reality, he tapped a team of people who knew little about Silicon Valley and had never worked on the E-ring. Given a blank canvas on which to paint something grand, they defaulted to the easiest and least imaginative option. As Ash Carter later wrote in his memoir, "Initially, I allowed DIUx to be organized and staffed by the Pentagon's research and engineering arm. This quickly proved to be a mistake."

Instead of renting a modern office in Palo Alto with open space, unfinished brick, and dual monitor workstations, the Pentagon hid DIUx's Silicon Valley office in a vacant wing of a National Guard armory. The armory sat on the edge of Moffett Field, a decommissioned naval air station so sleepy that few even knew it was there. The armory and the dirt fields that surrounded it had become a black hole, something people drove past every day on their way to work without ever noticing what was inside. Even Google Maps didn't have DIUx listed—we ultimately appealed to our friends at Google to add it so visitors stopped getting lost.

Upon arriving in Silicon Valley, the Pentagon team botched the initial setup so badly that DIUx couldn't even get furniture or a working Internet connection. For six months the first team worked at folding card tables and used 4G hotspots bought at Best Buy. It took less time than ordering coffee at Philz for Silicon Valley insiders to discern that the new outfit had no money, no clout, and no viable plan to buy technology at scale. Instead of encouraging startups to take meetings at DIUx, venture capitalists told them to run away.

When word filtered back to Carter that DIUx was floundering, he sent Todd Park, President Obama's chief technology officer, to visit and find out what was wrong. Park, a veteran tech entrepreneur, had built multibillion-dollar businesses in Silicon Valley and was known in Washington as the man who fixed the failing website HealthCare.gov. He took one look at the card tables and Best Buy hotspots, talked to the two guys in charge—and understood the problem. Back in Washington, he gave Carter an unvarnished assessment of DIUx: "It's fucked," he said, delivering the kind of tough talk a Valley venture capitalist tells a failing startup. "You need to get rid of the people in charge and find new leadership. Give them real resources and real authority. And don't do this quietly. You need to make a big deal of it. Show everyone in the Valley that you're starting over." In Silicon Valley, Park told Carter, it is better to fail fast and reboot than to try to hide failure behind incremental fixes.

In the Secretary of Defense's mind, the stillborn office would be known as DIUx 1.0—the initial release. Carter would personally oversee an upgrade to DIUx 2.0. The new version would have many new features, including the two of us at its helm, with Raj as managing director and Chris as founding partner. Two other partners would join. Not only would Carter remake DIUx, he'd fly out to Silicon Valley to re-christen it.

In Washington it counts as crazy to turn over the keys to the Pentagon's newest unit to a thirty-seven and thirty-eight-year old. Most of the graybeards that dominated the civilian and uniformed military looked at us as mere kids, fifteen years too young to run anything serious in the building even as we were fifteen years older than many first-time founders in the Valley. Yet we both had overlapping strengths purpose-built for the turnaround job that lay ahead.

Chris was the National Security Council's director of strategic planning and previously had been the senior civilian aide to the Chairman of the Joint Chiefs of Staff. His Ph.D. focused on technology breakdowns in national security. He'd helped craft the Pentagon's first cyber strategy, helped champion DARPA breakthroughs, and helped open the military's eyes to how rapidly commercial technology was evolving. When Ash Carter decided to create DIUx, he and Bob Work asked Chris to chair the Pentagon working group that developed the concept.

After Raj graduated from Princeton, where his senior thesis was titled "The Efficacy of Coercive Airpower," he flew F-16s in combat in Iraq and Afghanistan, learning firsthand the awesome power of military systems as well as their antiquated quirks. He then went on to business school and a stint at McKinsey & Company before becoming an entrepreneur himself, building a successful cybersecurity software startup. All the while, he served in uniform in the Air National Guard, strapping into F-16s on weekends. Growing up in rural Georgia as the son of immigrants from India, Raj always had flying on the brain. His childhood room was full of model airplanes he'd assembled and painted.

We'd known each other for years. We first met at the Council on Foreign Relations when we were each term members, a junior status granted to young professionals in government and business. We liked each other and started lunching each time Raj came into D.C., often meeting at Founding Farmers, three blocks from the White House. We were on opposite sides of the political spectrum—Chris an Obama Administration appointee, Raj a former Bush Administration appointee—but saw the world much the same, united in our conviction that Washington hadn't yet awakened to the tectonic shifts in technology emanating from Silicon Valley. Together, we might just be able to pull this off. Raj had experience discerning real innovation from vaporware and could read a balance sheet with eagle eyes. Chris could walk blindfolded around the West Wing and the Pentagon and was on a first-name basis with the national security advisor and the Secretary of Defense. The Pentagon had acronyms, Silicon Valley buzzwords. Together, we could navigate both worlds.

And yet—we were reluctant. Raj had recently sold his first startup, to Palo Alto Networks, and was on his way to founding another. Putting those plans on hold to go work for the government would delay his entrepreneurial ambitions. Worse, if DIUx failed again, he might never be able to raise capital and start another company in the Valley. Chris's credibility in Washington was likewise on the line. Too many missteps in such a high-profile role and he'd be looking for a new career.

The mission was two-pronged. In Silicon Valley we'd have to overcome deeply rooted skepticism that the government could ever be a good customer, and persuade top executives as well as rank-and-file engineers that the military would use the technology they developed in morally acceptable ways. On the other side lurked an even more entrenched fight. The military brass thought Silicon Valley programmers were spoiled and had no idea of the hardships men and women in uniform endured to keep them safe. They were appalled that some tech firms were willing to sell to China but not to the Department of Defense. Many still doubted that Silicon Valley could do a better job than big defense contractors. Deep down, they thought the iPhones their kids clamored for might look cool but weren't something you took into combat. Even in 2016, there was little understanding on the E-ring of the profound shift that had taken place. In sum, we'd have to break an enormous amount of glass in the Valley and in the Pentagon to have a chance at success.

"Okay," Raj said, over dinner with Chris. "I'll do it, but only if you do it."

"And I'll only do it if you do it," Chris said.

But we also knew that reporting to an office in the Pentagon's equivalent of East Siberia would cement our failure. If the Pentagon's middle management, which consisted of thousands of people, could tell us no, we could not honestly tell a startup CEO that yes—DIUx could deliver contracts on a timeline that mattered. So we made a wish list of necessary authorities, without which we knew DIUx 2.0 would fail.

The Secretary of Defense oversees 3 million people, 4,018 nuclear warheads, and 800 bases in 70 countries. Only the President is higher in the military's chain of command. The Secretary of Defense doesn't negotiate with terrorists, dictators, or his own subordinates, let alone two thirty-somethings to whom he just offered plumb jobs. Carter was an intimidating figure with a towering intellect and a prickly personality. However, the Secretary's office *would* have to negotiate with us, as we weren't going to take the job unless Carter set the conditions for success.

Carter's chief of staff Eric Rosenbach became Raj's interlocutor to draw up a "term sheet" detailing how DIUx 2.0 would operate. Over phone calls and one-on-ones in Rosenbach's office adjacent to the Secretary's suite, the two worked out a way forward.

"Raj, I can give you most of the things you're asking for, but I can't lend you an air force Gulfstream for your travel to D.C.," Eric said.

"Negotiating 101," responded Raj. "Always include one giveaway provision so your opponent has the illusion you are compromising."

The funniest moment happened at the end.

"The Secretary doesn't sign term sheets, especially with future hires," Eric told Raj.

"Well, someone has to sign it," Raj said. "How else do I know you're serious?"

The Secretary's lawyers debated for over a week about whether anyone could or should sign. In the end, Rosenbach lent his signature on May 5, 2016.

It was an impressive set of terms.

First, we would report directly to the Secretary. We would have a weekly call with his chief of staff, and he would assign one of his special assistants to support us. We would control our own budget and hiring. We would not deal with the Pentagon's ordinary administrative support staff—the people who left our predecessors with card tables and Wi-Fi hotspots. Instead, the chief management officer of the Pentagon would personally oversee the setup of the rebooted office. Every part of the DoD would lend support if requested. If some policy got in our way, we could request that the policy be waived. If the request was denied, the Secretary would decide immediately—we would not waste time going up and down the chain of command. And nobody from the Pentagon would visit Silicon Valley unless they coordinated with us.

Finally, and most important, the Secretary would put this in writing, in a directive-type memorandum—the DoD's most important decree, which carried the force of policy—and he would sign it.

We weren't being difficult for the sake of being difficult. We needed to do business at Silicon Valley speed. We had to get contracts signed quickly. We had to promise companies that we'd pay them on time and in full, and we had to keep those promises. If we couldn't do that, we'd end up failing, just like our predecessors.

Five days after the terms were finalized, the Boeing 757 that ordinarily serves as Air Force Two flew from Andrews Air Force Base to San Francisco, with Secretary Carter on board. The next morning, May 11, 2016, a convoy of armored Suburbans and staff vans, escorted by the California State Highway Patrol, whisked him and his phalanx of aides, advisors, and the traveling Pentagon press corps to Moffett Field.

Two hundred guests awaited, including unicorn company founders, some of the biggest venture capitalists in Silicon Valley, and many who would become close associates and partners for years. The night before, we'd been inundated with calls from Silicon Valley admins asking about the words "formal attire" on the invitation. Did this mean "East Coast" formal—a suit and tie? No, we assured them. While the Secretary would most certainly wear a suit and tie, they didn't need to. Neither did we. In fact, showing up in a suit in Silicon Valley immediately gets you written off as a clueless outsider. The very fact the invitation listed a dress code at all signaled how little the Secretary's protocol office knew about the audience the Secretary was trying to court. So we wore jeans and sport coats. Doug Beck, the Apple executive being announced as the commander of our new Reserve Unit, even left his shirt untucked.

The Secretary, true to form, wore a dark suit and bright blue tie. He walked in with an armed security detail and a dozen uniformed military aides carrying top-secret communications gear and binders with ready-to-go battle plans. One of the military aides, as always, would be carrying a locked briefcase with equipment for nuclear command and control. With rows of TV cameras filming, and the ceremony broadcast live to military bases worldwide on the Pentagon Channel, Carter introduced the two of us and our leadership team. We stood in a line, an American flag on one side and the blue battle flag of the Secretary of Defense on the other.

In his remarks, Carter acknowledged that just months before he'd been out here announcing the first version of DIUx, and that it had fallen short. But DIUx 2.0 would be new and improved, he vowed. "One of the most important things since starting DIUx is how much we've learned over the last eight months, not only about what works, but also what can make it work better," he said. "So armed with this knowledge, we're taking a page straight from the Silicon Valley playbook. Today we're launching DIUx 2.0, and there's several new features I'd like to tell you about."

He closed by explaining why Valley technologists should work with us. The point was not that startups could create value by doing business with the Pentagon—which they most certainly could. It was that in the global struggle between democracy and autocracy, we were all on the same side. "It has to do with our protection and our security, creating a world where our fellow citizens can go to school, dream their dreams, live their lives, and one day give their children a better future," he said. "Helping defend your country and making a better world is one of the noblest things a business leader, a technologist, an entrepreneur, or a young person can do."

With that, Carter flew back to Washington on Air Force Two. We stayed behind and mingled with the Silicon Valley elite, who, despite DIUx's rocky start, seemed enthusiastic about giving us another chance.

The team ended the day at the Space Bar at NASA Ames, enjoying a beer in the shadow of Hangar One, one of the world's largest freestanding structures, whose eight acres of inside space was used in the 1930s to house the navy's first zeppelin, a giant airship that met the same fate as the *Hindenburg*, with Admiral Moffett—the father of carrier aviation—on board. The real work would start tomorrow, after the camera crews had left, when we met the team.

Our first all-hands meeting was a critical moment to earn the trust of the people we'd lead—a motley crew of technology enthusiasts who'd come from all corners of the military. Though none of those on active duty wore their uniforms to the office, close-cropped hair and a certain bearing gave the place the feeling of a startup run by neatniks. Most were chipper except for one stern Special Operations guy, who never broke character. We only had a few proper technologists at first. Most everyone else bought a military skill—flying jets, driving tanks, leading infantry battalions, serving in combat.

The thirty-odd military and civilian personnel now in our charge had already had a rough go, having been announced to the world by the very same Secretary eight months before only to lack the tools they needed to succeed. With all the subtlety of a flashbang grenade, we'd arrived on scene and their former director and his leadership team had been sent home. Because the announcement had been kept under wraps until the last possible moment, very few knew the full details. The uniformed officers and enlisted personnel, civilians, and contractors who actually worked at DIUx were, quite literally, the last to be informed that their nascent organization was being rebooted and that we'd be the ones doing the rebooting.

In the weeks leading up to this moment Raj had quietly interviewed sitting team members without being able to fully explain what was about to happen. He'd picked up on a toxicity emanating from a small part of the org chart and decided to make decisive changes. Assessing the personnel who'd been detailed to DIUx from across the military, Raj kept most but asked that some be let go before the new leadership team arrived. We worked out a precise timeline with the Secretary's office of how the transition would occur. Two weeks before the Secretary's announcement, personnel identified for transfer were notified and given a last day in the office. Shortly after, all DIUx staff were made aware of the pending leadership change. A transition official was named to help the outgoing director hand off key responsibilities. Understanding that good people are sometimes put in unwinnable situations, the last thing Raj did before Carter landed for the announcement was take the outgoing director, George Duchak, out for a drink.

They met at the Four Seasons in Palo Alto, the hotel where Carter and his delegation were staying. Duchak—a Naval Academy graduate, P-3 pilot, and former head of an air force R&D lab—huddled with Raj for a private conversation at an out-of-the-way table while members of the Secretary's staff kept walking by, not noticing the handoff that was happening. George radiated disappointment at the Pentagon for not providing basic support such as Wi-Fi or furniture, and left Raj with a warning: "Watch out for the antibodies in the building. They'll come for you too."

After Todd Park recruited us, we recruited two others to form a core leadership team and also retained the commander for DIUx's Reserve Unit. Following the model of a venture capture firm, the core leadership team would be known as "partners" and share decisional authority. Raj, our managing partner, would have ultimate responsibility. But the idea was to embrace the flat structure of a startup.

A blitz of recruiting across the Valley led us to Isaac Taylor, a Harvard-educated Google X executive. Isaac had run operations for some of Google's biggest bets. Early in Google's self-driving car project, he'd been seriously injured on the highway just south of Google's campus when one of his fellow engineers pushed the car's algorithms beyond their breaking point. Unfazed, Isaac went on to a leadership role in Google Glass, one of the first attempts to build augmented reality glasses for consumers. Isaac would be our in-house hardware guru, bringing with him experience from the catalog of Google moonshots.

Our fourth partner was Vishaal "V8" Hariprasad, a decorated cyber operations officer in the air force who'd been a cofounder at Raj's cybersecurity startup. Vishaal, or V8, the military call sign he went by, was born in the Bronx to immigrant parents from British Guyana. He rose to be included among the first cadre of the USAF's cyber warriors, deploying to Iraq and working on some of our military's most clandestine missions. He'd be our in-house expert on software and oversee any project with code at its heart.

We secured Doug Beck's commitment to continue leading the DIUx Reserve Unit, a group of part-time military personnel who held civilian jobs in the tech sector while supporting DIUx a weekend a month. Beck, a naval reserve officer who'd deployed to Iraq and Afghanistan and like Carter was a Yale-trained Rhodes Scholar, was one of Tim Cook's direct reports at Apple. Doug had been part of the informal team behind the idea of DIUx and saw "dual fluency" reservists like Raj and himself as a central part of the solution. He had a knack for evangelizing to the military brass about the opportunity that existed in Silicon Valley and had charmed Pentagon officials during the run-up to DIUx 1.0 by showing them the original Apple Watch before it was released to the public, with Apple's permission.

We were meticulous in our preparation for the first all-hands.

Todd Park fired up the team with opening remarks. Raj then began with an energizing slide deck.

Part of the reason DIUx 1.0 had foundered was that it had become all things to all people. A matchmaker. An embassy. A technology scout. Raj's first slide was three carefully chosen pictures, each of a current DIUx team member—a Navy SEAL, a fighter pilot, and a cyberwarfare officer—deployed in a war zone. "Our mission," Raj said, "singularly and above all else, is to deliver commercial innovation to the warfighter." We would place in their hands new tools and technology they didn't have today. Success would be helping them accomplish their mission in better ways. Whether they were more effective would be our metric of success.

Raj's first directive was to stop all meetings, since the previous group had conflated success with the number of meetings they could secure. We had carefully read the weekly updates the inaugural director sent back to the Pentagon, which resembled a "meetings taken" scorecard, recording get-togethers with companies, investors, and academics. The Pentagon office overseeing DIUx 1.0 must have liked this, because as time went along each subsequent update focused more and more on meetings. The updates were a case study in how outputs can be mistaken for outcomes and how headquarters can reinforce low-yield behavior.

Raj's second directive to the staff was that DIUx 2.0 was going into stealth mode. Much like a startup that had just raised a big round of funding, we needed time to figure out what we were doing. Though our goals were now clear, how exactly we were going to achieve them was not. We needed to find focus and build an apparatus.

Raj then unveiled the new tools we'd been given to carry out our mission—the extraordinary set of authorities the Secretary had granted us.

"How are we going to deliver innovation to the warfighter faster than any thought possible?" Raj began. "We're going to need superpowers. There are going to be antibodies. So we negotiated, directly with the Secretary, a set of authorities no one else has."

Raj then put up on-screen the term sheet signed by the Secretary's chief of staff. It was an awesome sight to behold, dramatically signaling to DIUx's rank and file that they now had more operational authority than many generals and admirals.

First, as Carter had mentioned, we'd report directly to him as well as having regular meetings with the Vice Chairman of the Joint Chiefs of Staff and Deputy Secretary of Defense. Further, we'd receive administrative, logistical, and personnel support from the chief management officer and additional assistance or support as requested from any DoD component. This clause was important because it meant we had the Secretary's imprimatur to ask for whatever help we needed from whomever we needed it from, and that they were expected to give it. The next term concerned hiring. The Secretary wanted personnel decisions made by DIUx leadership to be executed in fourteen days. Most civilians waited seven to nine months to be hired. Fourteen days was unheard of. The term sheet also included provisions for an O-7 billet—military-speak for assigning a general or admiral to work at DIUx.

Raj saved the most transformational authority for last—waiver authority.

"I'm now going to talk about our nuclear weapon," Raj said. "This authority is what truly sets DIUx apart. What it means is that if we run into a regulation or policy that impedes our mission, we can ask the owner of that policy to waive it for our purposes."

"You mean they have to change the rule just for us, and all we have to do is ask?" exclaimed Trek, one of DIUx's six original team members.

"Yeah," Raj replied. "They do. We can't break the law. If it's in a statute, we have to follow it. But we can deliberately break rules set by others if we have a good enough reason."

"Wow," Trek said. "I've never heard of anything like this."

"There'll be a process. The partners will approve each request. The rule owner has fourteen days to respond. But if they turn us down, it goes immediately to Secretary Carter for review. He's encouraged us to use waiver authority if we need it. It's not just for show."

This was the bureaucratic version of the nuclear option. The fight would be far from fair. The minute some official wanted to throw a wrench in our gears just because they could, we had a powerful antidote. Carter was a no-nonsense guy. He wasn't about to endorse normal procedure for its own sake. Following normal procedure was exactly what had precipitated the slow-burn crisis in military power that DIUx had been created to help solve.

These authorities, especially waiver authority, were unheard of in the Department. The director of DARPA didn't have them. Nor did the head of the Pentagon's nuclear, biological, and chemical programs. Nor did any of the combatant commanders running our wars around the world. The director of a DoD agency couldn't even take an interview with a reporter without receiving permission from the relevant undersecretary. Yet we could do all these things and more because of the terms we'd negotiated.

To make full use of our authorities, we announced an additional personnel appointment. Crane Lopes, the legendary general counsel of DARPA, widely known as the most skilled technology lawyer in the Department, volunteered to be DIUx 2.0's interim general counsel. Crane would do this while still serving in his DARPA post. It was the legal equivalent of announcing Muhammad Ali as the interim boxing coach. Throw the rule book at us, and Crane would use it to punch you in the face. There was no better signal that we meant business.

Looking out at the staff, and seeing the floored expressions on their faces, we knew we'd solved the Pentagon version of the irresistible force paradox—what happens when an unstoppable force meets an immovable object. DIUx was the unstoppable force, and the Pentagon the immovable object. There was now no doubt the Pentagon would budge when we collided. Or so we hoped.

The outpouring of energy in the hours that followed was a validation of what we had all come to do. Everyone started to think bigger.

It turned out the person thinking the biggest that day was one of the smallest in stature. Her name was Lauren Dailey. Literally half the size of our stone-faced Special Operations officer, she came to Raj to share an idea. It was only partially formed and written down in a short paper Lauren had worked on in her spare time. But if true, it would change everything. Raj, Lauren, and Chris soon huddled to discuss how to turn her hunch into reality. It would be DIUx's first big break.

CHAPTER TWO
ZEROIZED

The halo that Carter's visit gave us didn't last.

Two days after the announcement, a friend on Capitol Hill called Raj with catastrophically bad news.

"Hey Raj," our source said, "there's something I need to tell you."

Raj, reading the tone, knew he was about to hear a whopper.

"I just got out of a meeting," said our personal Deep Throat. "They just whacked your budget for next year."

"Okay," Raj said. "How much did they shave off?"

"That's the thing," Deep Throat said. "They shaved all of it."

"All of it?" Raj asked.

"All of it," Deep Throat said.

For reasons unknown, our $30 million budget for the upcoming fiscal year, which started in only four months, was reduced—to zero. In Washington they call this getting "zeroized." It is the strongest way for the first branch of government, Congress, to tell the second branch, the Executive, to go to hell.

The Pentagon press was still busy penning fawning stories about the new whiz kids who were about to revolutionize military technology. They had no idea that we were on the verge of being dead in the water.

—

Our first trip to Washington was supposed to be a victory lap. Fresh off the Secretary's announcement in which he'd personally vested his authority in us and our mission, we were going to press the flesh with the brass, meeting with the Department's entire military and civilian leadership. This included the civilian secretaries that oversee each military service—the navy and marines, air force, and army—as well as the top uniformed four-star military officers—the chief of naval operations, commandant of the Marine Corps, and chiefs of staff of the air force and army. We were also seeing the head acquisition officials of each service—the officials whom we could presumably help the most.

While these meetings were crucial for us to get off on the right foot, the focus of the trip was now damage control. Our grand voyage would be over before it began if we didn't claw back that budget.

Congress wasn't the only one already taking shots. Halfway through the flight, our government credit cards stopped working. Our hotel informed us we'd need to rebook with a new form of payment. This welcoming present came from the crack administrative support team that had left our predecessors without office furniture. As payback for being removed from our chain of command, they canceled our cards rather than transferring them to the new team.

Dead travel cards were only a whizzing BB compared to the heavy artillery already arcing toward us from the Appropriations Committee. Carter and Rosenbach hadn't warned us that our next fiscal year's budget was at risk. They didn't even know. Had they known, they wouldn't have trotted us out on stage in Silicon Valley. They'd have postponed the announcement and sent their legislative staff to battle stations.

The timing couldn't have been worse.

At this late stage in the convoluted budget process, "zeroizing" wasn't something Carter could unilaterally fix. The DoD doesn't control its purse; Congress does so by systematically narrowing what it will and won't support in decisions that, once made, can't be reversed. When most people think of spring in Washington, they picture cherry blossoms and school trips. What they don't think of is thousands of budget officials huddling inside government buildings putting together a giant jigsaw puzzle, piece by piece.

We did some quick sleuthing and learned that the decision to zeroize DIUx had been made by two congressional staffers on the House Appropriations Committee, whom we'll call Evelyn and Ed. We had no idea who they were. And we couldn't imagine how these people had even found our tiny $30 million line item in a $770 billion defense budget, let alone why they wanted to erase it. Why had two Hill staffers dared to poke the Secretary of Defense and cripple the organization we were now leading? This was our first taste of how skillfully the empire would strike back and how we would have to artfully battle to achieve our mission.

Murder mystery theater is a familiar occurrence along the Potomac come budget season. Its rules derive from the Founding Fathers, who created the Executive and Legislature as co-equal branches of government. To ensure the elected representatives of the people can hold the Executive Branch to account, Congress approves every last penny the Executive spends on its programs. What the "power of the purse" means in practice is that a small number of staffers on the Appropriations Committees of the House and Senate wield enormous power over the federal budget. While the biggest decisions are worked out between the White House and congressional leaders, much of the nitty-gritty is decided at the committee level. And it is here that committee staffers accrue vast and functionally unchecked power to micromanage, so long as they aren't egregious in their individual decisions and are able to keep the trust of the members of Congress they serve.

Only a handful of staffers—about twenty—manage the Pentagon's $700 billion dollar budget. That's one staffer for every $35 billion—an astonishing scope of responsibility for one person. In their view, they are doing the Founders' work, keeping fast-talking administration appointees in check and balancing the initiatives they advance with the steady, institutional wisdom of committee staff. While most staffers bring broad experience to their work and are excellent stewards of their outsize responsibility, on the whole the institution is full of people who have not worked outside the Beltway and are less interested in pursuing a career elsewhere. A good number previously worked in the agencies they oversee, often in lower-level roles years earlier, a sometimes dangerous combination that gives them a false sense of overconfidence even as they view their convictions as hard-earned. The worst of these staffers wait years to reign over a slice of the federal pie and take joy in pushing around the military and civilian officials who were once their superiors. At least, it can feel that way.

It had begun to dawn on us that while Carter valued us, his sphere of protection only extended so far in Washington—perhaps far shorter than we'd bet on. We'd just announced to Silicon Valley that DIUx was open for business. Yet rather than scouting for deals, we were fighting a rearguard action 2,435 miles away. If this was our first week on the job, what would next week bring? We didn't know it yet, but one or both of us would end up flying to D.C. almost every week for the next year—so numerous would be the fires to be put out. Raj counted fifty-five red-eyes over his two years as managing partner, plus five more setting up DIUx 2.0, every flight in coach. We became such frequent flyers that once when Secretary Carter walked past us twice in two weeks in the E-ring, he stopped and bellowed, "Hey, I'm paying you guys to work out west." "I know, sir," Raj uttered without skipping a beat. "We keep having to come here to get your bureaucrats out of our way."

Thus began a routine of landing at Dulles, showering at the Pentagon gym ($8, cheaper than paying for early check-in at the hotel, which the government doesn't reimburse), changing into suits, and heading out as the sun rose to knock down the latest hurdle someone had put in our path. So on that first trip to D.C., with too little sleep and no way to officially pay for the Uber we took to Capitol Hill that morning, we found ourselves opening the door to Hart House Office Building Room 405, "Appropriation—Defense Subcommittee."

"Hi, we're with DIUx," we said to the receptionist. "We're here to meet with Evelyn and Ed."

"Just a minute," she said, giving us a chilly appraisal.

The receptionist eventually ushered us into a room off the lobby. Our antagonists walked in a few minutes later.

Evelyn was a retired army officer who had worked in the Pentagon before becoming a congressional staffer. While in the Public Affairs Office, she once oversaw the army's annual birthday celebration, a spirited affair with cake and military bands. Ed—also ex-military—had been on the Hill even longer. They were old enough to be our parents. We knew them by reputation to be among the most aggressive overseers on Capitol Hill.

As we were shown into a conference room with worn paneling and tired furniture, the meeting had a pretense of going all right for just longer than you could hold your breath. Before we made it five slides into our deck, Evelyn cut straight to the point. She informed us that she had killed our next year's budget because she worked for a congressman from Indiana and DIUx was not spending any money in Indiana—a statement which was, to put it politely, insane.

"The money's all going to California," she said. "That's all you guys care about, the West Coast. You're not paying any attention to the Midwest."

We tried to explain that California is where the startups are: 92 percent are founded there, so it's not surprising that much of our budget would ultimately be spent in the Bay Area. If Indiana had a thriving startup scene, we'd spend money accordingly.

"We have tech companies in Indiana," she said.

"And we'll talk to them," Chris promised. "But we can't do it if you cut our funding."

Evelyn gave him a withering look. She'd taken an immediate and intense dislike to Chris. For what it's worth, the feeling was mutual. A meeting that began with restrained anger now became openly hostile.

Evelyn let us know that she wasn't impressed by our Ivy League degrees. She actually said aloud the names of our alma maters—as if this was the reason why Indiana wasn't in on enough of the action. Where we went to school suddenly had become relevant to whether Congress would fund DIUx.

It turned out Evelyn was only warming up.

"You've never even had a real job in the Pentagon," she told Chris. "You know, working in the acquisition systems or running a program office."

"Excuse me?" Chris said.

"I wore the uniform," she said, "and I had real jobs in the Pentagon, doing the real work of the institution."

We were impressed: at least she'd done her homework. But Chris, who'd worked for six Secretaries of Defense, wasn't used to getting dressed down like this, and his fury showed.

Raj made an excuse to stop the meeting and managed to drag Chris out before the exchange devolved further.

"So that went well," Chris said, out in the hallway.

"Yeah. Really well. She seems to really like you."

Raj suggested that he go it alone for the remainder of the meeting.

Back in the conference room, he tried everything he could think of, including offering to explore establishing a branch office in Indiana. Later that year, DIUx opened additional offices in Boston and Austin because those cities are important innovation hubs and in part to avoid the very perception Evelyn held. Subsequently, as Raj got more savvy, DIUx began identifying military reservists in all fifty states who were interested in the innovation mission. We started calling them "Points of Presence" to show we had boots on the ground in most states and many legislative districts. Evelyn would ask Raj in a future meeting whether the Secretary would fly to Indiana to announce DIUx's team there. Raj pointed out that he worked *for* the Secretary, not the other way around, and couldn't make promises for his boss.

For Ed it came down to a grudge. He was peeved because Carter had once refused his request to use an air force Gulfstream to take a congressional staff delegation overseas. These trips were one of the few perks of the job. Visiting overseas military bases on congressional recess is decidedly less glamorous when flying coach. Now Ed was getting his revenge by killing Carter's pet project.

"Hey, I feel bad for you," he told Raj. "I really do. You seem like a good guy. And I know you just started and now it's going to get shut down. That kind of sucks."

Raj was a business guy. He knew how to find common ground and work out a way for both sides to win. He and Ed had served in the military. Ed knew our military needed better gear. "Think of those front-line service members," Raj said. "Think about what's at stake."

"I know we can find a way to work this out," Raj added.

Ed gave Raj a look that said, "You're new around here, aren't you?"

———

It looked like Ed and Evelyn had us in checkmate. It was time to make some calls. In the hallway, we escalated the impasse to top budget officials at the Pentagon and alerted the Secretary's office to the trouble we were now in. But for the moment, backstabbing, score-settling, and small-mindedness had won the day. Chris vented to Raj the whole ride back to the Pentagon. Here he was, paying for an Uber on his personal credit card, having been double-crossed by fellow public servants, one of whom had just told him he never had a "real" job in the Department of Defense. "I guess she didn't read the part of my bio that said 'served in Iraq,'" Chris fumed. Raj was more even-keeled, but still caught off guard. "So this is why you wanted to move to California?" he joked.

We were vulnerable to people like Ed and Evelyn because we didn't yet have an officially approved budget. DIUx came together so rapidly that the Department had cobbled together funds for the first year and just assumed, wrongly it turned out, that Congress would approve the small line item the Secretary's staff rushed into next year's budget bill.

Carter was moving fast because he knew the average tenure of the Secretary of Defense was under three years. Nominated with less than two years remaining in Obama's second term, Carter could only count on one year and 338 days in the job. With sand rushing through the hourglass, he sometimes moved with a speed that felt like whiplash.

One of the consequences of Carter's moving so quickly was that DIUx's budget had not been approved through normal processes. Nor were DIUx 2.0's new mission and resources previewed by the congressional committees that oversee DoD. In fact, to get DIUx 2.0 money before it was announced, the Pentagon comptroller had had no choice but to resort to a budgetary sleight of hand designed to avoid seeking congressional concurrence.

"It goes back to the way Mike set us up," Chris said, in reference to comptroller Michael McCord. "He was trying to do the right thing, and now we're paying for it."

It had all started in Mike's office before our announcement as DIUx's leaders. Raj was in town for a few days of frantic planning. Carter had agreed we needed "walking around money" to remedy the perception in the Valley—which was accurate—that DIUx 1.0 had had no ability to close a deal. The idea was to use funds under our own control to prime the pump, bridging to larger pools of funds that would flow from other parts of the military. DIUx 1.0 had also been run by a skeleton crew—eight people to be exact, including the director, plus two dozen military and civilians sent on detail from other departments and branches. More people worked in the Secretary's mess. Carter also agreed to beef up our operation so we could have real technical muscle on staff as well as more liaison officers from relevant parts of the military. By the time we stepped down from our roles DIUx had over one hundred people in its ranks. But even though the Secretary had agreed to resource DIUx 2.0 in this way, the plan wasn't coming together fast enough in the beginning.

Chris used to sit three chairs down from Pentagon comptroller Mike McCord each morning at the senior staff meeting, which started promptly at 7:30 a.m. Though years apart in age, they were both from Columbus, Ohio, and both endurance athletes—Chris an accomplished runner and Mike a triathlete who finished an Ironman while serving as comptroller.

To settle the matter of DIUx's budget before the coming announcement, Chris asked Mike if he and Raj could see him. On a Tuesday morning we found ourselves sitting on Mike's couch in his imposing E-ring office. He had a view to the north, toward the Pentagon's helipad, with Arlington Cemetery in the distance.

"Well, Mike," Chris started, "the Secretary wants us to have some walking around money, so we can show good faith right away in the Valley. We also need to hire a larger team. I know we're off-cycle with the budget. What's the best approach given we're three weeks away from being announced?"

Mike knew how much of a priority DIUx was for the Secretary. As comptroller of an $800 billion enterprise, he also knew how to find money. In fact, he'd probably never before had a meeting to discuss so small a budget item.

"All right," he said, after thinking for thirty seconds. "I have an idea. The Senate put through a large technology fund in last year's NDAA," referring to the National Defense Authorization Act, the one bill Congress must pass each year. "We can draw from that to get you guys R&D funds. Now, we can't risk a reprogramming"—the lengthy and often contentious process by which the Department seeks approval from Congress to move more than $15 million of funds from one account to another. "But I can get you $14 million this fiscal year and another $14 million right after the new fiscal year starts in October. That will get you guys around $30 million. We can figure out what happens after that in the regular process."

We were relieved. Mike had just addressed our greatest concern—being able to sign deals on day one. "Now on O&M," Mike said, referring to operations and maintenance funds, which covers salaries, travel, and facilities expenses, "you guys know this place. Tilt a couch and a couple million bucks spills out," he said, gesturing to the couch we were sitting on. "How about I get you guys another $5 million of O&M to plus you up through October, then get you $15 million for fiscal year 2017."

We spilled out into the hallway like kids exiting a candy store. After Mike shut his heavy vaulted door behind us, Chris turned to Raj and said, "See, I've got your back in this building. We can make things happen." Raj was astonished. A major who'd come up through the ranks doing things by the book had just witnessed the Department's top fiduciary officer handing out tens of millions of dollars on the basis of a verbal ask. Changing the tires on the F-16 Raj flew required multiple levels of approval and a paper trail to match. In less than fifteen minutes, McCord had gassed up the tank of DIUx 2.0 with a simple nod. The Secretary would soon announce that DIUx 2.0 had $30 million to acquire products from startups, establishing our credibility in the Valley.

Little did we know how much trouble this would land us in with Evelyn and Ed. Not only were they out for us, but so too was the small circle of Senate staffers who'd created the technology fund Mike raided. They hadn't put in all that work to see someone pull out amounts just below the threshold that would have triggered a veto.

Now, riding in an Uber after our drubbing by Evelyn and Ed, and deprived of funding for the next fiscal year, we still weren't ready to give up. Since even Carter might not be able to bail us out of this one—Congress controlled the purse strings—our best hope was to quickly lock down as many deals as possible using the initial funds McCord had transferred to DIUx. If we had SEAL teams and air force and army generals counting on us to deliver them products, we'd make ourselves indispensable. Evelyn and Ed would have to back down; they'd be shamed into restoring our funding.

Back in Mountain View, we assembled the team and told them that we needed to shift into warp speed. Stealth mode was out. Dealmaking was in. Without explaining the depths of the crisis we were facing, we instructed the team to start taking pitch meetings. They didn't fully realize that signing contracts and delivering solutions to warfighters was the only way to keep our unit alive.

The credit card fiasco and the tussle with small-minded congressional staffers were only the beginning of our troubles. Those first weeks at Moffett Field, even the easy things got hard. No one had fully thought through how an extension of the Secretary's office would function across the country from the Pentagon. The near-term result was that we had control of neither our website nor our email.

Washington Headquarters Service, a four-thousand-person field activity that provides Pentagon agencies every kind of equipment, from paperclips and staplers to emergency gear that is donned during a chemical attack, had yet to work out a way to provision us with the same email system used by the Office of the Secretary of Defense (OSD). This was actually a *lucky* break, because we didn't want it.

OSD's email system experienced outages and security breaches so often that the joke was: if we ever lost a war, it would be because we couldn't email each other. We'd met the enemy, and it was us. The system was so bad that when Chris was working with Vint Cerf, who had cofounded the Internet while at DARPA, one of Cerf's own emails bounced back. You know your IT system is in trouble when the founder of the Internet can't get through.

So, we thought, why not just use Gmail? Every startup had long ago figured out that it's far cheaper and more secure to let the enterprise professionals at Google, Microsoft, or Amazon run your network for you.

Using a modern enterprise provider rather than the Office of the Secretary's email servers meant we could issue Apple laptops and iPads to employees on day one, while the rest of the Department was stuck with government-issue Dell laptops four inches thick. Our colleagues had been shackled for their entire careers to an IT system they hated. All their IT was ugly—their laptops, the apps on them, the BlackBerries many were still forced to use. We were signaling that it didn't have to be this way, that we could do better.

A RACE TO SIGN DEALS

It was now time to sign contracts, deliver on the mission, and save our necks.

We had the money McCord had transferred, working email, and a direct report to the Secretary. A month in, things were looking up. What we didn't have was a way to buy technology at Silicon Valley speed.

DIUx 2.0 was set up to operate like a venture capital fund, making bets in five "portfolio" areas: artificial intelligence, autonomy, human systems, information technology, and space, each of which had a dedicated team. These teams would meet with military units wanting to carry out their mission in a better way, canvass startups that might help them, decide which matches between mission and technology were most promising, and then pitch them at a weekly "deals" meeting. There, by matching opportunity, technology, and available funds, we decided what projects to move forward with, and which to kill. And we were finding a lot we wanted to move forward with. But the same fatal flaw that had hamstrung DIUx 1.0 was about to afflict us too—the creaky contracting machinery that buys all the military's stuff once everyone agrees to do business together.

It turned out that before Silicon Valley tech could be used on the battlefield, we had to go to war to buy it. We had to hack the Pentagon itself—its archaic acquisition procedures, which prevent moving money at Silicon Valley speed. In Silicon Valley, deals are done in days. The eighteen- to twenty-four-month process for finalizing contracts used by most of the Pentagon was a nonstarter. No startup CEO trying to book revenue before their next venture capital raise can wait for the earth to circle the sun twice. We needed a new way.

One of our team members figured out a hack that could cut the contracting process down to little more than a month or even faster and make it possible to seamlessly go from buying one to a thousand or more of whatever piece of technology we needed, with no further renegotiation needed.

Lauren Dailey, a twenty-nine-year-old acquisitions manager, had transferred from Washington to work for DIUx when it was launched. She was a civilian who came from an army family—her dad worked on the crew of a tank. Working at the Pentagon was her way of serving.

In our introductory meeting, Lauren told Raj that she'd been looking through the Pentagon's rules and regulations for acquiring products and believed she'd found a loophole—a new authority in legislative language just passed by Congress—that we could use to sign contracts in weeks rather than months and then turn pilot projects into full production contracts, immediately.

"How come nobody else ever thought of this?" Raj said.

She shrugged. "I guess they didn't look."

Which really meant: nobody else spent their spare time poring through thousands of pages of newly passed legislation.

"Is it legal?" Raj said.

"Maybe?" she said, smiling.

Raj decided that he and Lauren were going to get along.

"Okay, so write me up a memo explaining how it works," he said.

"Actually," she said, "I already did."

She handed him a twenty-page white paper. Now Raj was sure that they were going to get along. Lauren was a Pentagon employee with the mind-set of a Silicon Valley growth hacker. Not only would Lauren's hack help DIUx 2.0 move past the failures of DIUx 1.0. It would change the way the entire Pentagon bought technology.

Lauren had arrived at Moffett Field in October 2015 to find six people sitting at card tables using Wi-Fi through hotspots. "Welcome to DIUx," one of the team said. "You're employee number seven. The topic of our meeting today is how to get Internet and get more people out here."

"I didn't know what the mission was," Lauren remembers of those early days. "Are we the customer who is supposed to be buying things? Are we connecting other customers in the military to startups? Our role wasn't clear in the early days. There was this sense that we'd go meet startups, introduce them to warfighters that have problems, and magic will happen." But magic didn't happen. "We quickly found that a startup and a customer would talk, but nothing would happen because there was no easy way to test out a prototype and try the technology."

In Silicon Valley, deals are agreed upon a handshake. Paperwork flows quickly. A few DocuSigns later, it's done. In government, deals begin with a warranted contracting officer, who is legally allowed to assume fiscal liability on behalf of the federal government. No one else, not even the President of the United States, can sign on the dotted line for Uncle Sam. The first problem was that DIUx didn't have any warranted contracting officers of its own. Most military units that initially worked with DIUx didn't either. They had to reach back to higher headquarters, which in turn put them in their contracting office's queue. The second problem was that warranted contracting officers default to the standard way the Department buys technology, via the Federal Acquisition Regulations, the government's acquisition bible. The FAR's defense supplement, or DFAR, is over thirteen hundred pages long. It reads like the Old Testament. Whole schools of interpretation have built up over decades to make sense of its conflicting provisions. Even in the hands of the most nimble contracting officer, FAR-based contracts can take twelve to eighteen months to negotiate, or longer.

The real slippage between the Pentagon's technology buyers and Silicon Valley entrepreneurs was one of mind-set. "DoD is used to buying aircraft carriers, missiles, tanks," Lauren says. "As the single buyer, it ordinarily has the power in the market relationship." The economic term for this is monopsony, when a buyer controls all the demand. As with a monopoly, ordinary rules of a free market don't apply. The buyer gets to call the shots. While this holds in defense markets, it's the opposite in technology markets. When you look at Silicon Valley, startups are chasing the $25 trillion global market for consumer and enterprise technology. The Pentagon's $200 billion acquisition budget is a rounding error in their business plans, and an unattractive one at that.

Not only do FAR-based contracts take eons to negotiate, but they impose obligations small firms can't support. DoD contracting practices have evolved so far away from commercial norms that non-defense businesses have to create separate accounting, audit, and compliance systems if they want to do business under the FAR. The cost and hassle are simply not worth it in most cases.

Over one thousand people work in the Office of the Undersecretary of Defense for Comptroller. The force that keeps DoD's coffers in order also includes the Defense Contract Audit Agency and the Defense Finance and Accounting Service, DCAA and DFAS. DFAS employs 11,000 people. DCAA has a workforce of 3,500 spread over 230 offices around the world.

The Pentagon has created an entire army of contract enforcers to ensure that when it buys aircraft carriers, it can control costs in very specific ways. This oversight is needed because even though the Pentagon is often the sole buyer, in the defense market there is often only one seller as well. Detailed financial accounting and intrusive audits are the only way to ensure the taxpayer is not being overcharged. (Think $400 hammers and $600 toilet seats.) This system works well enough for stealth bombers and nuclear submarines but is a disaster when it comes to startups.

"In Silicon Valley," Lauren explains, "DoD faces a very different market than what their acquisition tools, rules, and culture are built around. We fundamentally had to find a way to change that paradigm to allow DoD to become a better and more attractive customer."

DIUx 1.0 wasn't sure how to square this circle. Their first instinct was to admire the problem. "Maybe we should do studies of how Silicon Valley does business" was the thinking. Lauren knew right away that DIUx had to toss out the FAR. It would never work. A more promising strategy would be embracing a little-known authority called OTA, for Other Transactions Authority. Developed during the space race to enable NASA to buy parts from mom-and-pop suppliers, OTAs were still used in a few corners of the Department, including DARPA. The OTA is a tool and a mind trick all in one. By avoiding the FAR's ossification, it gives hardened contracting officers and the lawyers that support them permission to shed the routines they have clung to. But OTAs already had a bad name in the Valley. The most common example of them was the consortia model. In this, a defense lab or other entity would contract with a group of companies that would share technology they had in response to a request for proposal. To startups whose most valuable possession is their intellectual property, consortia OTAs were insane. They gave your competitors full insight into your technology and its pricing. The consortia model wouldn't work for anyone at technology's bleeding edge.

OTAs had a second problem. They were only for technology pilots, not for actual contracts that could scale technology across the military. If the pilot worked, you ended up right back at square one, having to issue a new solicitation using the FAR to win an actual deal that would generate revenue. The prize for proving your technology worked was another twelve to eighteen months of competition that you could lose if someone else swooped in with similar technology at a lower price, or worse, with better lobbyists.

DIUx had to escape this loop. Yet so abysmal is the Pentagon's record for developing new procurement tools that the official history of that search is titled *Defense Acquisition Reform, 1960-2009: An Elusive Goal.* The eureka moment came when Lauren was reading the 2016 National Defense Authorization Act. Passage of the NDAA, usually in November, was like Christmas for acquisition nerds—the final bill usually contained new authorities hidden within it. Deep in the act, in section 815, Lauren found an astonishing passage that was just a few sentences long. She had to read it several times to make sure she got it right. The passage gave the Department permission to advance successful OTA prototypes directly to production contracts, without requiring companies to go through another round of competition. This was the contracting equivalent of the Declaration of Independence. It allowed military customers who found technology that worked to scale it immediately without going back to square one. As soon as a tech company's pilot program succeeded, they could start selling products Department-wide and in volume.

The new authority had been inserted into the bill by a renegade Senate staffer named Bill Greenwalt, who for years had been trying to shake up defense procurement. It had limits—it could only be used for contracts under $250 million, though that ceiling too could be waived if the undersecretary of defense for acquisition assured Congress in writing the contract was "essential to meet critical national security objectives." Greenwalt hoped someone in the Department would discover his handiwork and run with it. That person was Lauren Dailey.

Lauren immediately began conceiving of a whole new kind of OTA, one she named a "Commercial Solutions Opening." CSOs, as they came to be called, would allow DIUx to engage directly with a company and buy its technology at scale as soon as a successful pilot was complete. What's more, the prototype-to-production language in section 815 allowed anyone to add on to an already negotiated production contract. If a drone pilot program at DIUx succeeded, and the army wanted to buy an additional ten thousand or one hundred thousand drones, it could, using the production contract DIUx had worked out with the vendor. For the first time a mechanism could be built to mainline the technology of startups straight into the Department without the usual barriers to entry. Lauren, leveraging Bill Greenwalt's gift, had found a way to leap over the Valley of Death.

The only problem? This idea was in Lauren's head. The twenty-page paper she'd written was a blueprint for a revolution. We had to find a way of carrying it out, and fast.

Chris flew to Washington and obtained time with every senior leader needed to approve this landmark shift in policy. Chris and Lauren's first meeting was with the Pentagon's head of acquisition policy, Claire Grady. A serious operator who'd cut her teeth on the Coast Guard's acquisition staff, Grady had a warm and welcoming personality.

Lauren already had an ally in Grady's operation. Victor Deal, a senior procurement analyst, had, like Bill Greenwalt, been striving to make it easier for the Department to better engage startups. An Air Force Academy graduate who went on to get his MBA, he and Lauren had been talking ever since the new NDAA came out. Deal spotted the same new authorities Lauren did, was floating proposals for how to apply them, and had greased the wheels with Grady. So had Chris, who'd already won over Carter to Lauren's idea and let it be known that the Secretary wanted to see it become policy, pronto.

Before Lauren walked into Grady's office on the Pentagon's third floor, she'd only seen her on stage at DoD procurement summits. Grady was functionally her boss's, boss's, boss's boss. Now Lauren sat across the table from her, a marked-up copy of her white paper in Grady's hands. Lauren did all the talking and got everyone's heads nodding. Grady embraced the idea. The trick now was to get it through Legal.

Our next stop was Susan Raps, the Pentagon's top acquisition lawyer. Susan was well acquainted with Chris from late night and early morning phone calls as they worked to clear an endless stream of documents, speeches, memos, and charters for the Secretary's reboot of DIUx. After tweaks, Susan gave her blessing. Chris, not one to leave things to chance, then walked the draft framework, now over one hundred pages, into the office of the Pentagon's general counsel, who gave it her enthusiastic endorsement. With the puff of white smoke now visible to all, we told our boss, the Secretary of Defense, about our first big policy win.

This was a land speed record on the E-ring. In little more than two weeks, DIUx had invented a whole new way of buying technology that superseded seventy years of how OTAs were structured. We did this by putting our hands on the pen that wrote the new guidance and making sure it suited our needs. Because the Secretary wanted it done instantly, a process that would have taken years took weeks.

The white paper Lauren wrote became a how-to manual for using the new contracting method. With DIUx's seal on the cover, we posted the white paper on our website, where it was downloaded by DoD acquisition cells all over the world. Two months later, our how-to manual was rebranded as official DoD policy, with the Department's seal replacing our own as it became the first update to the Department's guidance on OTAs since 2004.

What we needed now was warranted contracting officers to wield this new tool we'd created, which, as mentioned previously, Lauren had dubbed the Commercial Solutions Opening (CSO). We got the first volunteers from a unit known for being willing to work outside the FAR, a group of army civilians based at Picatinny Arsenal in New Jersey, led by Paul Milenkowic. This off-the-beaten-track unit specialized in OTAs. Their lawyer, a sunny woman named Denise Scott, was game to enact the first CSO—a nontrivial responsibility since it would be Picatinny assuming the legal risk if anything went wrong. We had Carter ring up the head of Army Acquisition and the head of Picatinny Arsenal to share his enthusiasm for giving this CSO thing a go. Carter later visited Picatinny, and in a military tradition he gave everyone in the contracting unit his personal coin—heavy, round, and embossed with the Secretary's seal.

Before we knew it, warranted contracting officers were flying to Mountain View from New Jersey in rotation. Someone was always on hand to sign a deal. While the process was fast, it had dozens of legal steps that had to be executed with precision. It was a team effort. One such team member whose selfless dedication to the mission was central to DIUx's success was chief operating officer Ernie Bio. Ernie was a former F-16 pilot who'd flown in combat with Raj before he earned his MBA at NYU and became a management consultant and cyber expert. He was one of the original DIUx members who had relocated to CA to help launch the initiative. Ernie kept the trains running smoothly and on time for our entire tenure, enabling Lauren and the rest of us to make astonishing progress.

Lauren's breakthrough let us start signing contracts almost immediately. In the years that followed, the military went on to use Lauren's hack to buy $70 billion worth of technology. She became a rock star in the acquisition community overnight, and eventually was invited to a meeting with President Trump.

But all that would come later. What we needed now was to deliver game-changing technology for the warfighter, ideally before October, when the fiscal year—and our funding—would end. Otherwise, we might cease to exist.

CHAPTER THREE
THE GONKULATOR

The Combined Air Operations Center (CAOC) is the command post for all U.S. military air operations across the Middle East. The nondescript windowless building sits on the sprawling Al Udeid Air Base, which is situated on a desert twenty miles west of Doha, the capital of Qatar, a nation on a spit of sand the size of Connecticut jutting out into the Persian Gulf. The CAOC commands anything that flies, from military flights to missile launches, across twenty countries in Northeast Africa, the Middle East, and Central and South Asia—an area bigger than the lower forty-eight states. Construction began in July 2002, spurred by the increasing American presence in Afghanistan after the attacks of September 11, 2001, and was completed in February 2003. A month later U.S. forces invaded Iraq to overthrow Saddam Hussein and scour the country for WMDs in Operation Enduring Freedom.

The decision to plant a substantial command and control facility in the region signaled American forces were going to be present for a long time. It was also a diplomatic gesture, demonstrating our commitment to Qatar. Twenty years after opening, the Al Udeid CAOC is still the primary hub for the combined branches of the U.S. and allied airpower from the Mediterranean to Kabul.

In October 2016, five months into the DIUx job and at the height of the air campaign against ISIS in Iraq and Syria, Raj visited this once-secret base with members of the Defense Innovation Board (DIB), an advisory group led by former Google chairman Eric Schmidt. The DIB's members, all top-tier technologists, were traveling to military outposts around the world, asking service members what technology they needed, and reporting their findings to the Secretary of Defense. The DIB and DIUx were complementary groups. The DIB spotted places where technology could be transformational; DIUx delivered solutions. By going out into the field, we were taking a Silicon Valley approach. In the Valley, you don't start with a product. You start with the customer. You find a problem and work backward from there.

Inside, the CAOC at first glance seemed impressive: a vast two-story open room that looked like NASA Mission Control, with giant screens on the walls and a few hundred people sitting at rows of desks, tracking hundreds of fighter jets, tankers, drones, and AWACS planes in the air above Syria, Iraq, and other hot spots. On closer inspection, however, the CAOC turned out to be not so cutting edge. In fact, its technology was woefully obsolete. Systems patched together with duct tape and Band-Aids were making it unnecessarily difficult for our service members to do their jobs. Technology is supposed to make things move faster, to let people do more with less, to be more efficient. The technology at the CAOC was the opposite: it was holding people back, slowing things down, and—it's not too much of a stretch to say this—putting lives at risk.

The CAOC is a modern-day digital version of the Controller's Cabin, the underground bunker outside London where Britain directed its air forces and interception radar systems during World War II, connected through an old-fashioned landline phone network to Fighter Command HQ at Bentley Priory. The Controller's Cabin was where military leaders crafted each day's plan to intercept German fighter planes during the Battle of Britain. It was the nerve center managing an array of systems, including anti-aircraft batteries, barrage balloons, radar stations, aerial observers, rescue boats, and fighter groups. In the tiny room, members of the Women's Auxiliary Air Force pushed markers around with paddles over big sector maps to update the position of the enemy and the fighters scrambling to intercept them. Colored lightbulbs gave the controller an at-a-glance picture of the situation.

The CAOC in Qatar served a similar purpose, though it was built on a much grander scale. The facility cost $60 million and involved more than sixty-seven miles of high-capacity and fiber-optic cable, creating what the air force called the most advanced operations center in history. On the second day of the assault on Iraq, the CAOC coordinated seventeen hundred coalition sorties and missile launches against Iraqi targets—seventy-one strikes each hour. America's control of the airspace was absolute. Judged by the money spent and the results delivered, the CAOC was a resounding success.

Thirteen years later, the CAOC was still operating nonstop, doing the job it was designed to do and in fact handling substantially more traffic. It's just that by 2016, the technology that had been cutting edge in 2003—when flat panel displays were a novelty, Wi-Fi and Bluetooth were just starting to catch on, and Windows XP was the dominant operating system—had become terribly outdated. The DIB group felt as if they'd traveled back to an era when people used AOL and dial-up modems. Airmen were still using systems with command-line interfaces. Programs were running on minicomputers and mainframes. "Some of this software might be older than the guys who are using it," Raj quipped.

Carter had created the DIB in 2016 charging Eric Schmidt and the board's other members with the mission of assessing the DoD's technical capabilities and giving recommendations on what should be done to modernize the military and prepare it to fight the wars of the future. Schmidt was a supporter of President Obama from the 2008 campaign's start.

The Obama administration arrived in Washington determined to freshen up the government's use of technology and steer it toward fixing complex problems. That technocratic optimism soured, though, in the fall of 2013 when HealthCare.gov, the portal for Obama's Affordable Care Act, crashed the day it was launched. The ongoing struggle to fix the website was an embarrassing counter to the administration's tech-savvy image and prompted Todd Park's rescue mission years before he helped Carter reboot DIUx. The original budget to develop HealthCare.gov was $93.7 million, and yet one year after its launch the Office of Inspector General reported that the total cost of the website had reached $1.7 billion. Something was very wrong with the way the government procured software.

Enter Eric Schmidt, who moved easily between Silicon Valley and Washington since stepping down as CEO of Google in 2011 to become its executive chairman.

More than most, he understood that one technology was on the verge of breaking out and changing the rules of warfare—artificial intelligence. From early in its history and throughout Schmidt's tenure, Google had been pouring money and talent into AI research. Most of the improvements that made searching easier for users—auto-fill of search boxes; spoken searches and commands; image recognition on Google Translate that allowed a tourist to point their phone at an object and find out its name in a foreign language—had their roots in AI science that had been under development for decades but came to market only after further pioneering work. Google led the way in the technology that led to autonomous vehicles, and its work in AI was considered ahead of most other institutions in the world.

By the time Eric convened the first meeting of the DIB in 2016, he was keenly aware of the shock and awe some AI innovations would have on the public when they rolled out over the next decade. Schmidt was a software engineer who had started his career as a coder at Bell Labs, the legendary R&D factory where the transistor, laser, and photoelectric cells were invented along with Unix and programming languages C and C++. As head of software engineering at Sun Microsystems, he was deeply embedded in the dual worlds of code and hardware. And he learned bare-knuckle business lessons battling against Microsoft in his years as CEO of the once powerful networking giant Novell. Schmidt rose to prominence in the Valley in 2001 when Sergey Brin and Larry Page hired him at Google.

Fifteen years later, at the helm of the DIB, he did the first thing a software engineer does before designing a new system: go out and talk to customers and find out what problems they need solved. This time the stakes were higher. Eric was working to protect lives, strengthen national security, and defend democracy against authoritarian regimes, especially China, whose advances in AI and other technologies had caused him to grow increasingly concerned.

Eric and the board, accompanied on their trips by either Raj or Chris, and the board's energetic executive director, Josh Marcuse, spent much of their first year traveling to American military outposts around the world, talking to the soldiers, sailors, airmen, and marines who were the end users of the weapons platforms developed by the defense industry and purchased by the Department of Defense. The DIB's recommendations would go directly to the Secretary of Defense. When the DIB identified opportunities where commercial technology could be transformational, DIUx would often go find companies to build solutions.

So it was that one day in the fall of 2016, as the DIB group toured the CAOC at Al Udeid, Raj turned a corner, glanced into a side room, and saw something that stopped him in his tracks. "You've gotta be kidding," he said to Eric. "That can't still be here."

BATTLE CABINS

Remember those members of the Women's Auxiliary Air Force in the bunker under London during the Battle of Britain, pushing markers around on maps? Here, in 2016, in the CAOC—an air command center operated by the largest and most advanced military in the world, coordinating thousands of flights a day, from more than a dozen air bases, sometimes in combat conditions, over an area the size of the United States—two airmen were standing at a whiteboard moving magnetic pucks around in a grid. The pucks on the whiteboard had names of fighter jets and refueling tankers written on them. This was how they scheduled midair refueling flights, using more or less the same system their predecessors had employed during the Second World War, seven decades ago. This modern-day abacus was how the logistics team performed the dizzyingly complicated calculations required to enable dozens of tankers to cross paths with hundreds of fighter jets and refuel them in mid-flight. To make things trickier, different jets have different fuel connectors and can only "mate" with certain tankers. Also, different jets refuel at different speeds, at different altitudes, and in different configurations. The air force was doing more than fifteen hundred refuelings *each day* over Afghanistan, Syria, and Iraq, and using this clumsy, manual process to manage all of it.

Every Fortune 500 company in the world—airlines, manufacturers, shipping companies—uses computers to do the mind-boggling math required to work out the logistics that power its operations. UPS and Fed-Ex don't have teams of people moving pucks around on whiteboards. But here in the CAOC, members of the world's most advanced air force were doing the work by hand. While the two airmen moved pucks around, two others sat at laptops using Excel spreadsheets, with one reading out numbers from his screen while the other typed the numbers into the second laptop. They literally could not share data electronically. A third person watched the two laptop operators and double-checked the numbers. The airman in charge was called the Thumper. The airman typing data into a laptop was called a Gonker, typing info into a "gonkulator," a name from the old sitcom *Hogan's Heroes*, meaning a useless device. This bit of dark humor showed that even the airmen knew the system was a farce—as did Lieutenant General Jeffrey "Cobra" Harrigian, the three-star who led air force operations in the region and whose remit included overseeing the CAOC. "I was down in the trenches. I saw the crap that these guys were working with, and I was like, 'Are you kidding me?' They were using fourteen apps to do something that should have been done machine-to-machine," recalls Harrigian, who later became commander of U.S. Air Forces in Europe and retired as a four-star general.

It's difficult to comprehend the enormity of the CAOC's mission. In 2016, the year Raj visited, the air force flew more than twenty-six thousand strike aircraft sorties into Afghanistan, Iraq, and Syria—more than seventy per day. It was the most intense bombing campaign in the air force's history—at its height ISIS targets in Mosul were struck every eight minutes. Sustaining these strikes required more than eighteen thousand tanker sorties and nearly one hundred thousand air refuelings, amounting to over 200 million gallons of jet fuel delivered airborne each year. The team at the CAOC also managed tens of thousands of airlift and airdrop sorties into Afghanistan, Iraq, and Syria. In addition to all that, they had seventeen other countries to worry about.

"I'm not sure that a lot of people understand the complexity of it," recalls General Harrigian, who was directing air operations for the U.S. and twenty-two coalition partners across 19 million square miles. "We were supporting the U.S. Army troops on the ground, and our Special Ops guys, and also the Iraqis. We were doing everything we could to protect civilians, to protect women and children, these families, and we're operating in this very complex environment that required us to not make mistakes due to human error. And that was one of the biggest things I worried about, because the tools we were providing to our airmen drove up that risk. I wanted to fix the tools they were using and drive down that risk because it was going to save not only Americans but also save Iraqis and any of the friendly forces we were supporting."

Scheduling those refuelings by hand took a team of trained specialists a combined sixty hours every day. And the process was far from perfect. When the unexpected happened—bad weather, a mechanical problem, a fighter rerouted to a different target—the puck-and-whiteboard calculations could not be done fast enough to accommodate the change. Instead, the CAOC had to scramble a spare tanker down the runway and send it up to refuel a single jet. Tankers, the size of a Boeing 767, are loaded with 212,000 pounds of fuel. Each scramble cost $250,000. They were doing this three times a day to ensure that ground troops received 24/7 air support. Doing the math by hand was causing the air force to waste more than $5 million each week.

Worse, this inefficient system was putting lives at risk—those of U.S. Special Forces and the allied militias they were embedded with, along with millions of civilians caught in the crossfire who we were trying to protect. Our air strikes were targeting ISIS fighters, who were committing atrocities in Iraq, using chemical and biological weapons against prisoners, carrying out genocide, and enslaving thousands of women. In Mosul, ISIS held more than seven hundred thousand Iraqi civilians hostage in their own city. Our fighters and drones were pounding ISIS forces twenty-four hours a day. The CAOC had even stopped the largest attempted genocide of the twenty-first century, saving fifty thousand Yazidi women, children, and men from certain death in 2014. ISIS had targeted members of this minority Kurdish religious group because they were viewed as heretics for adhering to a pre-Zoroastrian faith.

How many people we would save as the air campaign continued depended not just on the firepower of our jets and the capabilities of our pilots, but also on the skills of a dozen airmen stuffed into a windowless room a thousand miles to the south on an air base in Qatar who were doing their work by hand, moving pucks around on a whiteboard.

The airmen who were gonkulating the math by hand knew a basic optimization program would be relatively simple to create. They'd been clamoring for someone to do this work. Instead of battling the enemy they were battling a broken system. The fix would have to wait, though, since the CAOC was undergoing a top-to-bottom technology overhaul of every app and system it used, overseen by a team at Hanscom Air Force Base, in Massachusetts, which was sixty-five hundred miles and eight time zones away. It's typical for the military to hire defense contractors to run tech projects—in this case Northrop Grumman—spending far more than what similar commercial solutions might cost. Unfortunately, it's also typical for those defense contractors to deliver too little and too late, particularly when it comes to software, which is exactly what had been going on at the CAOC since 2008.

Northrop Grumman's ten-year tech overhaul was managed by Steven Wert, a twenty-five-year air force veteran turned government executive. By the time Raj visited Hanscom, the overhaulers were in year eight, and three years behind schedule. The original estimated budget of $374 million had bloated to $745 million, without much to show for it. Nevertheless, the air force was asking Congress to appropriate another $65 million.

We encountered this situation frequently during our years at DIUx—someone had a simple problem that could be fixed with relatively little effort, but a quick fix proved impossible given how the military and its defense contractor partners develop technology systems. Pentagon project managers were still using an outdated systems engineering approach that Silicon Valley had tossed out twenty years before. In that old model, the project was designed from the top down—meaning instead of asking the people who'd use the software what they needed, a group of product managers decided what the software should look like and what it should do. The product managers might spend a year or more drawing up the specifications. Then they'd invite contractors to submit bids, and they'd choose a winner—and that also could take a year or more. Then the chosen winner would spend another year or more writing and testing the code. The whole process took so long that by the time the software was put into production, it was already obsolete. In the case of the CAOC project, the requirements had been set by Wert's team at Hanscom, and the code was being written by programmers who were using old-fashioned development methodologies and, worse yet, rarely set foot inside the CAOC, limiting their firsthand knowledge of how the airmen did their jobs.

In Silicon Valley, coders had long ago ditched that way of doing things and adopted what's known as a "lean" methodology, pioneered by a DIUx supporter, the entrepreneur Steve Blank. That's how DIUx did things. In the lean approach, coders start by talking to the people who will use the software. They break big products into small pieces and attack each one separately, working in six-week sprints. Coders crank out a "minimum viable product," show it to the users, get feedback, create a new iteration, get more feedback, and so on. Coders can finish a program and get it into production in months or weeks—not years—and they can do it for one-tenth the cost.

Eric saw the absurdity of using whiteboards to schedule logistics and recognized this as something that in military slang would be called FUBAR—effed up beyond all repair. Eric also knew how quickly a team in Silicon Valley could build a solution. He watched in disbelief as the two airmen dictated numbers into the gonkulator.

"Raj," he said, "this is the most egregious misuse of IT that I've ever seen. You guys need to fix this—and right away."

Harrigian concurred.

So we decided to build an app.

The tanker refueling project gave us a chance to show what DIUx could do—and to give Congress another reason not to zeroize us. The app was a small project, we could do it quickly and cheaply, and it would have real impact. Raj didn't even wait to get home. That night, at his hotel, he called Enrique Oti, an air force colonel and member of the DIUx team back in Mountain View. "Start tomorrow," Raj told him. "Let's get something built as soon as we can, bring the engineers to the CAOC to meet the tanker planners, and get it launched."

"I'm on it," Enrique replied without missing a beat.

Enrique was the perfect person for the job. He was in his early forties, a career air force officer and a graduate of the Air Force Academy with a specialization in cyberwarfare. The next morning, he began assembling a team. There were already a handful of active-duty airmen at DIUx who were skilled software engineers. One was Wayne Starr, who'd just graduated from Rochester Institute of Technology and joined the air force as a second lieutenant. This was his first official air force posting. The air force had sent him to DIUx after learning that he had a background in software engineering and had spent a year working at Microsoft. Wayne was a rarity in the armed forces, which categorizes people into one of more than 150 military occupational specialties, or an MOS. There are plenty of technical MOS positions, but nothing specifically for programming software. He arrived at a time when the military was realizing that it needed coders and starting to look for them among its ranks. "There are a lot of people who can code in the air force," Starr said. "But the air force doesn't really know how to recognize them when they enlist."

In addition to Starr and a few other DIUx coders, Enrique hired a handful of software engineers from Pivotal, a software development company in San Francisco. Enrique, though not an engineer, was a brilliant manager. He was also an expert in Chinese technology strategies, including its cyber capabilities, and had studied in China and spoke Mandarin. Enrique had been assigned to DIUx under its original leadership in 2015, before we took over, and was one of the team members we retained.

By the time Raj returned to Mountain View a week later, Enrique's team was already scoping out the app. The fact that Schmidt himself had demanded the solution boosted the urgency of the project. "That put a little thrust behind fixing the tanker refueling systems," Starr said. "Even if all we did was make the whiteboard and the Excel spreadsheet more efficient, we were adding value."

One tenet of the lean software methodology is that you start by talking to the people who will use the software, which in this case meant we had to send the Pivotal and DIUx coders to Qatar. Under ordinary circumstances it would have taken months to get security clearances to send a bunch of scruffy San Francisco coders into an overseas air force command center executing the highest-tempo air operation in military history. But we had our "Secretary of Defense says so" card, which let us push quickly through the clearance process. On top of that, we needed to get a special waiver so that the Pivotal coders could use the Macs they were accustomed to instead of government-issued Windows computers which came loaded with Pentagon-certified apps and security software. No outside devices are allowed into the CAOC. Personal phones, iPads, laptops—they all get stored in lockers while service members are working. So it was a big deal when General Harrigian approved our request to let coders bring their Macs inside. A young airman at DIUx spent an entire day buying, packaging, and then FedExing iMacs from our office to the air base in Qatar.

We weren't bending rules just for the sake of bending them. We had to get the Pivotal coders onto the base, because our air force coders couldn't do the work on their own. Also, we wanted our air force coders to learn from the Pivotal coders, who were using modern development tools and methodologies. Bringing Silicon Valley coders into an air force base served another purpose. Part of our mission was to shake up the culture of the military—to start drilling those holes between the military and the commercial sector, as Ash Carter had put it in his 2015 speech at Stanford. Carter wanted us to infuse the Pentagon with the fast-moving ethos of Silicon Valley—to teach a giant organization how to think and act like a startup. This means moving decisively, being open to new ideas, taking risks, and tolerating failure. It means not getting so stuck on the way things have been done in the past that you get locked out of the future.

The DIUx and Pivotal coders spent a week in the CAOC making sure they understood the problem. This is how a half dozen shaggy (by air force standards) San Francisco coders in jeans and T-shirts ended up sitting around a table with a team of uniformed airmen in a combat center, solving a problem together, in the middle of the military's most intense modern combat operation. The experience was a bit of a culture shock for the Pivotal coders—not just the weirdness of being on an air force base but also having to deal with the directness and rough edges of the airmen. The "Pivots," as they called themselves, carried little signs with their motto—"Always be kind"—and were polite in their dealings with each other. "The airmen thought the Pivots seemed like cult members," Starr recalls. "They'd all get up and go to lunch at exactly the same time and start and stop work at exactly the same time." For their part, the Pivots thought the air force's technology had even rougher edges than its airmen.

"We were shocked by how badly things were broken in the command center," Starr remembers. "I mean from the outside, you see these high-tech ads for the air force, and they're saying, 'It's not science fiction, it's what we do every day.' But then you go inside and they're using Microsoft Office to run weapons systems. There was a lot of disappointment. It's not this fancy high-tech thing. It's just workflows and Microsoft Office."

Harrigian recalls hanging out with the Pivotal coders and their air force counterparts. "I used to go back there and ask, 'Hey, show me what you guys have got going on.' And they'd say, 'Oh, cool, here comes the commander. Three stars here can come back and hang out with us.' They'd show me what they were doing and I was like, 'Whoa, this is really cool.'" Harrigian was most impressed by how the Pivotal team became committed to the mission. "Some of these folks went in pretty native, trying to understand what we were trying to do. They became part of the war effort, part of the team, that's the only way I can put it.

They understood that this was serious and we needed to do the right thing, that they were part of the solution and I needed them to lean into it. And it was clear to me by the look in their eyes that they got it."

Before they left the base, the DIUx and Pivotal team members were already doing some of the basic coding. Back in Mountain View they spent six weeks creating a minimum viable product—a rough version of the app, basically a user interface and menu structure that the airmen could evaluate. The coders took their feedback, wrote some more code, uploaded the new version, and got more feedback. As Starr recalls, they had an advantage because the tanker app wasn't dependent on any other systems in the CAOC's technology stack. "The great thing is we didn't need to touch their system. We could get a stand-alone app, and it wouldn't have any third-party dependencies that we'd need to rely on."

After a few months—132 days, not that we were counting—the coders had a working product. At first the airmen kept using the whiteboard while running the software concurrently, but after a few months they stopped using the whiteboard completely. Wayne Starr and his airmen buddies in the CAOC celebrated with cigars.

The software could match a fighter to the optimal refueling tanker in under a minute, after which the planners would take less than an hour to double-check and refine the solution if needed. The airmen loved it. So did General Harrigian. The software could build the daily plan so quickly that when things changed, the airmen could recalculate the schedule on the fly, which meant the CAOC didn't need to scramble tankers as often. Before this tool, anytime our troops came into contact with insurgent fighters, they'd need to find "surge" tanker support. The U.S. had tankers and crews stationed on the ground around the region, ready to launch at a moment's notice, which they did two to three times a day on average. As mentioned previously, each scramble cost about $250,000, not including the wear on the airplane or crew. With our new tool, all it took to recompute was the press of a button and sixty seconds. We did the whole project for $1.5 million, which meant the app paid for itself in three days of air operations. The Air Force Office of Operational Energy later calculated the app increased operational efficiency by 10 percent, saving 25 million gallons of jet fuel per year.

Soon, the CAOC was putting DIUx to work on other broken apps, including a dynamic targeting tool that helped the air force optimize real time targeting given available assets. Maybe now, instead of trying to shut us down, the Pentagon bureaucracy would increase our budget and turn us loose on more and bigger projects.

Well, no.

THE MILITARY INDUSTRIAL AUTO-IMMUNE SYSTEM

Unbeknownst to us, while we were working on the refueling app, Steve Wert, the veteran air force officer who was the program manager running the Northrop Grumman project from Hanscom Air Force Base, was trying to shut us down. Wert ran a 3,500-person tech procurement organization at Hanscom. He knew his CAOC program was in trouble. He probably believed, perhaps correctly, that if the air force allowed us to get a toehold by installing the refueling app, this might lead to his losing the entire project.

To save his program, Wert sent a three-page memo to General David Goldfein, the chief of staff of the air force, it's most senior officer, trying to persuade him to boot us out of the CAOC. We might never have known about this except that at about this time Goldfein happened to visit the DIUx offices in Boston and showed the memo to Raj. Raj persuaded him to let us finish the app, if only to show what we could do. But since the bureaucrats had taken a shot at us, Raj decided to shoot back: he suggested that if our app was a success, Goldfein should move the entire CAOC project away from Hanscom and give it to DIUx.

"These guys have been working for eight years and they have little to show for it. They've burned three-quarters of a billion dollars. We can hire coders in Silicon Valley and get this whole thing done in one-tenth the time and one-tenth the cost," Raj said.

Goldfein wasn't willing to go that far. But he let us finish the tanker app. And once it was up and running, everyone in the CAOC loved it. While Wert was not thrilled at the time, he later became a true believer and supporter of the DIUx method. The incident highlighted the lack of trust and understanding between the two worlds and the time it would take to build a working collaboration.

"Raj, we really appreciate your help," Wert said. "Your guys have done a great job on this product demo."

"It's not a demo," Raj said. "It's live. It's working. The guys love it."

"Sure. But it's a one-off. It doesn't fit with the rest of what we're doing. That said, you've got some great ideas. We'll definitely incorporate some of those ideas into our broader program."

We were furious. So were the airmen who were using the app, and so was General Harrigian. Our software was helping his airmen manage the highest-tempo air force operation in history. There was no way he'd let them turn it off and go back to using whiteboards. But the air force was loath to switch away from their established program. To be fair, we weren't entirely surprised by the way things were playing out. We'd been around the Pentagon long enough to know how the game was played. It was a place where if you built a better mousetrap, the world did not beat a path to your door but instead might nail your door shut. Wert's team was three years behind schedule and over budget, but had spent eight years on this massive enterprise and wasn't going to let a bunch of outsiders derail their program.

A *Star Wars* fan, Raj liked to think of DIUx as part of the Rebel Alliance. When we delivered the tanker app, we felt like Luke Skywalker dropping a proton torpedo into an exhaust port of the Death Star. But the exhilaration was short-lived, and we now found ourselves at the remote edge of the galaxy on a planet covered in ice and snow.

PIZZAGATE

It didn't help that at this very moment Chris was quoted in the press calling the sitting chairman of the Joint Chiefs of Staff "weak on strategic thinking." The AP news story broke on a Sunday evening, the latest from a trove of hacked emails from John Podesta, Hillary Clinton's campaign chairman. "Stolen emails released by WikiLeaks on Sunday revealed a March 30, 2015, email from Christopher Kirchhoff to top Clinton campaign aide John Podesta that offered stark opinions about the nation's top military leaders," the story began.

The "WikiLeaks" episode was in fact a Russian disinformation operation designed to influence the 2016 election. A Russian cyber spy group nicknamed Fancy Bear had hacked Podesta's Gmail earlier that year. Thirty minutes after the *Access Hollywood* tape broke—in which candidate Trump used derogatory language about women—Wikileaks dumped twenty thousand pages of Podesta's emails into the public domain. It was a classic distraction play. Rather than reporting solely on Trump's "locker room banter," as the candidate called it, the press was now having a field day with everything from Podesta's campaign strategy memos to his tips for making creamy risotto.

It took reporters three weeks to find an email Chris had long planned to send only to Podesta's White House account. Chris had worked for Podesta when the latter was President Obama's counselor. Podesta was someone who took an interest in military affairs. He had asked for Chris's honest opinion of the four finalists to be the Chairman of the Joint Chiefs of Staff. Chris wrote up a memo, knowing Podesta would likely share it with President Obama, and possibly also Hillary Clinton, who, if elected, would inherit Obama's choice for chairman.

It was a mad dash for the exit on Podesta's last day at the White House. He was leaving in the morning to become chairman of Hillary's campaign. Burning the midnight oil, he was still furiously trying to close out White House business. Chris sat in his NSC office that evening waiting for him to skim the memo, which was full of frank observations Chris had gleaned from watching the four candidates up close. Eight o'clock came, then nine, then ten, then eleven. "Chris," Podesta's assistant finally said, "he's not going to get to it before midnight. Just send it to his Gmail."

Chris paused and thought to himself—cursor hovering over the send button—"This is a very bad idea." It was a no-no to send such a sensitive assessment to a non-government account. Chris was already over his skis sharing his views with Podesta, his old boss, without clearing it with his new boss, the national security advisor. But it was late, he was exhausted, and what was he to do? Podesta was both President Obama's closest advisor and Hillary's campaign chairman. He wanted the memo.

As the AP story generated others and reporters began to ring Chris, alarmed friends from all over Washington reached out. "Obama NSC staffer meddling in military affairs" is not the kind of accusation the brass takes lightly.

"Raj," Chris began when his DIUx partner picked up the phone, "we have a problem."

"Okay," Raj said after hearing the details. "Guess we'll be hiding you from Dunford's office for a long time."

With real and doctored emails dumped all at once, Podesta was by that point encircled by QAnon conspiracy theories. Chris now got a taste of the dark currents coursing through American politics. Death threats poured into his inbox and threatening calls to his personal cell phone. The election, seven days away, would be won by Trump. Podesta would no longer have influence, and now General Joe Dunford, whom President Obama had selected as Chairman, had read stories about what the DIUx guys really thought of him.

Could DIUx survive this?

Would Goldfein forget about our tanker project so as not to upset Dunford, his new boss?

But then, after a few tough months, the CAOC project—and DIUx by extension—caught a lucky break—a very Washington turn of fortune. One day in the spring of 2017, Matt Donovan, a senior aide to Senator John McCain and former fighter pilot—call sign "Gorilla"—happened to be visiting the CAOC. General Harrigian, a savvy operator, showed Donovan our software and explained that while he'd been waiting eight years for Hanscom's team to deliver, our DIUx crew had finished a product in three months and for just over a million bucks, and it was up and working and the airmen loved it. When Donovan asked Harrigian what he thought about the overhaul that Hanscom and Northrop Grumman had been running, the general didn't mince words: "It's time to kill that thing," he said. Harrigian was adamant about keeping our code running. "We're going to save lives. We're going to make the user experience better, and ultimately we're going to be more effective. And I don't know why people are fighting me on this." Harrigian also told Donovan that he'd like us to do more projects in the CAOC. "This is good, and we can take it to the next level. This is giving us the opportunity to see what the future could look like."

MEETING A MAVERICK

Donovan returned to Washington and told McCain who we were and what we'd done. McCain was the ranking member of the Senate Armed Services Committee, which controls the Pentagon's budget, and as it happens was in the middle of weighing the request from Wert and the air force to pony up another $65 million to keep the CAOC overhaul project alive.

"You should talk to this guy Raj who's running DIUx," Donovan told McCain. "He's a fighter pilot. From what I hear he's a guy who is not afraid to bend rules to get things done."

"All right, let's get him in," McCain said.

For DoD employees, speaking with McCain was like getting an audience with the Pope. Under ordinary circumstances such a visit would require weeks of preparation. Legislative aides on the senator's side and the Secretary of Defense's side would negotiate the parameters of the meeting, and who would be in attendance. People in the Secretary of Defense's office would determine what information could be released by the Pentagon. Given McCain's iron grip on the Pentagon's purse, an entire binder full of talking points and background materials would be created to ensure no one went off script. Minders would take copious notes.

Most significant: under ordinary rules of engagement, the Secretary of Defense's legislative affairs staff would run everything by the air force's legislative affairs staff. But if we'd done that, the very people who were trying to block us would have tried to cancel the meeting or send enough "handlers" that our message wouldn't have been delivered unvarnished.

So we didn't do any of that.

Instead, without coordinating with anyone, Raj simply flew to Washington and walked into McCain's office in the Russell Senate Office Building at the appointed time, by himself. The only other person in the room was Christian Brose, McCain's top defense aide. The walls were hung with photos of McCain's family, portraits of his father and grandfather, both four-star admirals, and the famous images of McCain returning from captivity in Vietnam, where he was held prisoner for six years, beaten, tortured, and left with lifelong disabilities. McCain had been a senator for thirty years and was one of the most powerful figures in government. But there was still some sailor in him.

"So, Brose tells me you're a fighter pilot," McCain said.

"Yes, sir."

"Navy?"

"Air force."

"Air force? Well, don't be too embarrassed. You guys aren't as soft as people say."

The stereotype about air force pilots is that they're well-mannered gentlemen who have cushy lives, play by the rules, and serve in the "Chair Force." Navy pilots, meanwhile, are foulmouthed yahoos who can slam a fighter jet down onto the three-hundred-foot pitching deck of an aircraft carrier at one hundred and fifty miles per hour. At night. In a monsoon.

"And you've got those pretty air bases," McCain said. "And nice golf courses."

"And long runways," Raj said. He'd heard all the jokes before.

"Right," McCain said, smiling. He turned to Brose. "I like this guy. He's all right."

McCain gestured for Raj to sit down on the leather couch across from him. "So tell me what's going on. Who are you guys? What do you do?"

Raj gave a little background on DIUx and the mission that Ash Carter had given us to find ways to modernize the military and get things moving at Silicon Valley speed. Then he explained how the tanker refueling app worked, and how the airmen and General Harrigian in charge of the CAOC loved it.

"But the guys at Hanscom who are running the tech program at the CAOC want to boot you out."

"That's right."

"And they're taking what you did, trying to call it a demo, take it offline, and want to do the rest business as usual."

"Yes, sir."

"So what do you want?"

Raj wasn't sure whether to press his luck. But then he figured, why the hell not? "Honestly, sir, what I want is for us to take over the whole project. Not just this app, but the entire overhaul of the CAOC. We can overhaul the whole place. We'll do it in two years, and for one-tenth of what they're spending."

"You can do that?"

"Absolutely. But at the very least I want you to stop them from rolling back the work we've done, and make sure the rest of the overhaul proceeds using modern software engineering practices, not the obsolete approach the taxpayer has bought so far."

McCain looked at Brose. Brose shrugged. McCain thought for a moment, then said, "Okay."

"Really?" Raj was taken aback.

"I'm frustrated with these guys. They've spent more than a half billion dollars, and now they're back asking for another $65 million, so they can keep doing whatever it is they've been doing for the past eight years, which as far as I can tell is a whole bunch of nothing. So that's it. They're done."

McCain stood up—the signal that the meeting was over.

"You keep delivering on what you're doing, and I'll make sure you get all the resources you need," he said.

Raj walked out of the Russell Building feeling a little bit dazed. *Did that just happen? Was it really that easy?* To be sure, he was going to get an earful from the legislative affairs folks for sidestepping the rules and protocols and having the temerity to walk into a senator's office without telling anyone. Maybe he could play dumb. Or maybe he could point out that by going rogue he was doing exactly what Ash Carter had hired him to do. This was the Silicon Valley way: better to beg forgiveness than to ask permission.

A week later, McCain oversaw a budget hearing of the Senate Armed

Services Committee. Acting secretary of the air force Lisa Disbrow ran through her presentation. When she got to the request for an additional $65 million, McCain put the hammer down. There would be no extra money. The overhaul could continue, but only if Wert and his team worked with DIUx and learned to do things our way.

That was in April 2017. A few months later, in July, the decision to keep the DIUx app was made public. McCain and Senator Jack Reed issued a statement slamming the program: "It is unfortunate that the Air Force had already spent more than half a billion dollars over the last ten years . . . and yet the program has not delivered any meaningful capability. Even more unfortunately, this program is only one example of the Department's troubling record on software-intensive systems."

This was a big win for us. To be sure, McCain wasn't putting us in charge of the CAOC overhaul. Wert and his team were still in charge, but they had to work with us. And this was going to be awkward. Wert disliked us for going behind his back to McCain. At the same time, we resented Wert for lobbying to kick us out of the CAOC in the first place.

To smooth things over, we turned to Enrique Oti, the career air force officer at Moffett Field who'd assembled the team of engineers that built the tanker refueling app. Enrique had been in the air force for twenty years, and he was skilled in the art of Pentagon diplomacy. Though we had a lot to teach the air force about writing software, Enrique knew we'd only get that chance if we helped Wert pick up the broken glass, together. To broker the peace, he invited Wert and his team to San Francisco and rolled out the red carpet for them at our offices at Moffett Field. We wanted them to see that we came in peace, and that we could be useful to them. Our offices looked like a startup, not an air force facility. Enlisted air force programmers in jeans and hoodies (not exactly military dress code) worked at open tables instead of in cubicles, collaborating on projects using modern software tools and a lean startup methodology. Chris's golden retriever roamed the halls. The woman who ran our software demo had blue hair, which most definitely didn't comply with the military's grooming and appearance standards.

Maybe Wert figured he had no choice but to work with us, since Senator McCain had taken our side. Or maybe he truly became born again in the waters of Silicon Valley and was impressed by how quickly we could write apps. Whatever the reason, Wert and his team agreed to work with us, to adopt our methods and start writing software the way startups do.

Going significantly further, Wert and his team sat down with Enrique and decided to create an air force "software factory," based in Boston, that would operate like a tech startup, with a mix of airmen and civilian programmers using modern software development tools and the lean methodology. Wert quickly transformed from our nemesis into one of DIUx's strongest supporters and collaborators, further evidence that most people in the Department are true patriots trying to do the right thing but trapped in a bureaucracy that creates perverse incentives. Wert and Enrique named the team Kessel Run, a reference to the speed record that Han Solo brags about in *Star Wars*: "You've never heard of the *Millennium Falcon*? It's the ship that made the Kessel Run in less than twelve parsecs!" General Goldfein, the chief of staff of the air force, was so impressed by our tanker refueling project that he tapped Enrique as Kessel Run's first leader. Over the next few years, with Wert's support, the Kessel Run coders and other coders inside and outside the Department of Defense collaboratively rebuilt the entire CAOC system, finishing toward the end of 2022.

In August 2021, during the evacuation of Kabul, an Afghan woman named Worahmeena and her five-day-old son, Mustafa, were airlifted on a C-17 transport aircraft out of Hamid Karzai Airport and flown to Ramstein Air Base in Germany, headed eventually to the United States. They'd just spent four days—the first four days of Mustafa's life—sleeping outdoors among thousands of refugees who were hoping to escape the Taliban as the U.S. withdrew its forces from Afghanistan. Now they were sleeping on the floor of an aircraft hangar, but soon they would begin a new life. "I plan to build a life for my son and his siblings in America," Worahmeena told a National Public Radio reporter.

She couldn't know this, but she and tens of thousands of others who managed to get out of Kabul owed some of their thanks to a small team of coders at Kessel Run, and a software app called Slapshot, a "mission and air-combat sortie flow organizer" they created to handle planning operations in the CAOC in Qatar. Like our tanker refueling app, Slapshot replaced a kludgy manual process in which airmen previously had used Excel spreadsheets and Gantt charts. That piece of software enabled the CAOC to coordinate the largest noncombat evacuation in history, when more than 120,000 Americans and Afghans were airlifted from Kabul. For two weeks, aircraft were leaving Hamid Karzai Airport every forty-five minutes. Slapshot tracked planes in crowded airspace and maintained passenger manifests.

To be sure, the U.S. withdrawal from Afghanistan was marred by mistakes. But lost amid all the finger-pointing that took place in Washington was that fact that rank-and-file U.S. service members had performed one of the greatest logistical feats in history, under tremendous pressure and constant risk of attack by ISIS terrorists and other adversaries of the U.S. Those service members didn't get the thanks and recognition they deserved.

Six thousand miles from Kabul, programmers at Kessel Run in Boston were working around the clock during the airlift, updating the Slapshot app and iterating on the fly to accommodate new needs and the sudden increase in demand. Those software engineers had the rare and indescribably gratifying experience of seeing their work saving lives, in real time. Software engineers can make a lot of money at Google or Facebook, but they'll never know that feeling.

Kessel Run is headquartered in an office building near Boston's

Financial District, in a space that a VC would mistake for an early-stage startup. Since launching in 2018, Kessel Run has opened offices at Hanscom and Langley Air Force Bases, and now employs twelve hundred people, of whom four hundred are programmers, well beyond the scale of what our original forty-member team at DIUx could have dreamed of. Some coders are air force reservists who were working in tech but returned to active duty to serve two-year stints at Kessel Run. A whiteboard in the Kessel Run engineering room bears a reminder of the group's ambitious—perhaps audacious—vision: "Deliver combat capability that can sense and respond to conflict in any domain, anytime, anywhere."

The commander of Kessel Run during the Kabul airlift was air force colonel Brian Beachkofski, aka "Beach," who has a Ph.D. in engineering, an MBA from MIT, and experience working as a tech venture capitalist and startup advisor. When Chris visited Beach toward the end of 2021, the Kessel Run commander tried to sound positive but admitted that he often felt frustrated. He and his team constantly ran into the "frozen middle" that we'd encountered—where the generals at the top and the coders at the bottom agree on a plan, but the people in between get in the way. Battling with Pentagon bureaucracy is exhausting. Even when people have good intentions, it's hard to get anything done with so much complexity and so many layers. When people don't share your intentions, that frozen middle provides limitless opportunities for obstruction.

A few months after Chris visited Beach, in April 2022, the Kessel Run commander, after just two years at the helm, left to became chief technology officer of a sports betting company. Like us, Beach had gone in wanting to make a difference—and he *did* make a difference—but eventually a role that by design cut across the institutional grain wore him down.

For our part, we tried to stay focused on the positives and hoped the culture would gradually change.

Simultaneous with DIUx's work at the CAOC, dozens of other projects were, in fact, underway, from space to cyber, from robots to human performance. In that first year, we were laser focused on putting points on the board, delivering innovation to warfighters, and justifying our existence to our budgetary overlords in the four congressional committees that had purview over DIUx. After signing contract after contract, in 2016 we opened new offices in Boston and Austin. Raj continued his charm offensive with Congressional staffers, flying to Washington weekly.

The U.S. fiscal year starts in October of every year, and each department needs its appropriations bill passed by Congress and signed by the President by October 1. But the DoD budget is rarely passed on time—it's happened in only four of the past eighteen years—and Congress usually passes a continuing resolution, legislation that forestalls a government shutdown but also prevents things called "new starts." This unfortunately hampers the DoD's ability to start and fund new weapons programs on time.

The budget battle in 2016 and the ensuing continuing resolution gave DIUx a crucial few extra months to overturn the proposed zeroization. Raj fundamentally believed that congressional leaders wanted and understood the need to modernize our military, but that DIUx had been caught between misunderstanding and mistrust, much of it driven by the unwillingness of the Secretary's legislative staff to have direct and transparent conversations with Congress before DIUx 2.0 was launched.

In the fall of 2016, Raj scored a coup: he secured a one-on-one with Mac Thornberry, a Republican congressman from Texas who chaired the House Armed Services Committee. Thornberry hadn't been a big fan of DIUx initially. He questioned why the DoD needed it when they already had DARPA. His staff had told him it was a vanity project with limited ability to make a difference for our troops. Thornberry asked Raj to come over for a one-hour meeting with just the two of them, no staffers from either side. Raj explained our vision, our initial successes, and why engaging with commercial innovation was so important to national defense.

It worked. On the spot Thornberry pledged to help overturn Evelyn and Ed's zeroization of DIUx. He agreed to support us and ensure our budget grew so we had the opportunity to put our vision into reality. As with the McCain meeting, Raj had had to go rogue and engage the Hill on his own.

In recalling that meeting, Thornberry said, "I appreciated Raj's vision for the organization and his willingness to come by my office and explain to me directly why this was a good investment for the American taxpayer. I'm proud to have supported him and proud of what DIUx has done for our men and women in uniform."

CHAPTER FOUR
A NEW KILL CHAIN FOR NORTH KOREA

In the summer of 2016, DIUx was called into a mission so secret we could only talk about its full contours inside a SCIF, or sensitive compartmented information facility, an enclosed area built to resist surveillance and prevent electrical or radio signals from leaking to the outside world. The mission involved finding new technology that could stop a nuclear missile before it was launched, saving an American city.

"The President himself is pushing for this," Reuben Sorensen, an advisor to the Vice Chairman of the Joint Chiefs of Staff, said, kicking off the meeting. "It's a top five national security priority."

Sorensen and Ryan Farris, a navy commander serving as a military assistant to the Deputy Secretary of Defense, had both supported the stand-up of DIUx. They were meeting with Raj in a SCIF deep inside the Joint Staff offices in the Pentagon.

"The problem is North Korea," Farris said. "We know they have nukes. Now Kim Jong-un is developing ballistic missiles that can strike the West Coast of the United States."

"This," Sorensen said, putting an image onto the screen on the wall, "is the KN-08. It's a road-mobile intercontinental ballistic missile that can carry a nuclear warhead. With it, Kim can potentially wipe out Seattle or even Los Angeles." Sorensen clicked to the next photo: an image of a missile on its flatbed launcher, nestled in North Korea's steep, plentiful mountainous terrain. Stashing truck-mounted ICBMs in bunkers dug from granite was a low-cost way to hide their position from a pre-emptive enemy strike.

"The problem is that we can't see exactly where the North Koreans are keeping the missiles, how often they move them, and when they're being readied for launch. We're basically flying blind."

Sorensen and Farris were part of a special task force, created in an office called J-39, to find a solution to the problem of pinpointing KN-08s. They were reaching out to DIUx hoping that we could find a company in Silicon Valley able to launch a constellation of microsatellites to keep North Korea under constant surveillance. These satellites needed to have something that hadn't yet been invented—a miniaturized synthetic aperture radar (SAR) sensor that provides highly detailed images by bouncing radar waves off the earth's surface from space. SAR sensors can spot mobile missile launchers through all weather, day and night.

Sorensen was a boyish-looking guy in his late thirties, a civilian who had a Ph.D. in nuclear engineering from the University of Michigan. He'd been one of the wizards who developed technical countermeasures for the SEALs in Virginia Beach, until being asked to take over some of the most sensitive operations on the Joint Staff. It was a promotion, to be sure, but a mixed one, moving from the hardest-charging unit in the military to the headquarters of what his command called "the consultants of slow."

"I figured we could see North Korea all the time," Raj said.

"You mean like in the movies?" Farris said, smirking.

Farris reminded him that North Korea was covered in clouds roughly two hundred days a year.

Raj was shocked when Farris gave him exact figures about how poor our satellite coverage of North Korea was. Raj had known it wasn't like a James Bond movie, where you zoom in on any location and watch people moving around in real time. *But really?* Raj sat there thinking, *North Korea is mostly a black hole to us?*

The rogue state obtained Pakistan's nuclear technology in the late 1990s. In 2006 it tested its first bomb in tunnels dug into seven-thousand-foot Mount Mantapsan. By 2014 the intelligence community believed the North Koreans had created a nuclear warhead small enough to be carried by a ballistic missile. In 2016, North Korea fired five missiles in a test of its capabilities. In 2017, North Korea claimed to have detonated a hydrogen bomb—a device a thousand times more powerful. Officials in the U.S. and South Korea were skeptical of the claim, but whatever kind of detonation it was, a study published in the journal *Science* determined the test "made the mountain bulge sideways by about twelve feet and collapse vertically by a foot and a half."

The real problem began when North Korea developed the ability to build multiple missiles that could carry warheads over the Pacific Ocean and potentially defeat our missile defense system if they were launched all at once. Kim Jong-un could decide to wake up one morning and nuke the West Coast. The worry became a preoccupation of the National Security Council and the President, who regularly engaged Vice Chairman of the Joint Chiefs Paul Selva about it.

Finding the right technology to spot the location of these missiles was only part of the challenge that DIUx would face. The other was that a cadre of powerful players inside the Pentagon and intelligence community became determined to kill the project we ultimately backed. It's not that they wanted North Korea to succeed. Rather, our project arose at an inconvenient time. The National Reconnaissance Office had already funded a separate program to build new SAR satellites that could surveil North Korea. But that project had begun to flounder. Influential people inside the DoD, including Stephanie O'Sullivan, the principal deputy director of national intelligence and a longtime CIA veteran, worried that a request to fund an untested microsatellite constellation might unsettle Congress as it was about to approve a long-debated spy satellite program.

We'd also eventually find ourselves up against the Pentagon's built-in bias against relying on technology from the commercial sector. That was especially the case with things like spy satellites. The Pentagon liked to use exquisite "bespoke" solutions, meaning equipment that was funded entirely by the Pentagon and built to its exact specifications, and only for its use. The Pentagon's intelligence community was uneasy buying imagery from a commercial company that could sell the same products to other customers. Most of the intel brass also believed that Silicon Valley products were prone to failure, something you couldn't afford in a high-stakes-use case like monitoring nuclear weapons.

At the same time, Silicon Valley offered some advantages. Their products cost less and were completed in much less time. Sorensen and Farris believed the new approach they were building would surpass all expectations if DIUx could help them find microsatellites able to hunt missile launchers.

There was no time to lose.

"The primes are projecting that their solution will cost a few billion dollars," Sorensen said.

"Which probably means six billion," Raj interrupted.

"Or ten," Farris said, nodding.

"And they're saying it will take seven to ten years," Sorensen said.

"Which probably means never," Farris said.

"Anyway, we can't wait ten years to solve this problem," Sorensen said. "We needed this capability yesterday."

As it happened, the head of DIUx's Space Portfolio, Colonel Steve "Bucky" Butow, had already stumbled on a tiny startup that was designing a SAR satellite that could solve the KN-08 problem.

"We can do this for you," Raj said.

"Seriously?"

"And our solution will cost one one-thousandth of what the primes are doing, and we can deliver it in a year."

"Honestly," Farris said, "that sounds impossible."

"That's what DIUx does," Raj said. "We make the impossible possible."

What Raj didn't know—what none of us could have imagined—was the ferocity of the opposition we were soon to encounter.

Spying from the sky has been at the center of national security for seventy years. The United States Air Force started developing reconnaissance satellites in 1955, two years before the Soviets launched Sputnik. The first U.S. reconnaissance satellite, the KH-1 Corona, took photographs that were ejected in film canisters which floated back to earth under parachutes and were caught in air by specially modified air force aircraft. Spy satellite technology soon went digital and beyond optics, to include sensors that detected the launch of ballistic missiles or a nuclear explosion and eavesdropped on the other side's communications. Spy satellites remain one of the most powerful technologies in superpowers' arsenals, so much so that their development, and exact capabilities, remain cloaked in the highest levels of secrecy.

The U.S. had long invested in ballistic missile defenses for just the kind of scenario North Korea now presented. The Nike air defense system, dating to 1953, was the mainstay of early approaches, with many variations and new programs launched over the decades that followed. The most ambitious came to be known as "Star Wars." Announced in 1983 by President Ronald Reagan, the Strategic Defense Initiative was a program to put lasers and particle-beam weapons into a fleet of orbiting killer satellites that would blast incoming missiles out of the sky. Four years later, after some thrilling artist renditions of what Star Wars could do, the American Physical Society issued its opinion that the whiz-bang technologies at the heart of Star Wars were decades away from being ready to use. A key figure behind exposing that the program was too good to be true? Our benefactor, Ash Carter, the creator of DIUx.

By the late 1980s Star Wars had evolved into "Brilliant Pebbles," a concept that used small orbiting missiles fired out of killer satellites like smart buckshot. This too never achieved operational capability. However, by 2016 the U.S. had deployed a new system that comprised ground stations and interceptor missiles, mainly in Alaska, and a network of space-based satellite systems that detected a missile launch. Unlike Star Wars, this system worked. Not every intercept was a success, and it was incredibly expensive, but there was a high percentage of successful intercepts.

Even so, when Raj was meeting with Sorensen and Farris, the worry was that the North Koreans might be able to deploy ten or even twenty KN-08 missiles at the same time, which raised the possibility of our defenses being overwhelmed. Our interceptors might take out most, but we probably couldn't get them all.

The best way to ensure nothing got through our missile defense system was to find a way to kill every KN-08 missile before it got off the ground. In Pentagon parlance this is called a "left-of-launch" solution. But the window to detect the North Koreans moving mobile launchers out of concealment and preparing to launch was incredibly brief. The time it takes to bring the missile out of hiding, fuel it, and then fire it is measured in minutes, not hours. Over the years North Korea had become highly skilled at evading detection of its impending launches. It hid its missiles and artillery batteries in caves carved into mountainsides and frequently moved them from location to location, with many more hiding places than launchers, creating a kind of shell game that U.S. and South Korean intelligence would attempt to pierce. Over decades of paranoid preparation for another war, North Korea had become better at playing the shell game than our intelligence agencies were at decoding it.

As the urgency ramped up, North Korea became a priority for military leaders like Admiral Sandy Winnefeld, Selva's predecessor as Vice Chairman of the Joint Chiefs.

"We had a good 'right-of-launch' solution, namely, ballistic missile defense, but we were worried that they would outpace us in quantity," Winnefeld recalls. Winnefeld's staff had created a graph that compared the potential growth of KN-08 quantities to projections over time of how many missiles we'd be able to counter. The graph showed that in a short period of time, North Korea would have sufficient KN-08 missiles to overwhelm our defenses. It was the same issue that decades before had caused Secretary of Defense Robert McNamara, in the mid-1960s, to sour on the Nike anti-ballistic missile system when it became apparent that given the interception rate, the Soviets could simply flood the zone by launching more missiles.

Winnefeld believed our only recourse was to perfect a left-of-launch solution, giving defenders a brief opportunity in which to "get in the way of the North Koreans pulling a missile out of a tunnel, preparing it, and firing it," he remembers. To create a successful left-of-launch solution—to kill North Korean missiles before they could be launched—we needed to build better intelligence systems that could track them.

Instead of relying on a small number of "exquisite" satellites—the kind of beautiful, highly engineered, and enormously expensive devices that were built by the primes—Winnefeld thought the solution should involve a large number of low-cost satellites that might not have all the capability of the billion-dollar satellites but could be developed rapidly, be operational for a few years, and then replaced by upgraded versions with even better sensors and technology. What he cared most about was the ability to have satellites fly over North Korea more frequently, which in Pentagon parlance was called having a high "revisit rate."

Besides, the world of aerospace was changing. Space launch and satellite operations had once been controlled by NASA and the military, but the success of new players such as SpaceX, Planet Labs, Blue Origin, and others was already disrupting and transforming the fundamentals of the space industry. The government no longer shouldered the cost of building spacecraft as it had done with the Mercury and Apollo missions in the 1960s. By the 2010s, the government was just another customer of commercial launch companies that could get payloads into space cheaper than NASA. SpaceX could even do it for a fraction of the cost of United Launch Alliance, a consortium of Lockheed Martin and Boeing. Every month there seemed to be a new well-financed launch or satellite startup with a novel technical approach that was on its way to providing capabilities that hadn't previously existed. This trend has continued, and in 2023, SpaceX launched 80 percent of all mass to space globally.

That's why Winnefeld had assembled the J-39 SWAT team led by Sorensen and Farris to comb the globe for alternate solutions, after realizing that the solutions proposed by the intelligence community weren't keeping up with the speed with which the North Korean nuclear strike capability was advancing. Sorensen and Farris could tolerate less exacting technical standards than the intelligence community sought, as long as they were collecting a lot of data with a high revisit rate.

To defend against an attack by North Korea, the Joint Staff had first turned to big data and machine learning, using newly powerful computer chips and algorithms to mine massive data sets compiled from many different sources, including unclassified commercial data on North Korea that revealed the daily pattern of life. The tireless machines that ingested this data looked for signals that correlated with North Korean preparations for launch. The experimental system was called Datahub. Sorensen stood up Datahub within J-39, and drawing on technologies from DIUx portfolio companies, he had worked for over a year to refine it. Now that Datahub was up and running, the next step was to supercharge it by feeding lots of imagery data into the model, which would enable us to detect even faint signals of launch preparation in North Korea.

Near-continuous real-time surveillance through snow and clouds is impossible to accomplish with conventional optical satellites. But SAR can do it by collecting echoes of electromagnetic signals and processing them into visual data. Like bats making pictures of their surroundings with sound, SAR "sees" by bouncing radio waves off the ground, and extrapolating the shape and position of objects on it through the measure of the time it takes for those outgoing signals to reflect back to its sensors.

SAR was not new. Research on it began at Goodyear after World War II, when the typical radar antenna was the size of a house. Lockheed Martin took over SAR R&D in the 1950s and tested an airborne system called "Douser," which was the first to create an image of terrain features, initially being able to discern those over five hundred feet across and soon picturing fifty-foot objects through darkness or cloud cover. In the 1960s Lockheed deployed a SAR sensor on its SR-71 Blackbird, which gave the plane the ability to "see" thirty-foot-diameter objects one hundred miles away while flying fifteen miles above targets at three times the speed of sound. Further improvements in SAR could penetrate the foliage of a jungle and distinguish between a tree trunk and an enemy howitzer.

What was missing in this long available technology was affordability and miniaturization. The sheer size of the SAR satellites made them expensive, which meant very few could be built. "The biggest problem was that we needed more SAR data, and the intelligence community wasn't providing enough of it to feed the Datahub project," Farris remembers. Out in Palo Alto, California, there was a young energetic entrepreneur who was trying to build that exact thing. His name was Payam Banazadeh, and he'd just finished graduate school at Stanford and raised seed funding for a company he named Capella, the sixth brightest star in the night sky. This was the startup DIUx Space Portfolio leader Bucky Butow had discovered.

Butow was a fifty-ish Air National Guard colonel. He had started his career as a Special Operations C-130 pilot and eventually commanded the air wing that ran all rescue missions for military personnel in Afghanistan, but had also worked at the Search for Extraterrestrial Intelligence Institute (SETI) and done a stint at the NASA Ames Research Center developing instrument concepts for Mars surface soil analysis. One of the first to see value in applying Silicon Valley technology to military missions, he'd been hosting monthly beer sessions with investors, entrepreneurs, and military leaders since 2010. When DIUx was created, he was the first senior military officer to sign on. His brilliant work leading the Space Portfolio ultimately earned him his first star—a promotion to brigadier general, and his second star, to major general, in 2023.

"Can Capella deliver a product in a year?" Raj asked Butow when he returned from Washington.

Butow explained that Banazadeh had come up with a great idea, and if it worked it would be a major breakthrough. "But he hasn't even built a prototype. He doesn't have a final design yet. He's never built a company. And he's twenty-four years old," Butow said.

"He sounds perfect," Raj replied.

Banazadeh is an Iranian-born immigrant and brilliant engineer who studied Aerospace, Aeronautical, and Astronautical Engineering at the University of Texas in Austin and as an undergraduate worked as an intern at the legendary NASA Jet Propulsion Laboratory (JPL), which put rovers on Mars and sent probes to the edges of the solar system. Upon graduation, Banazadeh joined JPL to lead deep space exploration missions. From there, he moved to the Stanford Space Rendezvous Lab, which does cutting-edge research in small satellite design, while simultaneously getting a master's degree in Management Science and Engineering.

Banazadeh's interest in SAR satellites was sparked by the March 2014 disappearance of Malaysia Airlines Flight 370 in the southern Indian Ocean with 227 passengers and 12 crew members aboard. Investigators spent three years searching unsuccessfully for wreckage of the plane before giving up. Banazadeh, who was working at JPL on space satellites when the plane went missing, was astonished. "The question that I was asking, as a space guy, was 'Hey, what are we doing to monitor our planet from space today? What is the state of the art, and why is it that I'm not seeing multiple pictures of that area every day all the time, and why is the search and rescue not really involving the space assets or capabilities?' And as I pulled that thread, what was very clear to me is that we're actually not that great when it comes to surveillance from space."

Indeed, even with hundreds of satellites in orbit that look back at earth, the aerial surveillance of the planet was spotty and crude. To Banazadeh, the disappearance of Malaysian Airlines Flight 370 and the fruitless attempts to determine its fate in the weeks that followed felt like a challenge. "I knew there's a bunch of optical-based satellites and there's more and more of them going up all the time. But there are significant limitations to optical satellites. You can't see at night; you can't see through clouds." Instead of optics and light, Banazadeh turned to SAR, which allows you to do imaging much more reliably. Having spotted an opportunity, Banazadeh went to Stanford to learn more about SAR technology while also learning how to build a company. Stanford has one of the best SAR research groups in the world. Banazadeh started sitting in on their meetings to learn how the technology worked and what challenges existed. "It was a personal journey I went through," he recalls. "And at a very high level, I had a conceptual idea on how to do SAR with a small satellite as opposed to one of these massive, billion-dollar satellites."

Traditional SAR designs required a giant antenna and lots of power. As a result, SAR satellites had remained physically large and expensive to launch. Since the early 2000s, commercial satellite companies in Silicon Valley had launched thousands of small satellites, but only a handful had SAR imaging.

During his time at JPL, Banazadeh had specialized in finding ways to pack a lot of capabilities into small satellites. One project he worked on was called Lunar Flashlight, a mission to send a very small satellite, the size of a camping backpack, to the moon. The satellite would be powered with solar sails, which flip out and catch radiation from the sun, propelling the craft forward. Banazadeh reckoned he could use the same idea to make solar arrays powering tiny SAR satellites. Smaller not only meant cheaper, it meant you could launch more of them. If he succeeded, Banazadeh would bring the design features and cost structure of SAR down to the same economies of scale propelling the commercial space revolution forward.

Banazadeh had explained this concept to Butow at a coffee shop on University Avenue near the Stanford campus. Butow recommended Banazadeh take a course at Stanford called Hacking for Defense, which DIUx helped sponsor, and which was led by Steve Blank, the legendary entrepreneur who'd pioneered the Lean methodology for building companies. Banazadeh joined Blank's class in the spring of 2016, his final semester at Stanford.

Blank is an air force veteran who during the Vietnam War worked as an electronics mechanic on Wild Weasel aircraft, the counter-electronic warfare planes with the motto "YGBSM," for "You Gotta Be Shittin' Me," which, as the story goes, is what one pilot exclaimed after hearing his job was to attract Soviet-made SAM missiles, get them to lock onto his plane, and then fire a radar-seeking missile to take out the SAM battery before the telephone pole–sized rocket could catch him.

Returning home, without a college education, Blank began his career in 1978 at ESL, a defense contractor that supplied intelligence and reconnaissance systems to the military. He went on to help start eight successful companies in Silicon Valley, taking one public. Now seventy years old, Blank has a shock of curly white hair, a beard, and the slightly disheveled look of a professor. He is passionate about defense and loves to remind people that the original version of Silicon Valley mainly comprised companies that sold technology to the military and intelligence communities, a history he catalogs in a presentation called "Hidden in Plain Sight: The Secret History of Silicon Valley." "Our roots are in defense," says Blank, whose experience in Vietnam and at ESL instilled in him a respect for the role Silicon Valley played in the national security of the United States. It bothers him that so many bright engineers steer away from creating products that could contribute to national security.

Blank's class at Stanford has spawned countless startups that sell to both commercial and defense customers, and the Hacking for Defense model has spread to other universities around the country. The main thing Blank teaches students is to avoid the mistake of starting out with a cool product idea; instead, go talk to customers, interview them, listen to them, and then build the product they need. "Working backward from the customer" is what we call it in Silicon Valley. Blank wrote a book, *Four Steps to the Epiphany* (which is also the textbook for his class), in which he distinguishes "between existing companies that execute business models versus startups that *search* for them—search versus execution is the concept that launched modern entrepreneurship."

During his semester at Stanford studying under Blank, Banazadeh went searching for a business model by interviewing more than one hundred people in government to find out how they might use SAR technology and what they needed. What he heard led him to the idea of developing small, relatively inexpensive satellites and launching a few dozen to form a constellation of all-seeing electronic eyes that could canvass the planet. By the time the semester ended, Banazadeh had raised $200,000 from venture investors, enough to start his company, Capella Space.

Butow followed Banazadeh's progress and in June 2016, he and Raj sat in on Banazadeh's final class presentation, in which he explained his technology and his business model. Butow was impressed with what he saw, as was Blank. A few months later, Butow went to see Banazadeh bearing some good news. "The DoD wants to buy SAR data," he said, leaving out any mention of North Korea and the special task force in J-39. "We're going to issue a solicitation. I'd like you to put in a proposal. I think Capella will be competitive and could be awarded a contract by DIUx."

DIUx issued the solicitation in September 2016. Capella was one of several companies that submitted proposals. Butow and Raj returned to Washington, told Sorensen and Farris that DIUx had found a potential supplier, and tried to lock down additional funding to make a big bet that Capella's technology could provide the breakthrough on North Korea that the Joint Staff sought. Sorensen, in turn, commissioned an outside analytical firm to conduct due diligence on Banazadeh's design. The analysis confirmed the claims Banazadeh was making—his technology seemed capable of achieving the very breakthroughs in function, size, and cost that many in the small, tightly knit SAR community had thought weren't possible.

THE BUREAUCRACY STRIKES BACK

Early in 2017 Raj and Butow traveled to Washington again, this time for a meeting with top military and intelligence officials to seek funding for Capella. The meeting was cochaired by Deputy Secretary of Defense Bob Work and the Vice Chairman of the Joint Chiefs of Staff Paul Selva: they were the ones who would decide whether to fund Capella.

Also present were the undersecretary of defense for intelligence, representatives from various intelligence agencies, the air force, and DARPA.

Sorensen and Farris presented their case to Work and Selva, arguing that the Pentagon should grant Capella a contract for $15 million so the company could build a prototype satellite. They explained Capella would complement the Datahub AI system and enable surveillance of North Korea. If things went well, the plan was to invest $50 million all told.

Butow, our satellite expert, walked the group through the prototype that Capella was designing for a backpack-sized satellite powered by solar energy. Banazadeh had already successfully tested one of his SAR sensors from an airplane, Butow explained. The next step was to build a prototype satellite and launch it into space.

Raj pointed out that a $15 million contract was tiny for the Pentagon, a rounding error on a rounding error as compared to each of DoD's billion-dollar bespoke spy satellites. If we could promise Capella that the DoD would become a customer, Banazadeh could raise millions in venture capital to fund his development. In effect, we'd be getting Silicon Valley investors to foot the vast majority of the R&D bill for developing satellites that we needed. If Capella failed, we lost $15 million. But if Capella succeeded, we'd have a constellation of tiny satellites that could potentially protect us from a nuclear attack.

Opposition was instantaneous, and it wasn't over the money.

Many of those in the room had just participated in a lengthy and exhaustive review, requested by Congress, whose goal was to decide how much of the SAR requirements of both the intelligence community and the military to fund. Exasperated staffers on the House and Senate committees kept receiving conflicting accounts of who wanted what and how much everything would cost. As soon as they thought they had a composite picture, some new request would flow in seeking additional capability for an urgent mission. SAR capability was expensive. Congress, together with the administration, had to make trade-offs on which new capabilities to fund. Each time Congress reviewed SAR capability, they also reevaluated whether it was worth continuing the billion-dollar SAR satellite program that was over budget and behind schedule—the program whose capabilities Sorensen and Farris had to find a replacement for since they needed data about North Korea now. The intelligence community had just convinced Congress to stay the course with the mega-project, but only by a hair.

What did this mean for DIUx's efforts to unlock a tactical picture of KN-08s?

It meant most people in the room were against it, because our little $15 million dollar pilot, if successful, might cause Congress to second-guess its continued support for the foundering mega-program and instead see our program as a partial replacement, because it provided some of the same capability at a fraction of the cost. Besides, in the view of the intelligence community's high priesthood of satellite reconnaissance, a pilot effort using unproven, inferior commercial technology was bound to fail anyway. Why take a technical risk that for them had a big political risk attached to it?

Turning to a startup did in fact add an element of risk. With Capella, the DoD would be buying the rights to data from the satellites, not the satellites themselves. Unlike a traditional defense contractor, Capella could still sell data to other customers, which could include commercial companies but also, with the proper permissions from the U.S. government, intelligence services and militaries of partners and allies. To some in the Pentagon, that commingling was scary, and perhaps understandably so.

"It was just so radioactive," Sorensen said. "The smallest amount of money I've seen cause such a huge headache."

Unexpectedly, all of the arguments *against* Capella failed.

Deputy Secretary of Defense Bob Work was not dissuaded. In his mind, space startups in Silicon Valley were where the action was, or at least where it was headed. Work endorsed the DIUx proposal to move to a full on-orbit demonstration of Capella's technology. "I'm in favor of moving forward," Vice Chairman Selva chimed in. Work and Selva were the two most powerful people in the room, and two of the most powerful people in the Pentagon—in the entire U.S. government for that matter. There'd be no more discussion: the Pentagon would send Raj the money.

As Raj and Butow rode in an Uber to the airport, Butow called Banazadeh, telling him he had a green light. "We'll have the contract paperwork for you soon," he said.

Banazadeh was ecstatic. So were we. This was a huge win for DIUx. We were doing what Ash Carter had enlisted us to do: harnessing the power of Silicon Valley to deliver critical new capabilities to the warfighter.

We had no idea at the time that a trip wire crossed our path, and we were about to walk straight into it. We left Washington feeling victorious, but it turned out the battle was only beginning.

SOUTH KOREA

Halfway around the world, Chris was walking through the streets of Seoul on a warm Saturday evening, coming to grips with what he'd learned in a classified briefing earlier that day with General Vincent Brooks, the commander of United States Forces Korea and the R.O.K.-Combined U.S. Forces Command. Brooks was a thirty-six-year army veteran with a distinguished record that began at West Point, where he was the very first African-American first captain, the highest position a cadet can hold. Later he became the youngest general officer in the history of the army. He was soft-spoken in a way you wouldn't expect given the responsibilities he shouldered.

Chris was in Korea to get a firsthand look at the problem DIUx would be solving with Capella. He was traveling with the Defense Innovation Board, who were assessing technological opportunities on the Korean Peninsula.

In his secure, windowless conference room, Brooks explained the risks he was most concerned about, and why the Capella SAR satellites would be a game changer. Brooks was just one of many combatant commanders who were expressing their support for DIUx and Capella to the Pentagon. Brooks even talked about creating a branch of DIUx located at his headquarters in Seoul so we could make things move faster.

"The North Koreans have hundreds of rocket and artillery launchers aimed at Seoul," Brooks said. "They have missiles in mountain complexes. They have underground bunkers. They've spent decades on secret construction." Because our satellite coverage was inadequate, "we could get into a very fast escalation cycle, and we don't have information dominance," Brooks said. It was an unnerving prospect. After the session with Brooks, the group met with intelligence squadrons at Pusan Air Base, which still operates the U-2 spy plane using new sensors bolted onto a Cold War airframe older than the parents of the pilot who flies it. Chris and the DIB also flew to a Korean army base on an island on the maritime border with North Korea, which had been shelled by the North in response to a South Korean military exercise earlier in the decade. The next day the group visited the Demilitarized Zone (DMZ), the no-man's-land between South Korea and North Korea. The DMZ was established in 1953 with the Armistice Agreement that brought about a cessation of fighting between the North and the South, albeit without officially declaring an end to the war. It's a strip of land about two and a half miles wide, with opposing militaries stationed on each side, both on a hair trigger. It's considered the most heavily fortified location in the world. Each year defectors try to cross under gunfire, with often tragic results.

Since the mid-1990s tension with North Korea had been growing. In 1994, Kim Jong-il expelled international nuclear inspectors and threatened to turn South Korea into a "sea of fire." In March 2010 things heated up again, when a South Korean navy vessel, the *Chenoan*, sank in the Yellow Sea, with forty-six lives lost. North Korea denied responsibility, but a team of international investigators determined a North Korean torpedo was responsible. In November 2010, in response to a South Korean artillery exercise in disputed waters near Yeonpyeong Island, North Korean military fired 170 artillery and rocket shells at the island. South Korea fired back at North Korean forces. The back-and-forth led to four deaths and twenty-two injured, as well as damage to the island, which Chris and the DIB were able to inspect firsthand. The incident took place just days after North Korea unveiled a new uranium enrichment facility, a threat serious enough that the South Korean government pondered asking the U.S. to station tactical nukes in South Korea. Soon thereafter Kim Jong-il announced that his son, Kim Jong-un, would be his successor as supreme leader of North Korea.

By the time Chris visited in 2017, Brooks assessed that Kim Jong-un had become more dangerous than his father, Kim Jong-il, or grandfather, Kim Il-sung. "We have a more virulent form of Kim," Brooks said. "Things are never going to be stable with North Korea. It's just not who they are. It's a wicked problem."

The U.S. command had a good idea of North Korea's capabilities, which put Seoul, a city of nearly 10 million people only thirty miles from the border, in constant danger. Bombardment—the North Koreans could fire sixteen thousand rounds an hour at Seoul alone—was only one threat. "There's another thing that keeps me awake at night. That's the threat of biological and chemical warfare," Brooks said.

The U.S. command knew how many rocket launchers North Korea possessed. They also knew how long it would take to get South Koreans into underground shelters once an attack began. Based on those figures it was entirely possible that, in the first hours of conflict, civilian casualty numbers would be in the millions. The conversation shifted to another grim topic—the mortuary capacity that would be required if Kim Jong-un ever decided to carry through on his plans to attack.

"If we can't stop them before they get into position to attack, the cost to life is extraordinarily high," Brooks said. Brooks urgently needed the left-of-launch solution that the SAR microsatellites could enable.

That night, Chris and the DIB entourage were treated to dinner with U.S. embassy and military personnel in a fashionable part of Seoul. Afterward, Chris went for a walk along the river and through the streets, drinking in the energy of a vibrant Saturday night in Seoul, seeing thousands of people out enjoying the evening in this thriving democracy, even as the war between the North and South was technically ongoing.

How did people go about their day-to-day lives, knowing this gleaming, modern city could so easily be turned into cinders? While everyone knew of the danger, few people wrestled with the intricate details that Chris and the others confronted in classified briefings. Thinking back on that conversation with Brooks gave Chris the chills, but also affirmed the importance of DIUx's work, not only for Americans but for people around the world who lived under the security umbrella the United States provides.

LAUNCHING CAPELLA

Back in Mountain View, in March 2017 Raj and Butow drew up a contract with Capella. The terms of the deal were that DIUx would pay Capella $10.4 million in tranches as the company hit defined milestones such as delivering images and demonstrating the system would work. "It was crawl, walk, run, but we were compressing the timeline down to eighteen months or less," Sorensen said.

The DIUx payments weren't an investment in an equity position. They were payments on behalf of customers within the Department of Defense who'd be purchasing data collected by Capella satellites. For Capella, our contract represented a guaranteed revenue stream—one of the most valuable things a startup can show to investors when it raises funds. It would act as a turbocharger for the business. Soon after signing the deal with DIUx, Capella raised $12.7 million in a Series A round led by DCVC and Spark Capital, two prominent deep-tech venture capital firms. Capella got another boost in July when the company was included in a front-page *New York Times* story headlined, "Tiny Satellites from Silicon Valley May Help Track North Korean Missiles," in which Raj was quoted saying Capella was on track to have a satellite in use by the Pentagon by the end of 2017 or early 2018. "The company says its radar fleet, if successfully deployed, will be able to monitor important targets hourly," *Times* veteran national security correspondent David E. Sanger reported.

It was an exciting time for SAR technology. Capella was poised to become the first U.S. company to build a commercially available SAR capability. It spent the summer staffing up, and Banazadeh and his team were working around the clock to build a prototype satellite for us. A feel-good story seemed to be coming true but for the fact that Capella's one paying customer, DIUx, hadn't been given the funds it was promised.

Something strange was happening. The money we'd been expecting from Washington never arrived. At first, we weren't too concerned. Butow was tracking the issue closely and would sometimes be told that there was a paperwork hassle, or another approval that needed to be signed. Or he'd get bounced from one person to another. This was just bureaucracy, people told him. You know how things are. The Pentagon moves slowly.

The truth was that when Work and Selva overrode the objections of the intelligence community at the January 2017 meeting, they set into motion a swift and silent autoimmune response that began among the holders of the purse strings in the byzantine world of covert spy satellites. Despite letters of interest signed by three combatant commanders, despite support from General Brooks in South Korea, despite the direct order from Work and Selva, despite the mounting concerns over what could be happening on the ground in North Korea, Capella's money stayed put in Washington.

Gradually it became clear that we did have something to be worried about. Someone unseen was holding up the money, or at the very least slow-rolling its transfer. And, as we were going to find out, the delay was part of a scheme to trip us up.

In the spring, the Office of Management and Budget convened a meeting where we had to make the case for the $15 million all over again. Our adversaries had managed to roll our project into the larger tussle playing out over SAR funds, thus tripping the threshold for congressional reprogramming. That then required the military's four oversight committees to sign off on the funding change.

Everyone on the Hill was fine with the request except for the House Appropriations Subcommittee on Defense—HAC-D, the Evelyn and Ed crowd. These were the people who'd tried to kill DIUx in the cradle. Lieutenant General Tony Ierardi had seen combat in both Iraq wars and in Afghanistan, commanded the army's First Cavalry Division, and culminated his career as the Joint Staff's director for force structure, resources, and assessments, known as J-8. Nearly a thousand people worked for him. An official government sedan chauffeured Lieutenant General Ierardi and Butow to Capitol Hill. They walked through the same House Appropriations Committee office doors we had when we were fighting for DIUx's existence. "It was the most miserable experience I ever had in my life," Butow recalls. "General Ierardi opens his deck. We never got past the first slide. For three hours, they berated DIUx and the whole department. For three hours, nonstop."

This was Raj and Chris versus Evelyn and Ed all over again, only this time it was the Joint Staff's top program officer asking for help targeting North Korean nuclear missiles. "General Ierardi goes, 'Hey, this is clearly an emotional thing for you.'" They'd planned to be there only forty-five minutes, but the meeting went on for so long that by the time they finished, their driver had gone home for the night, leaving them to take an Uber back to the Pentagon, "all jammed into the back in our class A uniforms. It was just the most ridiculous thing ever," Butow recalls.

An even bigger hurdle arose in July. A high-level Pentagon meeting was called on such short notice that we had to get on a red-eye with only four hours' warning. In the Deputy Secretary of Defense's conference room the next morning, Stephanie O'Sullivan, the principal deputy director of national intelligence, made a direct plea to Work and Selva to pause all work on the Capella project for even longer, as she still felt moving forward would risk upsetting the congressional committees. O'Sullivan was asking a four-star military officer and the deputy Secretary of Defense to stop progress on a tactical program to hunt KN-08s because she needed more time to carry her own water on the Hill. Chris looked at Raj, who looked at Sorensen, who looked at Farris. We were stunned. All four of us had never seen anything like this. Yet balancing many considerations, including the relationship between the Pentagon and the intelligence community, and their own personal working relationship, Work and Selva honored her ask. The wait would continue.

Waiting in war is almost always the wrong answer. Our first week at DIUx, we had met with James "Snake" Clark, the gung-ho operator who, during the search to kill or capture bin Laden in the months before 9/11, figured out how to put a Hellfire missile on a Predator drone in sixty-one days. The first test fire occurred on February 16, 2001. Clarke could have fielded the capability faster but was slowed down by bureaucratic barriers. He and his team came tantalizingly close to giving the U.S. the ability to take bin Laden off the battlefield before 9/11. Had they achieved operational capability just a few weeks earlier, world history would be different. Clark told us two things. "Shoot for the moon. And know everyone will come after you for doing so." Talking like the former F-4 fighter pilot he was, he told us exactly how it would feel when our enemies came after us, using an unprintable analogy involving an appendage of the male anatomy and a Cuisinart food processor.

This more or less described how we were feeling as we dragged ourselves back to San Francisco after the meeting with Work, Selva, and O'Sullivan. The coup de grâce happened in October 2017, when we were still waiting for the money transfer that Work had originally ordered. Someone in Washington—again, as with so many of our battles, we didn't know who—threatened to have us investigated on a technicality. Because we'd signed a contract with Capella without having the money transfer in hand, we were technically in violation of a Pentagon procurement rule called the Anti-Deficiency Act. This is an act passed by Congress in the 1870s to stop the Executive Branch and military from creating "coercive deficiencies," meaning signing contracts with the commercial sector without having the funds already approved and set aside by Congress to pay the obligation. In the 150 years the act has been in effect no one has ever been charged with a violation.

Nevertheless: we were being threatened with legal repercussions. And that's when we folded. DIUx had to issue a "stop work" order to Capella. Until the funds actually transferred, we couldn't expose ourselves to further risk.

Were we set up? It sure felt like it. As with so many things, we'll never know.

The stop work order caused bigger problems for Capella.

Banazadeh had raised venture funding based on the promise of getting revenue from DIUx, but now revenue was going to be delayed indefinitely and might not come at all. How was he going to explain that to the investors who'd put millions into Capella? Butow offered to talk to Capella's investors and assure them that the problem had nothing to do with Capella's technology and was entirely caused by Pentagon shenanigans—though that wasn't exactly reassuring, either. If the DIUx couldn't keep its word on contracts it signed, why should anyone believe anything we said?

"It was really bad for Capella," Banazadeh recalls. "It was difficult. I don't want to say that the company was put on an existential path, but in those early days when money's super tight and you're trying to really deliver on promise, any sort of setback has some sort of an existential feeling to it, and this definitely had that feeling. And there was some mystery around the stop work order. Why was this happening? It's not even that much money in the grand scheme of things. So there was a cloud around it, and that cloud created a lot of uncertainty. We're getting a stop work order from what we believed to be the most important customer for this product, so it was tough for sure."

In addition to delaying Capella's technology, the stalled contract meant the company had to go back to investors for another round of venture capital funding at a lower valuation and give up more ownership of the company. "So we got diluted more, and we had to delay our first launch. And that launch delay was really painful because if you don't have the satellite up, then you can't raise the next round of funding. All these things are tied together," Banazadeh says.

The fiasco was the first major reputational setback for DIUx 2.0 in the Valley. For years the conventional wisdom had been that you should never make a deal with the Department of Defense because they take too long to get a contract signed, and even if you got a contract you never knew when the money would actually arrive. But then we arrived and told everyone things had changed, that we were guys who could get things done at Silicon Valley speed. The Capella stop work order threatened to destroy our credibility.

Months later, in July 2018, when the funds still hadn't arrived, Raj and Butow supported Capella by dipping into the "walking around" money Carter had directed DIUx have at its opening. These were the funds that got DIUx so crosswise with Evelyn and Ed, the two congressional staffers who tried to "zeroize" DIUx's budget. The funds had already been allocated to other projects, but we needed to save face and, more important, get a promising technology off the ground. Butow was able to issue a "resume work" order, "which was great," Banazadeh says, "but it changed our view of how reliable the government could be for us. From then on, I had to be aware that I couldn't depend on them." With any DoD contract, "I assume that the money is not going to be there, and if the money does arrive, then that's amazing, but if it doesn't, it's not going to be an existential threat for me."

By then, Sorensen and Farris had left government to found their own satellite company, Orbital Effects. Bob Work left not that long afterward. The good news is that, for Capella, the fiasco was just a bump in the road. Toward the end of 2018, the company launched its first test satellite into space. In 2020, Capella launched its first commercial satellite, and landed its first customer—which was, ironically, the intelligence service of an allied country. (Banazadeh can't name them.) Since then, Capella has launched seven more satellites, and its business is booming. In 2022, Capella raised a $97 million venture capital round, followed only months later with $60 million more from another venture firm.

The Datahub pilot program first assembled to solve the North Korea KN-08 problem was eventually rolled into other even more advanced AI early warning projects, though Capella's imagery feeds weren't pulled forward into that ongoing work. Capella finally won more DoD business when Russia invaded Ukraine and the National Reconnaissance Office (NRO) started buying its satellite data. Butow is hopeful the decisive use of commercial space capabilities in the Ukraine conflict will usher in the sea change he'd hoped the original Capella project might trigger.

As for that floundering billion-dollar satellite project that O'Sullivan and others fought so hard to protect, by 2023 the firm that had won the contract still hadn't delivered a working satellite, and the Pentagon was soliciting new bids from other prime contractors. Because it's a "black" program, we'll never know exactly how much money has been wasted, or what went wrong, or who screwed up—that's all classified.

Kim Jong-Un, meanwhile, continues to saber-rattle. In December 2022, five North Korean drones eluded South Korean air defenses and flew south. One traveled all the way to Seoul. South Korea's military issued a formal apology for its failure to shoot down the drone, and President Yoon Suk Yeol called for stronger air defenses and vowed to "bolster our surveillance capability."

That DIUx office General Brooks asked for may happen yet, as we continue to unlock more possibilities enabled by commercial technology.

CHAPTER FIVE
UNIT X LOSES THE X

By the end of 2017, DIUx had awarded contracts for forty-eight projects leveraging $84 million in funding from thirty military entities. By using our Other Transactions Authority (OTA) workaround, the DIUx team closed deals in sixty days on average. For startups, our contracts were just a first step—the firm received a small amount of money to develop a pilot project or proof of concept, and if that worked out they'd move to the next stage, where their pilot projects would turn into real production contracts with customers across the military. In the traditional Pentagon acquisition process, crossing from pilot project to production contract can take years. But we were doing it in months. In 2017 we moved two projects from pilot stage into production, including a $35 million contract for Tanium, a cybersecurity company, to provide services to the Army Network Enterprise Technology Command (NETCOM), which provides all the networking infrastructure for the army. In the world of the DoD, this was lightning-strike fast. As Carter had envisioned, when we gave portfolio companies the promise of future DoD revenue, they were able to convince venture capitalists to invest in them. All told, the companies in our portfolio raised $1.8 billion in venture funding. Carter's vision of enticing Silicon Valley to build products for the military was coming to fruition.

We made bets across our five portfolios: artificial intelligence, autonomy, human systems, information technology, and space. In artificial intelligence we were working with a company called C3.ai, whose software predicted maintenance for aircraft, saving the air force millions of dollars and keeping more planes airborne. Our AI team also helped orchestrate an initiative called Project Maven, in which Amazon, Microsoft, and Google were developing computer vision algorithms—computer code that can see—which enhanced the military's ability to track ISIS fighters. In human systems, we worked with a company that used wearables to monitor soldiers in reconnaissance platoons for dehydration—a major cause of mission failure. Another startup developed earbuds that used bone conduction to communicate, enabling warfighters to talk in high-noise environments. Our IT team got wins in network security and helped bring modern software development techniques to the DoD.

One of the standouts in our portfolio was ForAllSecure, founded by David Brumley, a computer science professor from Carnegie Mellon University, and several of his graduate students. In 2016, Brumley's team competed at the DARPA Grand Challenge, a competition in Las Vegas where teams of hackers ran autonomous cybersecurity software on supercomputers in a race to see which did the best job defeating cyberattacks without human intervention. Brumley's software, called Mayhem, could scour millions of lines of code, find vulnerabilities, and patch them—on its own. Work that would take months or even years for human cybersecurity experts to finish could be completed by Mayhem in hours, or even minutes. The DIUx cyber team immediately recognized Mayhem's potential to protect weapons systems. After the technology beat out dozens of other competitors to win the DARPA Challenge, they arranged for ForAllSecure to conduct pilot programs for several customers inside the DoD. One of those pilot programs eventually resulted in a contract worth $45 million under which ForAllSecure is providing Mayhem to the air force, army, and navy.

Another future winner was Shield AI, a company started by two brothers—Brandon Tseng, a former Navy SEAL, and Ryan Tseng, an MIT-trained engineer. Their first product was based on an idea that Brandon conceived during his time in Afghanistan, where SEAL units raided buildings without knowing whether enemy fighters were inside. Tseng believed it would be possible to build a small drone that could fly into buildings and transmit video of the interior before SEALs broke down the door. At DIUx we discovered Shield AI in 2016 when they were only a team of five, awarded them a contract from our autonomy portfolio, and by 2018 the company's Nova drones were being deployed in combat missions. The drones use AI to operate autonomously and find their way through buildings. Thanks to our support, Shield went on to raise hundreds of millions of dollars in venture funding and has been valued at more than $2 billion. The company has won contracts from the air force and navy, and the *Wall Street Journal* has hailed its technology as "the first autonomous robot of its kind used in combat."

Throughout 2017 DIUx was recruiting top talent from the commercial sector, and by the end of the year we'd built a staff of a few dozen full-time personnel across three offices—Mountain View, Boston, and Austin—as well as fifty-five reservists and guardsmen.

Meanwhile, investors and entrepreneurs in Silicon Valley were becoming more interested in working with the Pentagon, not only because DIUx had lowered the barriers to entry and moved so many projects forward, but also because other big defense-oriented startups were gaining traction. Palantir, which did big data analytics, and Elon Musk's SpaceX, which launched payloads into space, were growing quickly and winning government business. Anduril, a company whose leaders Raj met before they even incorporated and that planned to build drone-killing technology, raised funding quickly when it was founded in 2017—VCs were quite eager to invest. By 2019, VCs would value Anduril at $1 billion, making it a "unicorn," in Valley-speak.

Our ideas about innovation and operating at startup speed were spreading across the military. The air force's Kessel Run team, which was born from our "Gonkulator" project at the CAOC in Qatar, was gaining steam. The air force also opened a technology accelerator called AFWERX, whose mission was to identify service members with entrepreneurial chops, collaborate with tech companies, and find ways to use autonomous technologies. Inspired by DIUx and under the direction of army chief of staff General Mark Milley, the army launched its own public-private technology incubator, called Army Futures Command, to modernize the army. Headquartered in Austin, Texas, Futures Command would grow from twelve people in 2018 to more than twenty-four thousand in 2019, with billions of dollars in funding. It was all part of the movement to inject Silicon Valley technology and thinking into how the Pentagon did business.

The biggest highlight of our year—in fact, a make-or-break moment for us—was a visit in August 2017 by Secretary of Defense James Mattis, who toured the DIUx offices during a three-day visit to Seattle and Silicon Valley. His stops included Amazon, Microsoft, and Google. We'd been holding our breath ever since President Trump was elected and Ash Carter, our patron, left office and was replaced by Mattis. Transitions to new administrations are always tricky. For months we lived in fear that we might be shut down, just as we were getting going. All the support that we'd built up in the Pentagon was gone. It wasn't just Carter who'd left the building, but also his staff, his deputies, the secretaries of the military services with whom we'd built relationships. We were starting over, and it wasn't clear we would still report to the Secretary of Defense.

With Mattis there was an extra challenge. He'd left command in the Middle East for a fellowship at Stanford, exchanging the scarred battleground where his marines had fought and died in Ramadi and Fallujah for a sunny world where preppy undergrads on scooters zipped past stately Mission Revival sandstone buildings. After landing in Silicon Valley, Mattis became a board member of Theranos, a blood-testing startup eventually engulfed in scandal when its company's founder, Elizabeth Holmes, engaged in fraud. Mattis resigned from the board in January 2017 when he took the Secretary of Defense job. But the experience had left him wary of Silicon Valley, and he'd made some comments in public to the effect that the Valley was full of hucksters and charlatans.

The night before his visit to DIUx, we hosted Mattis at a dinner attended by some of the titans of technology. In a private room we had Mattis meet Marc Andreessen, the founder of Andreessen Horowitz, a top venture capital firm, and Sam Altman, the founder of Y Combinator, a startup incubator, who'd go on to found OpenAI, developer of ChatGPT, which launched an AI revolution in 2022. Andreessen assured Mattis that VCs wanted to invest in defense-related technology. While for many years the Valley had shied away from doing business with the Pentagon, DIUx had changed the prevailing view. Every week, Raj was fielding calls from venture capitalists eager to invest in our portfolio companies. Andreessen also assured Mattis that for the first time, the Pentagon had assembled a group that understood technology, could work with entrepreneurs, and move fast: "Support DIUx," he said. "This is the most important and valuable thing that we've seen out of DoD in decades."

That helped make Mattis a believer. We sealed the deal the next morning when he spent a half day at DIUx being briefed on our programs. He was especially impressed by the work we were doing with drones. Mattis had been hearing from commanders in Syria and Afghanistan that drones were becoming a real problem. ISIS and the insurgents were using cheap ones built by DJI, a Chinese company, which could be purchased for a few hundred dollars, to surveil our troops and direct fire at them. They even sent drone swarms into Mosul, dropping grenades on our troops. In at least one incident this led to fatalities.

Mattis knew we had to solve this problem. The primary drones in the DoD inventory were expensive ScanEagles, which were made by Boeing and cost about $1 million each, and Predators, which cost $30 million and required a fifteen-person team to run them from Nevada. These platforms were very capable in their own way, but they weren't something a soldier could pull out of his backpack in the middle of a fight with ISIS.

Another challenge was that we didn't want U.S. troops using Chinese-made DJI drones in combat because those drones could convey back to Chinese servers data about where U.S. forces were and what they were looking at. The army had issued an edict saying soldiers couldn't use DJI drones in combat or in training—but soldiers were buying them anyway, paying out of their own pockets, and using them to surveil ISIS positions. Troops were buying DJI drones because DJI had cornered the market for small drones, and there were no decent alternatives from American manufacturers.

We won Mattis over with a presentation made by a pair of tech wizards who'd assembled a DIUx drone team called Rogue Squadron. Mark Jacobsen was an air force lieutenant colonel who began his career as a cargo pilot and studied the Syrian Civil War before getting a Ph.D. in political science from Stanford. Ryan Beall was a young navy helicopter pilot, drone enthusiast, and software savant. Mattis lit up when they showed him the work they'd been doing.

Beall and Jacobsen had set up Rogue Squadron in an old warehouse next to our offices at Moffett Field. Nicknamed "the cages" for its labyrinth of chain-link enclosures once used to store weapons, the warehouse had no running water, air-conditioning, or heating. Blisteringly hot in summer, cold in winter, it was crammed full of lab benches, computer terminals, and real-time communications links to experimental drones and anti-drone equipment on the mock battlefield outside. Between them, Jacobsen and Beall owned nearly fifty drones of various models and makes. When they offered to donate them to DIUx to furnish the Batcave with a starter-kit of hardware, our lawyer informed them they couldn't. DIUx lacked "gift authority," so receiving free goods or services was against regulation. The lawyer never noticed that Beall and Jacobsen ignored her completely, replacing in time the drones they donated with ones purchased by DIUx.

Rogue Squadron's first mission was to help us assess technology claims from drone startups. Company representatives would claim certain capabilities. Jacobsen and Beall would take the prototypes out to our test range and engage in mock combat—with Rogue Squadron drones and counter-drone systems in the role of Red team, or bad guys, and the startup guys playing the role of Blue team. "Red-teaming" was fun, but from there Rogue Squadron moved on to their first real project, scouring the software inside DJI drones to discover backdoors and vulnerabilities in the code.

Nobody liked the idea of using Chinese drones, but battlefield operators knew DJI's were better than anything else on the market and generations ahead of the standard-issue portable drones the army and marines sent to front-line combat units. We needed to find a way to use the DJI hardware. One of the vulnerabilities in DJI's operating system enabled Beall to code a hack that could shut off the ability of a DJI drone to send data back to China—making it safe for U.S. operators to use in the field. Rogue Squadron published the hack on a secure government site and within a year more than two hundred organizations inside the DoD had downloaded the software and installed it on the DJI drones they used.

An even more ambitious Rogue Squadron project began with a fortuitous offhand conversation in the lobby at DIUx, the kind of thing that can only occur when one innovator meets another. On his first morning at DIUx, Beall happened to sit next to a Navy SEAL in the lobby. "I just rolled off a rotation from Afghanistan, and drones are becoming a big thing over there," the SEAL told him. "We're getting our asses handed to us, and the big problem we're seeing is sometimes we capture the drone, but we can't go get the drone operator." At the time, the only way data on captured drones could be exploited was by boxing them up and shipping them from the battlefield to a lab, which would send a forensic report weeks later. There was no way to recover in real time where the drone had been launched from.

The SEAL asked Beall if he could build an Android phone app that warfighters could carry in the field to locate the operator of a captured drone. Beall used a tool called Wireshark that reveals network traffic, byte by byte, to reverse engineer a DJI drone's communications protocol. In two weeks, Beall finished the Android app. "I just taught myself that tool, plugged in the drone, and started hammering on the software in the drone as hard as I could to figure out what it was doing." There were no manuals that described the DJI software's protocols. Fortunately for us, Beall possessed a kind of genius for combing through thousands of lines of code to decipher how a program worked, a talent that even he doesn't fully understand. "It was like reading the Matrix. I just figured it out," he recalls.

As Jacobsen points out, the need to locate the operator of an enemy drone was becoming more acute since U.S. military bases and ports all around the world were constantly being surveilled by drones. (In military parlance, a drone is called an "unmanned aircraft system," or UAS, and systems used to combat them are called "counter-UAS" solutions.) Jacobsen recalls an incident at a Fleet Week event—when the navy parks dozens of ships in a port for public display—where "we had forty drone incursions in a single day." These were presumably all hobbyist pilots poking around, but it's easy to imagine how weaponizing hobbyist drones could lead to a future Pearl Harbor event the navy would not be prepared to defend against.

The Rogue Squadron software that could locate a drone operator was a big deal. But in time a cat-and-mouse game ensued, since our enemies were constantly figuring out how we were hacking their drones then changing their software so that our hacks no longer worked. Then our hackers would have to start over. Essentially, our software programmers were waging an invisible war against their software programmers. This was a new kind of warfare, in which the battle is waged not with tanks and missiles but with laptops and lines of code. Whoever had the best coders would win.

Beall did a lot of the software hacking himself, but he also found a creative way to enlist help from outsiders, by joining online message boards where the world's best drone hackers were sharing their exploits. Beall didn't identify himself to the group as a member of the U.S. military; he was just a fellow hacker, sharing code that he'd developed and gaining the trust of others on the board. Eventually, he'd recruit some of them to work on DJI software projects. To be sure, our mission was to find ways to work with the commercial sector. But enlisting a bunch of shadowy hackers who lived in the gray zone between "white hat" and "black hat" was a pretty extreme version of that. If it meant we could get better technology into the hands of warfighters, though, we were willing to bend the rules.

As Jacobsen saw things, hacking DJI drones wasn't a satisfactory permanent solution. Beall had cracked the code on one generation of drones, but DJI constantly released new models, with new software. And it updated the software on its existing drones. This meant we'd be going through that same hacking exercise over and over. The preferred—but ambitious—solution was to persuade entrepreneurs in the U.S. to start new companies and build drones that would be better than DJI's. Essentially, jump-start an entire new industry. "We always viewed the DJI work as a Band-Aid, a short-term fix," Jacobsen says. "Long-term, it wasn't going to work. And we shouldn't be flying DJI drones as an alternative to using American products."

There once had been several U.S. drone makers, but DJI had put most out of business. Jacobsen believed that breaking DJI's monopoly would require heavy investment by the U.S. government, first in components like autopilots and datalinks and later in complete drones. DIUx worked with the army's new quadcopter effort to see if soliciting new drone designs suitable for military applications would lead U.S. manufacturers to bring new drones to market. It did. One of the companies DIUx funded, Skydio, became the primary supplier of surveillance drones to the U.S. military. Founded in 2014 by three young MIT grads, Skydio has grown to be the largest U.S. drone-maker, with a $2.2 billion valuation, supported by Andreessen Horowitz and other VC firms. We did, in fact, do the seemingly impossible: we helped bring a faltering U.S. industry back to life.

The Department of Defense scaled this effort into a larger program called Blue UAS, which published a list of drones that met DoD standards—a military version of the Good Housekeeping Seal of Approval—so that anyone across the U.S. government could place orders.

When Mattis visited in 2017 and Jacobsen demonstrated how Rogue Squadron's software could close DJI security vulnerabilities, making it safe for U.S. troops to use DJI drones, the Secretary of Defense knew we'd made a huge breakthrough that could tilt the balance of power on the battlefield—and he didn't hide his enthusiasm. "This is awesome. Make this your number one priority. Go fast, go big, and solve this. I'll fund it. Get going as soon as this meeting ends," he said. "I want you to scale this across the entire DoD."

As soon as the meeting ended, members of Mattis's entourage raced over to Jacobsen and told him he could have whatever resources he needed. Following the visit, Rogue Squadron would get $3 million in funding over the next three years—a big bump from the $25,000 it had been given to start. Jacobsen used the money to hire civilian software developers and scale the work with the urgency Mattis had requested.

In addition to Rogue Squadron, we showed Mattis several other projects, and we could tell he was impressed. At the end of the visit, Raj walked the Secretary of Defense to his motorcade, and Mattis assured him we'd have his full support. "I need you to keep doing what you're doing, but I need you to move even faster. I need you to scale. You can call me anytime you need me. And come see me in the Pentagon," he said.

Mattis then held a press conference and gave DIUx a very public blessing: "There is no doubt in my mind that DIUx will not only continue to exist, it will actually grow in its influence and its impact on the Department of Defense. I don't embrace it; I *enthusiastically* embrace it. And I'm grateful that Secretary Carter had the foresight," he said, to create the unit. He even affixed a decal of DIUx's logo to the front of the leather notebook he carried everywhere. In the weeks after, DIUx's staff took joy in seeing our logo appear in photos showing the Secretary of Defense meeting with the Crown Prince of Saudi Arabia and other world leaders. Not long after that, Mattis further cemented his support when he removed the "x" from our name, dubbing us simply DIU. The "x" had stood for "experimental." Mattis was sending a signal: the unit was no longer an experiment, but rather a permanent part of the Pentagon. Although Unit X had officially lost its X, in our minds it would always be Unit X, an ongoing experiment meant to take risks in pushing technology that other parts of the Pentagon couldn't.

Jacobsen and Beall reluctantly left Rogue Squadron after a couple years. The military personnel system, which doesn't value nontraditional assignments, insisted they move to new roles. "Imagine if a startup had to fire its executive leadership team every two years," Jacobsen lamented. He took a teaching job at the Air Force Education Center at Maxwell Air Force Base in Alabama, where he now runs a program that teaches entrepreneurship to air force officers. Beall, denied promotion twice because he was hacking drones instead of flying helicopters, left the navy to take a job at Anduril, the defense startup. In 2023 he launched his own startup to build military drones. Rogue Squadron eventually moved out from under DIU to be housed inside another part of the DoD.

As Jacobsen sees it, Rogue Squadron enjoyed mixed success. Like so many other initiatives, its progress was impeded by Pentagon bureaucracy and skullduggery. One example: another government agency asked Rogue Squadron for an app it had developed; Beall complied, and not long afterward his reverse-engineered code appeared in a competing app the agency paid a contractor to build—line for line. Another example: though Mattis had promised to provide Rogue Squadron with $3 million over the course of three years, most of the money never arrived because the Evelyn and Ed crowd at the House Appropriations Committee marked down DIU's budget from the amount the Pentagon requested. At this point, DIU no longer reported directly to Mattis. And it's difficult—and perhaps unwise—to try to get on the Secretary of Defense's calendar to squawk about a tiny budget squabble. DIU tried to secure other funds, but the request kept bouncing around. The problem wasn't malfeasance. It was just another example of how the Pentagon's convoluted apparatus sometimes made it impossible for even the Secretary of Defense's orders to be carried out. Jacobsen remembers hustling to pay contractors. "I spent a lot of my time just trying to help us survive," he recalls.

SAILDRONE

Another startup that impressed Mattis was Saildrone, one of our first portfolio companies, which was developing self-powered autonomous sailboats that could remain at sea for months, conducting ocean surveillance for a fraction of the price of building and deploying destroyers, which carry a price tag of $2 billion or more per ship.

Saildrone's founder, Richard Jenkins, is a colorful figure in his own right, a Brit who first made his name in 2009 by breaking the wind-powered land speed record. He did so with a sleek "land yacht" called *Greenbird* that hit 126.2 miles per hour in the Mojave Desert in California. He was a daredevil, an avid pilot and sailor who learned to fly at age fourteen and at age sixteen sailed across the Atlantic. Strapping himself into a flimsy carbon-fiber shell that was essentially an airplane wing with wheels attached was par for the course.

Greenbird was a kind of prototype for the wind-powered sailing drones that Jenkins would build after turning his attention to the ocean. He founded Saildrone in 2012 after moving to Alameda, California, and within a year built an unmanned ship that sailed from San Francisco to Hawaii in thirty-two days. In 2014 he struck a partnership with the National Oceanic and Atmospheric Administration (NOAA) to gather ocean data and conduct surveys of fisheries for conservation purposes. His original business plan was to study the oceans to measure the effects of climate change. But soon he recognized the value that autonomous ships could have for defense. Jenkins was eventually introduced to DIUx, who shared his technology with Carter, who then summoned Jenkins to Washington to make a presentation.

"I didn't even know who the defense secretary was," Jenkins recalls. "Someone told me, 'You're going to present to Ash Carter,' and I was like, 'Who's Ash Carter?'"

Jenkins arrived to find he was one of five entrepreneurs who'd be presenting to Carter and to Frank Kendall, the undersecretary of defense for acquisition, technology, and logistics (AT&L)—the Pentagon's lead weapons buyer. (Kendall is now secretary of the air force.) Carter was a brilliant scientist, but he was also known for his sharp edges and prickly personality—terrifying, basically. "Just as I was about to go on stage, a big guy in an air force uniform leaned toward me and asked if I wanted some advice. I said sure, and he goes, 'Don't suck,' then slapped me on the back and pushed me out onto the stage," Jenkins says.

Jenkins need not have worried. Carter and Kendall immediately saw the potential of what Saildrone was building, and within weeks Jenkins got a call from the Pentagon asking him what a fleet of drones to cover the northern Pacific might cost. Each drone would be equipped with communications equipment so they could operate as a network. Just weeks later Trump was elected, Carter and Kendall were out of jobs, and that project disappeared. But another DIU opportunity arose: in 2017 the company operated a pilot program for the U.S. Southern Command (SOUTHCOM). The project showed that Saildrones, towing acoustic arrays, could track the fast boats and submersibles used by narcotics smugglers, in effect providing the same capability as a navy destroyer for this particular use.

Jenkins soon realized that the drones themselves weren't the core of the business—the real product was the data that the drones could generate. His technicians put cameras on the drones that took a picture every five seconds, quickly amassing an enormous data set. They then trained machine learning software that could analyze the images. "People look at Saildrone and think we're a hardware company, but the hardware's just twenty percent of the puzzle," Jenkins says. He likens the drones to trucks—and even refers to Saildrone's three models as the F-150, F-250, and F-350, in a nod to Ford. "The trucks get you into the field. But it's the things you put in the trucks that give you the value. It's what you do with that data that gives you what you sell to the customer."

Today, Saildrone has amassed a data set that contains billions of images showing birds, marine mammals, whales, dolphins, ice—and ships. And its autonomous vessels have become more and more capable. In 2019, a Saildrone became the first unmanned vehicle to complete a circumnavigation of Antarctica. In 2021, Saildrone also sent a vessel into the eye of Hurricane Sam. While capturing historic video, it survived winds of up to 135 miles per hour and waves that surged above one hundred feet.

Bolstered by DIU contracts, Jenkins in Saildrone's early days was able to raise $30 million in venture capital funding. All told, Saildrone has raised nearly $200 million. DIU's OTA contracting system made it easy for government agencies to make contracts with Saildrone, and the company now provides services to a number of military and civilian agencies. Today Saildrone has 260 employees, many of them software engineers.

Saildrone found itself in the news in 2022 when Iran's navy seized a pair of Saildrone vessels that had been conducting surveillance in the Red Sea. Jenkins and his team could see the whole thing unfolding as they watched camera feeds from the drones in real time. After a tense standoff and some back-and-forth, the vessels were returned to the U.S. Navy. The temporary seizure of Jenkins's Saildrones was suddenly the top global news story, the latest tangle between the Iranian and American navies. It was ultimately great for the company's business, Jenkins explains, because "it gave us visibility throughout the government. A lot of people in the Pentagon had never heard of Saildrone, or simply believed the vessels were just prototypes being used in a pilot program. Four years ago, I'd try to pitch Saildrone to Big Navy, and folks just dismissed us. 'You guys, you're like toys. You're too small, just not useful. We have ships, carriers.' That has totally changed now. People appreciate what small unmanned seagoing vehicles can do."

The skirmish with Iran also bolstered an argument that Jenkins had been making which is that the vessels are absolutely going to be seized. "I'm surprised it took so long to happen," he says, but it's not a problem because there's nothing special in terms of hardware, and the data is encrypted or deleted. The seizure helped Saildrone learn what to expect when the drones are operating in "denied environments," as Jenkins puts it. "I've been saying for a long time that you should expect unmanned systems to get captured. Unless you're willing to actually protect them, there's nothing you can do. That's why they need to be built with off-the-shelf technology that isn't subject to export controls. You should be able to give your assets to your most sophisticated adversary," confident that they can't do much with them.

Jenkins's role has evolved from simply building technology to also advising on the role of unmanned systems in defense strategy. "For the first number of years, I was always presenting the technology and thinking, 'Who am I to tell you how to use it? You must be the experts.' I guess it was a dawning moment after three or four years when I was describing to an admiral the kind of things we could do, the problems we could solve, when he said, 'You guys are so far ahead of our thinking on where we need to go.' When things are moving fast, the government becomes almost hobbled by its inertia."

The war in Ukraine has also helped raise awareness of the power of oceangoing drones, which together with anti-ship missiles have been used to sink Russian ships in the Black Sea, including its flagship guided missile cruiser *Moskva*, a six-hundred-foot warship with a crew of 510. Ukraine, which doesn't even have a navy, essentially neutralized Russia's Black Sea Fleet, turning its forty ships into what naval strategists call a "fleet in being"—one that has been functionally defeated. The conflict has made a lot of people realize that the future of war at sea is changing. In a world where hypersonic weapons and anti-ship missiles can easily destroy a navy vessel, it no longer makes sense to spend billions of dollars building destroyers and battleships. Echoing comments made by former Vice Chairman of the Joint Chiefs Admiral Sandy Winnefeld and others, Jenkins said, "Until we have a solution to anti-ship hypersonics, you're just not going to deploy a ship in a conflict again against our most advanced adversaries. Ships have a useful peacetime power projection capability, but they're very vulnerable in a real conflict."

Just as aerial drones are increasingly doing work that previously required fighter jets, ocean drones will perform work that previously has been done by large navy vessels. Future conflicts, Jenkins believes, will rely heavily on submarines and long-range missiles, together with fleets of unmanned vessels on the surface and undersea, operating in a mesh network. As elsewhere, machine learning and AI will help make sense of the data and power real-time targeting.

JOBY AVIATION

In 2016, one of our partners, Isaac Taylor, a veteran of Google X, the company's experimental "moonshot" lab, discovered a young inventor, JoeBen Bevirt, and his team working in a barn on a ranch in the Santa Cruz Mountains. They were trying to build something that Bevirt had been dreaming about since he was a kid growing up in a remote hippie community in Last Chance, California: a flying car. In techno-language, it's called a battery-powered vertical takeoff and landing (eVTOL) aircraft. The cool factor was off the charts.

Taylor and DIU offered to help Bevirt's Joby Aviation by obtaining permission for the company to test its prototypes at Fort Hunter Liggett, an army base in Jolon, California, near Monterey. "We took an old remote site and installed a tent hangar and facilities where our test flight test team was able to operate," Bevirt recalls. The company started out flying "sub-scale" versions of its aircraft, but by 2017 they'd built full-sized aircraft in testing. "That facility materially accelerated the development and testing of our aircraft and formed the foundation for the growth of the company," Bevirt says.

Like a lot of DIU projects, Joby was designing a "dual-use" product, meaning one that could be sold to commercial customers as well as the military. It was one of several companies, including Uber, trying to create air taxis that could shuttle people on short hops to avoid traffic in crowded cities. But we also saw the potential for military applications, as did Navy SEALs and air force pilots, who soon made their way to Hunter Liggett to check out Joby's aircraft and see how they could use it, for example, to fly personnel and supplies into combat zones.

Depending on your perspective, Joby's aircraft looks either like a giant drone or a small helicopter. Its six electric motors are set horizontally to lift the vehicle off the ground, then flip ninety degrees and act like propellers. The craft can carry four passengers and a pilot and travel at speeds up to 205 miles per hour, enabling it to zip passengers from Midtown Manhattan to JFK Airport in seven minutes. It can travel up to 150 miles on a single charge. Also, the aircraft is incredibly quiet, making it even more appealing for stealthy military missions.

In 2018, Joby raised a $100 million venture funding round from Toyota AI Ventures, helped in part by the fact that DIU was lining up potential military contracts. Another round followed in 2020, in which Toyota and others invested another $590 million. By then the company had completed its vehicle design and set up a manufacturing facility at the Marina Municipal Airport in Marina, California. That same year, Joby acquired one of its rivals, Uber Elevate, the air taxi service that Uber had originated.

In 2023, Joby Aviation introduced its first production vehicle, and announced a $131 million contract to provide eVTOL aircraft to the air force—making the U.S. military Joby's first paying customer. Joby delivered its first aircraft in late 2023, and they're slated to go into service in 2025. It will have taken less than ten years to transition from a prototype in the Santa Cruz Mountains to an aircraft used by the military—a remarkably speedy rollout in the world of military aviation. Consider that Lockheed Martin's F-35 fighter jet, first conceived in the 1990s, endured significant delays and cost overruns before finally entering service in 2015. Joby went public in 2021 and now has a market value of $5.5 billion, making it yet another Silicon Valley success story and an example of an entrepreneurial startup outgunning big primes by producing small, nimble, relatively inexpensive products that can be fielded quickly.

PROJECT MAVEN

The Pentagon and primes weren't the only foes we had to conquer—sometimes we battled with the Valley's rank-and-file employees. This was the case with Project Maven, a joint venture involving DIU and a few commercial software companies, including Amazon, Google, and Microsoft, that helped raise awareness inside the Pentagon about the importance of AI in the modern military.

Officially called the Algorithmic Warfare Cross-Functional Team (AWCFT), Project Maven was launched by Deputy Secretary Bob Work in 2017 with a mission to create machine learning software that could study drone footage and imagery to protect U.S. and coalition forces and lower the risks of civilian casualties and collateral damage. The challenge the military faced was that the volume of video data being collected as part of counterterrorism and counterinsurgency efforts was so enormous that humans couldn't analyze it all on their own. The U.S. had done a great job creating sensors and cameras that could gather information—but hadn't figured out how to analyze the millions of hours of video that those devices collected. AI algorithms could rifle through petabytes of video data so that the military analysts could make better decisions. The software wasn't going to be operating autonomously; rather, human analysts would be reviewing data brought to their attention by the algorithms. The goal was to help our people be more accurate, which could give us a crucial edge in the war against ISIS and other adversaries. The software could, for example, track the location and movements of ISIS fighters, and thus help prevent attacks.

Project Maven's broader goal was to serve as a pilot that could push the DoD to use AI more widely, at a time when most people inside the Pentagon had little sense of how companies in the commercial realm were using AI and machine learning to improve their businesses. Air Force Lieutenant General John "Jack" Shanahan, a former F-4 and F-15 weapons system officer, oversaw the project. He explained that "Maven is designed to be that pilot project, that pathfinder, that spark that kindles the flame in front of artificial intelligence across the rest of the Department and accelerates DoD's integration of machine learning."

Our involvement began when Brendan McCord, a former navy officer who served on submarines and then left the service for civilian life, wrote to Raj describing work he was doing at Evolv Technology, a Boston-area startup backed by Bill Gates and In-Q-Tel, the CIA's venture capital arm. Evolv was using AI to scan massive amounts of imagery data for security applications like protecting sports venues. McCord, who was director of software and intelligence there, had an engineering degree from MIT and an MBA from Harvard. He'd heard about DIU and knew we were opening an office in Cambridge, home to his alma maters. Raj invited McCord to come to the ribbon-cutting for the new office, where Carter gave a speech that McCord recalls was "a clarion call for progress in AI and especially for computer vision," which was exactly what McCord was working on.

He was further inspired by a meeting in which Eric Schmidt and a handful of eminent Silicon Valley technologists—including John Giannandrea, a top AI scientist at Google who'd soon become the head of AI research at Apple—discussed the initiative that would come to be known as Maven. Warfighters in Iraq, Syria, and Afghanistan were getting trapped in situations where they had limited situational awareness on the battlefield. Another problem was that we simply didn't have enough human analysts to cover every area where the U.S. was operating. If a new problem flared up on the Korean Peninsula, analysts were called away from whatever they'd been working on. McCord and the others all knew that computer vision could solve that problem. And that's why McCord went back to Boston and convinced his fiancée to move with him to San Francisco so he could join our team. McCord, like so many others we recruited from the private sector, gave up a seven-figure compensation package to do this. Most members of our team were making a fraction of what they could make in the private sector. They were there because they believed in the mission.

McCord began by convening top computer vision and AI talent in the Valley—people who were in academia, big tech companies like Google, or tiny startups—and learning about the state of the art in computer vision research. Soon McCord and his team created a set of AI models that surpassed anything the DoD had done before. When McCord visited the Army Supercomputer Center at the Aberdeen Proving Ground in Maryland, he brought with him one of his engineers who'd helped build the infrastructure of Google Brain and OpenAI. "We were blown away by how far behind they were," McCord recalls. "All they wanted to talk to us about was how their old building was falling into the river."

At about this time, McCord joined forces with a grizzled marine colonel named Drew Cukor, who'd fought and lost comrades in the most violent struggles of the Iraq and Afghanistan wars. The hard-charging Cukor had enlisted the help of a team inside Google that was working on wide-area motion imagery, a tough challenge that involved gaining granular visibility of specific objects across an entire city at once—knowing the difference between a truck and an ambulance, for example—and being able to track them as they moved. One of the sensors they dealt with was Gorgon Stare, named after the three sisters in Greek mythology whose glare would turn those who beheld it into stone. Its spherical array of 368 cameras, flown at twenty-five thousand feet on a drone, collect 1.8 billion pixels each second of an area the size of Disney World. Before Maven, air force analysts could make sense of only 5 percent of this data in real time. When the software matured, Cukor, McCord, and the Maven team tested it with marines in Afghanistan. They packed a shipping container full of specialized computers filled with the 240 NVIDIA processors needed to run this power-intensive AI software and flew it to Kandahar. Sure enough, the software performed as advertised. Warfighters were able to track bad actors.

Back at the Pentagon, word was spreading about this tiny team of specialists at DIU who were working miracles with AI. Joint Chiefs chairman General Joseph Dunford, who never did seem perturbed by Chris's candor in the John Podesta memo, asked McCord to use AI to conduct a war-game analysis that would predict the first fifteen moves in a conflict with North Korea. One morning, fresh off a red-eye from San Francisco, McCord found himself in the Pentagon, leading a presentation to the entire Joint Chiefs about a strategy for fighting a war against North Korea—not a situation in which he'd ever imagined himself.

Project Maven had nothing to do with weapons. It was only going to identify objects like cars and people, using computer vision for "non-offensive" uses, in Pentagon parlance. Nevertheless, in 2018, when Gizmodo, a tech news site, broke news that Google was working with the DoD, all hell broke loose. The article explicitly stated that Maven involved image recognition software. But its headline—"Google Is Helping the Pentagon Build AI for Drones"—led many to believe that Google was building autonomous weapons. In April 2018, a month after the Gizmodo article appeared, three thousand Google employees signed an open letter demanding that Google withdraw from the project, because "we believe that Google should not be in the business of war. . . . Therefore we ask that Project Maven be canceled, and that Google draft, publicize and enforce a clear policy stating that neither Google nor its contractors will ever build warfare technology."

To us, this was ridiculous. For one thing, Google was not making weapons. Not even close. For another, Google and other tech companies absolutely should be in the business of helping to defend the United States and its allies, whether by building solutions for warfighters on the battlefield or protecting our people, corporations, government agencies, and military from cyberattacks. This was an argument that Chris advanced in an op-ed about the controversy for the *New York Times*, "Why Silicon Valley Must Go to War." To Raj, who had served in uniform, the three thousand employees protesting Project Maven were hopelessly naïve and even reckless—well-paid people who were reaping the benefits of Western democracy but didn't want to support the freedoms they enjoyed. In June, Diane Greene, the president of Google's cloud division, announced that because of the internal turmoil generated around Maven, Google wouldn't renew its contract with us when it ended in 2019. This happened despite objections from tech luminaries like Vint Cerf, who declared, correctly, that the project was about creating "situational awareness" and helping troops identify terrorists planting improvised explosive devices. "There is a lot of misunderstanding about the positive benefits of working with the public sector, the military being a part of that," Cerf said.

From our perspective, Google made a huge mistake in abandoning Project Maven. A lot of their engineers felt the same way. Unlike the employees who signed the open letter, the Google developers who were actually working on Project Maven believed deeply in the importance of the mission they were pursuing. On a visit to Google to meet with Project Maven engineers, many told Raj this was the most impactful work they'd ever done at Google, or even in their entire careers, because the software they were building would save the lives of U.S. and allied troops, as well as the lives of innocent civilians, by enabling analysts to make better decisions.

Some of these engineers had immigrated to the U.S. from authoritarian regimes, making this work deeply personal. The silver lining is that the work begun by Maven continued unabated after Google dropped out. Also, as General Shanahan had predicted, Maven served as a spark for further development of AI throughout the Department of Defense. In 2018, Shanahan lobbied to build an organization that could oversee AI development across the entire DoD. At the time, more than six hundred projects involving AI were being conducted inside various branches. Shanahan wanted to bring them all under one umbrella, called the Joint Artificial Intelligence Center—JAIC, pronounced "Jake"—and asked McCord to figure out how to do it. McCord talked to people in the private sector who'd built large-scale AI organizations, like Andrew Ng, who ran Google Brain. "From the people who built the machine learning platform at Uber to the head of computer vision at Facebook, I went right to the source," McCord recalls.

McCord pitched his ideas to every senior leader who'd listen to him, including Mike Griffin, the undersecretary of defense for research and engineering, who'd previously served as NASA administrator. Griffin, who is notoriously prickly, was not a big fan of the Maven Project or DIU generally, but did admire how fast the project proceeded. "Whatever you guys did with Maven," Griffin told McCord, "at least you figured out how to get stuff done quickly. I don't know if it's always done right, but you got it done really, really quickly. You need to just keep moving on that front and don't let people screw you up." McCord says Griffin was supportive, but their relationship was not exactly warm. He recalls Griffin pulling him aside in a hallway and telling him that he needed someone who understood AI. "I said, 'Are you saying that's me?' And he said, 'Well, I don't have anyone else.' So it was not exactly laudatory," McCord remembers. The next step was to win support for JAIC from Joseph Kernan, the undersecretary of defense for intelligence. McCord ran through his spiel, and remembers Kernan, a former Navy SEAL and not a technologist, giving his blessing: "Brendan, I don't know what you're talking about. But the Maven guys said you do. So let's go do it."

Thus, the JAIC was brought to life as yet another powerful motor of innovation inside the Pentagon. To ensure AI was deployed responsibly, the Defense Innovation Board devised a set of principles, developed in coordination with human rights groups, and published them in 2019. At long last, the DoD had become serious about building a military driven by data and artificial intelligence and doing so responsibly. In that sense Maven, from our perspective, was a tremendous success, as it went from a small project with a simple remit to transforming the entire Department. We chalked that up as a win.

PETER THIEL AND THE DEFENSE UNICORNS

In Silicon Valley, the anti-Pentagon sentiment among founders and investors was waning, helped in part by two big lawsuits brought by companies that were funded by Peter Thiel's venture capital firm, Founders Fund. The legal maneuvers were aimed at breaking apart the oligopoly held by traditional government suppliers. Thiel is an interesting and controversial figure. Born in Germany, raised in South Africa and then California, he studied philosophy at Stanford before earning a law degree from Stanford Law School.

In 1998, Thiel helped found PayPal and became part of the so-called "PayPal Mafia," a group of influential figures that included Elon Musk, another South African and the leader of Tesla, SpaceX, and other start-ups, and Reid Hoffman, who'd go on to found LinkedIn and become a prominent venture capitalist. Thiel used the money he made from PayPal to launch a career as an investor, scoring his first major hit as one of the earliest investors in Facebook, as famously depicted in the Aaron Sorkin film *The Social Network*. Thiel then founded Palantir to provide data mining capabilities to U.S. intelligence services, and created Founders Fund, which invested in Palantir and Anduril.

In 2014, Thiel helped SpaceX (founded by his longtime friend Elon Musk) sue the air force for issuing an $11 billion sole-source contract to United Launch Alliance (ULA) for the launch of military satellites. ULA is a joint venture between Lockheed Martin and Boeing, two big primes. That suit was settled in 2015 after the air force promised to open military launch missions to wider competition.

In 2015, Palantir sued the army after getting boxed out of a bid to provide software for the Distributed Common Ground System—Army (DCGS-A), an intelligence gathering and analysis system. The army wanted to develop the software internally, and had already spent billions on the project, but—in a story that was now familiar to us at DIU—the warfighters who were actually using the software hated it, claiming it was buggy. Some teams on the ground had been using Palantir software on small projects and loved it, but when they started asking for Palantir, the army rejected their requests. In 2016, a judge ruled in favor of Palantir, saying that its product, the Palantir Gotham Platform, filled the requirements of what the army needed and at a lower cost than developing the software internally. That enabled Palantir to compete for the project, vying against Raytheon. Eventually, in 2019, Palantir won the contract, worth nearly $1 billion over ten years.

Little by little, the lawsuits were forcing the Pentagon to rethink its acquisition process—in part by shaming the DoD and exposing to the public its outdated, oligopolistic methods. "I'll tell you, what SpaceX had to do to effectively do business with the United States Air Force embarrassed us in public. And no service secretary likes to be embarrassed in public," air force general John Hyten, who became Vice Chairman of the Joint Chiefs of Staff when Paul Selva retired, would later remark.

A third Founders Fund company, Anduril, also started shaking up the way the Pentagon acquired products. Its founder, Palmer Luckey, was only twenty-one years old when he sold his first company, Oculus Rift, a maker of virtual reality goggles, to Facebook for $2 billion in 2014. A few months later, Luckey attended a retreat in British Columbia hosted by Founders Fund, which had been one of the investors in Oculus. At the retreat he met Trae Stephens, a former intelligence analyst and Palantir executive who'd joined Founders Fund with the goal of investing in venture-backed companies aimed at the defense sector.

Like a lot of people in Silicon Valley, Stephens had taken an unusual route into the world of technology. He majored in Regional and Comparative Studies at Georgetown before going to work in the intelligence community on computational linguistics. Having imagined futurist command centers and real-time analytics, he became dismayed at the actual state of the tech that agencies were using. Just like what Raj had discovered at the air force command center in Qatar, Stephens was taken aback to see U.S. intelligence analysts working with incompatible databases that couldn't connect to each other. "I'd say twenty percent of my time was literally just running searches and merging database files. This was taking up a full day out of every week. I thought I was going to show up and it would be this James Bond thing—they'd give me a supercomputer and the keys to an Aston Martin. Instead, it was a joke," Stephens recalls.

Stephens pushed to bring in modern technology, like the software Palantir had developed. His requests were refused. When he kept pushing, he was told to shut up. So he quit and went to work at Palantir. That company had been founded in 2004 as a response to 9/11, when the founders read the 9/11 Commission report and realized that "it was just a failure to connect the dots. We had the data, but it was never pulled into a single place," Stephens says. The techies who founded Palantir knew how to do connect-the-dots work—they'd done it for years at PayPal, to counter fraud. "They knew they could take what they'd learned and build that into a product and sell that to the government," Stephens says.

The problem, Stephens discovered when he joined Palantir, was that though these were brilliant software engineers, they had no idea how to deal with the government. Palantir was funded in part by In-Q-Tel, which helped them sell pilot programs, but they struggled to move projects into production. For years they beat their heads against the wall trying to win business from the government. "In Silicon Valley we're used to a world where once you find product-market fit, you start winning customers. It's like *Field of Dreams*—if you build it, the customers will come. But with the government, there is no field of dreams. If you build it, they still won't come." Recalling how Palantir finally had to sue the army to be given the chance to bid on a contract, Stephens says, "Palantir had to go to war to get the chance to go to war. The army was in full-out fortress mode. They were just going to batten down the hatches and block Palantir."

When Stephens and Luckey decided to do something in the tech space, they visited Raj at the DIU offices and spent ninety minutes talking ideas. They hadn't named the company or even decided what product they wanted to build; they were just looking for problems to solve. They were also concerned about doing business with the DoD for fear that it would take too long to get contracts and start generating revenue.

"Should we even do this?" Stephens asked Raj. "Should we spend a bunch of energy on this? Because a lot of people seem pretty skeptical about dealing with the government."

"No, there's real change happening," Raj said. "We have fifty people here, but there's more to this than just DIU. The army is launching its own innovation unit, called the Army Futures Command. Other branches of the military are beginning to follow us."

Raj, who had been at DIU for more than a year, shared how much the DoD needed innovators like Stephens and Luckey. He gave them some advice and discussed their original idea, which was to deploy sensors along the southern border to stop immigrants from crossing into the United States—a digital version of the physical wall that Trump was trying to build. The idea was controversial. In liberal Silicon Valley, the Department of Homeland Security (DHS) border policies were seen as hateful. Now here were a bunch of techies enthusiastically joining the effort to "build the wall." The optics were unusual and led Bloomberg to describe Anduril as "tech's most controversial startup."

Another idea Luckey and Stephens wanted to pursue was to create a way to knock down enemy drones. In that first brainstorming meeting with Raj, they described a system that consisted of a box that would open, unleashing a swarm of drones that would shoot down enemy drones then fly back into the box to recharge or refuel. While it would take till 2023 for that idea to reach fruition, Anduril did achieve early success with its design of surveillance towers that could be placed along the southern border and on military bases. Anduril also developed a set of combat drones, including one called Anvil that uses computer vision to spot enemy drones and then destroys them by smashing into them at speeds of up to two hundred miles per hour. Another, a stealth drone called Ghost, can be lugged in a backpack and is used by the U.S. military as well as DHS and Customs and Border Protection. The crown jewel of Anduril's business is an AI software program called Lattice that can analyze enormous amounts of data gathered by sensors.

Stephens says Anduril benefited from the lawsuits that SpaceX and Palantir had brought. He recalls overhearing someone from the Department of Homeland Security at an In-Q-Tel conference talking about why they were going to do business with Anduril: "Anduril was founded by the same people who built Palantir and SpaceX. I don't want to get tied into a lawsuit for the next ten years. These people have teeth." Palantir and SpaceX needed five years to get to their first $10 million in revenue, "but Anduril did that in twenty-two months," Stephens recalls.

By the end of 2021, Anduril was doing $200 million a year in revenue. In 2022, the company won a $1 billion contract from the U.S. Special Operations Command, and later that year the company raised a whopping $1.5 billion venture capital round that valued the company at $8.5 billion. The company is by far the most successful defense-centered tech startup. Luckey's long-term goal is to build Anduril into the next huge defense prime contractor, displacing the likes of Lockheed Martin.

Anduril's success has sparked more interest from Silicon Valley investors in defense technology. Palantir's 2020 IPO, which valued the company at $16.5 billion, helped too. (The company is now worth $30 billion and generates $2 billion a year in revenue.) Further momentum comes from the fact that by 2023 SpaceX was valued at $137 billion. "There's more appetite now than at any time in the past two decades," Stephens says. "When VCs can see a clear pattern that they can invest in defense and make money, a lot of those emotional appeals protesting getting involved with weapons kind of go away. The successful new defense tech companies today are standing on the shoulders of Palantir and SpaceX."

Stephens has no patience for people in Silicon Valley who insist commercial tech companies like Google and Microsoft shouldn't work for the DoD. "There's a vocal minority, like the people who pushed Google out of Project Maven, who don't see why this matters," Stephens says. "But do you think global supply chains matter? Do you realize that rests on the power of the U.S. Navy? If you care about global supply chains, you should care about national security. If you care about cellular technology, you should care about national security. If you care about freedom of speech, you should care about national security. One thing DIU has accomplished," he adds, "is that it has created a forum for conversation, a 'convening power' for those ideas."

PRESSING THE EJECT BUTTON

Despite the progress we were making, the work was exhausting—and, in particular, Raj was beginning to worry that his window for becoming an entrepreneur again might be closing. The new president's freewheeling style was throwing institutionalists for a loop. The chaos of the Oval Office spilled downward and created confusion even down to the military units we were working with to buy game-changing technology. Raj had been invited to a meeting with President Trump. It was one of his stranger experiences. A few dozen of the country's biggest tech executives arrived at the White House to meet with the President and his cabinet, plus Jared and Ivanka. The event was supposed to last an hour, during which the President and his advisors would be briefed on important emerging technologies. Instead, the first twenty-five minutes were wasted introducing people and praising Trump, who soaked up the adulation. The President was less interested in the part of the meeting that dealt with actual technology—in fact, he wasn't interested at all.

The CEO of Kespry, a tech company in Silicon Valley, demonstrated a drone. Randall Stephenson, the CEO of AT&T, briefly presented on 5G. Halfway through the scheduled meeting, President Trump stood up to leave. There were more things on the agenda, but Trump wasn't staying. "You're doing a tremendous job. We're doing great technology. And next week we're going to announce our great health care plan." And just like that, Trump walked out, along with his entire cabinet, except for Wilbur Ross, the commerce secretary, who stayed behind and continued the conversation for twenty minutes with the CEOs who'd flown to D.C. for this meeting. There were no more presentations. The affair showcased the dynamics we had to wade through in the new regime.

But the Pentagon bureaucracy was a bipartisan feature, a fixture of life no matter which administration was in charge. It felt as if we and our fellow travelers in Silicon Valley were constantly squaring off against the Pentagon and the primes. We were trying to help. Our only goal was to make the U.S. military more competitive by arming our troops with the best possible technology. For Raj, this was personal. He had close friends, people he'd served with in Iraq and Afghanistan, who were still serving in uniform as warfighters. In a way our mission was ridiculously simple and straightforward: just do what's best for the military. We'd assembled a team of great people. We were working with brilliant technologists and entrepreneurs who were taking big risks by trying to start their own companies and trusting us to help them succeed. We knew the future of warfare would be built around technology, and we knew Silicon Valley was bursting with great ideas that could solve our biggest problems. The top brass knew this too. Yet at so many turns we ran into ferocious opposition. The Capella fiasco was just one example of a time when we brought the Pentagon a system that could save lives, and cost a tiny fraction of the alternative, only to have the gem we'd found tossed aside.

After thirteen straight years in some of the most pressurized jobs in national security, from Iraq to the National Security Council, Chris decided to exit DIU in November 2017, just after Mattis visited and blessed the unit. The kid from Worthington, Ohio, had begun a sprint in public service that turned into an ultra-marathon. His work across three presidential administrations had imposed terrible costs on his personal life. His thirteen-year marriage, already on the rocks, frayed further and ended shortly thereafter. It was time to step away. Four months later, in March of 2018, Raj quietly transitioned too, after hitting his promised two-year tenure, his emotional constitution similarly worn down. "You should leave public service before you hate it, so you'll return one day," one of his mentors had advised him. With the organization scaling and executing on contracts, its model firmly established, it seemed the right time to leave.

Raj's efforts to enact an orderly leadership transition plan were stymied by Mike Griffin, the new undersecretary of defense for research and engineering. In a bureaucratic demotion, DIU was about to be assigned to Griffin's organization. Worse, among the members of Griffin's team was a woman Raj had been forced to override on orders from Carter. Her moment of tit for tat at hand, she convinced Griffin that DIU was a rogue unit in need of overhaul. Before even meeting Raj or visiting DIU, Griffin refused to interview the candidates Raj put forward to replace himself. While choosing subordinates is the prerogative of any new leader, Griffin ran the process at glacial speed, leaving DIU in the care of a well-meaning navy officer hamstrung by his "acting" title and without the protection of the Secretary of Defense. New leadership finally arrived in the form of Michael Brown, the former CEO of Symantec, who signed on as managing director in September 2018. Despite bittersweet departures, we were proud of what we'd accomplished at DIU and committed to continuing the mission. But it was time to pass the baton.

After leaving DIU, Chris took a month off and then taught a class at the Harvard Institute of Politics. After that, he teamed with Eric Schmidt, taking a role as a senior director at Schmidt Futures. That role would eventually lead to his working with Schmidt to counter the rising threat posed by China, contribute to the efforts of the National Security Commission on AI, and help push forward the CHIPS Act, whose aim is to rebuild the American semiconductor industry and reduce our reliance on China.

Raj transitioned to becoming the founding CEO at Resilience, a cyber insurance company that he started with DIU alum Vishaal Hariprasad. Raj also started doing some angel investing and was being approached by venture capital firms that wanted him to scout defense-related investment opportunities. Defense was getting hot enough that a lot of VC firms wanted to double down and needed a partner who understood the Pentagon and the military and could spot promising startups. The opportunity was tempting. Some firms were offering partner positions. But Raj hesitated. He was mulling starting his own VC firm in a few years rather than working for someone else, but now was not the time. He needed to immerse himself in his new startup.

As draining as the last two years had been, we both remained optimistic. The Pentagon was becoming more open to commercial technology. Silicon Valley was becoming more willing to work with the DoD. In fits and starts, the two sides were moving closer to one another.

DIU portfolio companies were making an impact, putting into wide use satellites, drones, and sensors that were becoming the digital eyes and ears of the warfighter, collecting vast oceans of information and feeding that data into powerful AI software that could analyze it in the blink of an eye. Things were still in transition, but you could feel the playing field starting to tilt. Saildrone vessels were roaming the oceans scouting for drug traffickers. Shield AI drones were looking promising in their early prototype stages, and it seemed likely the startup would succeed in building devices to help Navy SEALs knock down doors and take down terrorist hideouts. Drones built for the Blue UAS program were making their way into the hands of military customers. Ryan Beall's Android app was enabling Special Forces operators to turn the enemy's drones against them. Joby was setting up a manufacturing facility; we felt sure that in a few years its aircraft would be doing reconnaissance, carrying cargo, and even perhaps shuttling warfighters into combat zones.

Other DIU companies were modernizing the DoD's obsolete computer systems with better software, stronger cybersecurity, and smart algorithms that delivered huge savings on mundane but necessary chores like fleet maintenance. Software from ForAllSecure and Tanium was protecting weapons systems and other critical infrastructure. Palantir was empowering intelligence services to make better decisions. Anduril was devising new ways to provide perimeter security at military bases and dreaming up systems that could blow ISIS drones out of the sky.

Although Google had bailed out of Project Maven, Amazon and Microsoft had remained involved, and the commercial sector was making a long-term commitment to helping the DoD—if not out of a sense of patriotism then because it was good business. In Washington, the Pentagon was pumping real money—tens of billions of dollars, a far cry from our tiny $30 million budget—into technology. JAIC was building AI capabilities across all branches of the DoD. The air force had stood up Kessel Run and AFWERX. In Austin, Texas, the Army Futures Command was buzzing with activity, teaching modern software development techniques to DoD programmers, funding research at hundreds of universities, and teaming with commercial companies to assemble technologies for everything from hypersonic missiles to missile-killing lasers to robotic combat vehicles.

By the end of 2018, DIU and its portfolio companies were starting to breach the walls of the Pentagon fortress. Despite the inefficiency and sluggish bureaucracy, and all the slow-walking, foot-dragging, exhausting internecine battles, and obstruction by the primes and their lobbyists, the DoD was battling its way into the digital age. Ash Carter's vision of public-private cooperation was becoming a reality. If you squinted a little bit, and used some imagination, you could see the hazy outlines of a new kind of military—speedy, nimble, tech-driven—taking shape.

CHAPTER SIX
WASHINGTON AND THE RISE OF THE MACHINES

"The U.S. is fucked," Madeleine Albright said after a briefing about where the U.S. stood compared to China when it came to artificial intelligence.

America's first female secretary of state, whose elegant lapel brooches and sharp wit defined U.S. diplomacy in the 1990s, was sitting with experts in AI and geopolitics in her role as chairwoman of the National Democratic Institute. The colorful but rarely profane secretary was coming to terms with what those at DIU had been grappling with for years—that emerging technology and especially AI was turning the world upside down.

By the summer of 2018, it was suddenly dawning on policymakers in Washington that the tectonic shifts in technology weren't just an innovation sideshow. The rapid adoption of advanced sensors and processors was driving change in the global political system faster than any previous transformation. Not only did it begin to look like China might actually achieve its ambitions of overtaking the U.S. in multiple tech sectors, but the U.S. military no longer looked as dominant as it once had. AI was helping autocrats repress their own populations. In the words of one of the world's top AI researchers, "AI could create infinitely stable dictatorships."

In a sign of how urgently these questions were now being considered, the Aspen Strategy Group—a who's who of diplomats, lawmakers, and national security officials—selected as its summer meeting topic "Technology & National Security: Maintaining America's Edge." The bipartisan group of distinguished leaders meets for five days each summer with the national security team of whichever administration is in power. The sitting secretaries of state and defense or their deputies usually attend along with the President's national security advisor. The only clue that so many senior officials are in Aspen is a row of air force Gulfstreams painted like Air Force One at the airport. It's the kind of group where people sometimes excuse themselves to take a phone call from the President of the United States.

Attendees in 2018 included Condoleezza Rice, Madeleine Albright, Ash Carter, David Petraeus, and dozens of senators, ambassadors, and former cabinet members. Chris, a longtime participant in the Strategy Group, was joined that year by DIU reserve commander and Apple vice president Doug Beck. Eric Schmidt also flew in.

It was a special moment for Chris to see Eric as he'd just agreed to go to work for him the week before. Eric had asked Chris to help build his new philanthropic enterprise, Schmidt Futures.

The Strategy Group's opening session, "Tectonic Shifts: Technological Changes Shaping the Instruments of American Power," was meant to explain why technological change is exponential in nature and how this makes predicting future developments so difficult. Two seasoned experts led the discussion: Jason Matheny, director of IARPA, the Intelligence Advanced Research Projects Activity, and Richard Danzig, the polymath former secretary of the navy. They deployed an alluring analogy to illustrate how difficult exponential change can be to spot, even as it becomes a tidal wave that suddenly engulfs everything.

"Imagine," Danzig said, "that Lake Michigan was empty of water. Then in that vast basin, with its 1,600-mile circumference, we place one ounce of water at its center. Each year that water doubles. If we started in the year 1940, how long would it take to fill?"

The group of brainiacs in the room started squirming to figure out the answer. It was so close to one of those ridiculous management consulting interview questions about how many jellybeans can fit in a room that Chris figured the head of McKinsey's Defense Practice, sitting behind him, would raise his hand first. It turned out that everyone was too shy to venture a guess. After a pregnant pause, Danzig walked further down his analogy.

"By 1950," he said, "we would have a gallon. By 1960, we would have 150 gallons. In 1970 we hit 16,000 gallons—a swimming pool!"

Moving quicker now, Danzig said that "by 2000, you have a slight sheen on the lake floor and by 2010 you have a few inches of water here and there."

He then said what everyone was thinking.

"This is ridiculous. It's now been *seventy years* and you still don't have enough water to float a goldfish. Surely this task is futile? But just wait," Danzig said, his voice rising with excitement. "Just as you're about to give up, things *suddenly change*. By 2020, you have about 40 feet of water. And by 2025 you're done."

The room was stunned.

Danzig and Matheny had wowed their audience.

"After seventy years you had nothing. Fifteen years later, the job was finished," Danzig concluded.

Matheny and Danzig then moved through a series of slides on exponential shifts in technology sectors that were behind dramatic transformations in our lives. The moral of the story is that you never quite know when the law of exponential returns is going to cause everything to change.

Policymakers were learning what historians of technology had long known. We often live in what are called "the in-between times," the sometimes long pause between when a transformational technology is demonstrated and when its promise is fully realized through widespread adoption.

Twenty years after Edison's first lightbulb flickered, only 3 percent of the U.S. population had electricity. Not long thereafter electricity was ubiquitous around the world.

For this very reason we cannot take the linearity of the past as a given.

The U.S. pursuit of technological superiority that has held for each decade since World War II, through the Cold War, Gulf Wars, and beyond, could change if another actor on the world stage learned to harness the laws of exponential change faster than the U.S.

China now aspires to be that actor.

CHINA'S RISE

By the time the Aspen Strategy Group convened in 2018, we were a long way from Air Force One touching down in China in the summer of 1998, when Bill Clinton made the first visit of a U.S. president since the 1989 Tiananmen Square massacre and declared that the United States and China "have a special responsibility to the future of the world." The hope was that bringing it further into the international community would lead China to offer its people more freedom and to act harmoniously toward others. It was a beautiful dream—one started in 1972 by Henry Kissinger and Richard Nixon.

That dream was now dying in the minds of most policymakers and was completely dead in national security circles. China had become increasingly combative. President Xi Jinping had declared himself ruler for life, suppressed self-rule in Hong Kong, disappeared dissidents and businessmen who opposed his rule, and undertaken a campaign of genocide against the Uyghurs, a minority ethnic population in Western China.

And he was just as brutal abroad. He illegally possessed territory in the South China Sea, ran drills simulating the invasion of Taiwan, and used China's economic power to coerce allegiance from weaker nations. He even stationed Chinese police forces in Chinese embassies and consulates to chase down dissidents who fled abroad.

Xi was also amassing military power at an astonishing clip. By the time the Trump administration assumed office, a new bipartisan consensus had formed in Washington that China was shifting from frenemy to enemy, that our most significant trading partner might also be our most dangerous adversary. The switch happened so suddenly that Kurt Campbell, Obama's top China hand, wrote a mea culpa in *Foreign Affairs* titled "The China Reckoning: How Beijing Defied American Expectations."

China's ambitions were no secret. For years Xi had published plans outlining exactly how China would win the technology race with the United States. China hands across D.C. could reel them off from memory: the "Made in China 2025" plan, the "AI Global Leader by 2030" plan, the plan to dominate global standard-setting bodies by 2035. AI, next-generation networks, semiconductors, advanced manufacturing, synthetic biology, biopharmaceuticals, quantum computing, fusion energy—China had a plan for each. The U.S. had no plan at all.

China was putting serious money behind their strategy—increasing R&D spending thirtyfold between 1991 and 2015. While the dollar amounts were still modest by global standards, when adjusted for purchasing power—investments in China go twice as far—China was in fact spending 88 percent of what the U.S. was on R&D.

It wasn't just in scientific endeavors that the Chinese were achieving mastery. Following the strategy set by Xi, China was mobilizing the power of the state in every sector to create "national champion" companies that would dominate global market share. Already, China had Huawei in 5G, SenseTime in facial recognition, DJI in drones, and Alibaba in e-commerce. TikTok would soon become China's best known national champion.

All of these companies were already outcompeting their U.S. equivalents, in part because the Chinese state subsidized their growth, fueled them with data to improve their algorithms, and ensured access to massive customer bases at home and abroad. In 2015, two of the world's twenty most valuable companies were Chinese. Six years later there were seven. China's industrial production capacities were ten times the U.S. Even if U.S. teamed with its Asian and European allies, China would still outmatch them in manufacturing three to one.

While many technologies were important, AI was proving most consequential because it unlocks exponential progress in other fields. Human language processing, self-driving cars, modeling protein structures, controlling plasma in a cold fusion reactor—AI could potentially solve these seemingly intractable problems. The stakes of the game were quickly coming into focus. Whichever nation first mastered AI at scale would not only command scientific and commercial power. Its military capability would grow exponentially as well. Self-driving cars lead to self-driving tanks. Algorithms that detect signals can defeat stealth. AI will drive geopolitics in the same way other empires have risen and fallen on gunpowder, the steamship, and steel.

Here too China had had a plan for some time. Xi called it "civil-military fusion." He announced it on a day Chris was traveling with Vice Chairman Winnefeld in Silicon Valley. DIU hadn't even yet been created. Xi told his countrymen that the People's Liberation Army would now have access to any technology made by a Chinese company, place military officials on corporate boards, and ingest technology with military applications directly into the Chinese army and navy. In the Chinese system, the line where the Communist Party ended and firms began was fluid.

"You saw Xi's announcement, right?" Chris asked Winnefeld as they stepped into the motorcade at their Palo Alto hotel. Both had just read the Early Bird, the Pentagon's news clips pushed to senior officials each morning. Winnefeld, the military's second-ranking official, four stars on his shoulders and rows of medals on his chest, said, "Yeah, and here we are today just starting to talk with venture capitalists and startups."

Some in Washington now wondered whether the U.S. might suddenly lose its economic and military advantage in one fell swoop. China had flipped our own playbook on us, fueling its rise with the very paradigm of state-sponsored R&D we devised after Sputnik, but then forgot about after the Cold War.

What should we do now?

BACK IN ASPEN

The Aspen Strategy Group dedicated its entire 2018 meeting to the U.S.'s technology strategy because of an unnerving session the summer before. In 2017 President Trump's national security advisor, Lieutenant General H. R. McMaster, flew to Aspen to address the group just seven months into the Trump administration. A renowned military thinker, combat veteran, and graduate of West Point with a Ph.D. in American History, McMaster had authored *Dereliction of Duty*, a searing critique of how Lyndon Johnson and his advisors mishandled the Vietnam War. He arrived in Aspen just in time to catch the session before he was scheduled to speak. It was titled "The Technological Tsunami." Chris, then still at DIU, presented a paper to the group titled "An Even Flatter World: How Technology Is Remaking the World Order." The presentation explored how the diffusion of scientific discovery was changing the nature of power, and why the U.S. had the most to lose from this shift. Addressing the room of senior officials from a table at its front, he talked about how the global technology playing field had leveled—for example, how the AI behind Amazon's Alexa and Apple's Siri could be equally put to use mining geospatial data and identifying military targets. And he brought up how free trade and open borders, long assumed to draw global talent to the U.S. and Europe, had now begun to work in reverse, with foreign Ph.D.s and post-docs returning to Beijing or Shanghai.

The last line of Chris's paper summed up how the tide had turned: "Technology—once an unmistakable comparative advantage of the liberal world order—now almost equally empowers those who seek its undoing."

McMaster had traveled from Washington with Dr. Nadia Schadlow, the national security advisor's lead strategist. Schadlow, a brilliant scholar of the Cold War, was responsible for writing the Trump administration's national security strategy, the plan the U.S. would use to counter China. Everyone in the room wanted to know what it would say.

McMaster was then in the early stages of formulating what would become a landmark turnabout in U.S. policy on China and artificial intelligence, but at that moment his answers lacked the depth the group was hoping to hear.

They asked tough questions: "How do we think about a world in which war is cheap and not dangerous?" one person asked. "Should we admit failure and move to strategic adaptation?" another wondered. Most of the questions were about China and technology.

As McMaster was peppered by questions, Chris leaned over and asked Nadia, with whom he'd previously worked, if she'd seen the technology strategy he'd helped create as part of a joint effort between the NSC and White House Office of Science and Technology Policy in 2016.

"You guys did a technology strategy?" she said.

Chris flashed with anger. He suddenly realized how the disorderly transition between administrations had disrupted the flow of information to the NSC. Chris had co-chaired the technology strategy with U.S. chief technology advisor Megan Smith. A working group of almost one hundred people from eighteen departments and agencies had participated.

"There's a lot of stuff in there about AI," Chris explained.

The working group had solicited insights from world experts and even invited Mustafa Suleyman, the cofounder of Google DeepMind, to the White House for a day. In the Situation Room Mustafa had shown the President's national security staff videos of DeepMind's algorithms learning to play videogames better than humans. The NSC staff called the brief "the robots are coming."

Chris and Megan briefed the strategy to the National Security Council, White House chief of staff, and ultimately to President Obama. Chris now realized that his most important work at the NSC had been lost in translation.

"We left both reports in the 'A' transition binder," Chris said, referring to the compilation of key decision memos, studies, and findings the outgoing administration passes to the incoming. As McMaster continued speaking, Chris opened his laptop, got Nadia's NSC email address, and sent her the study's unclassified version.

It was a serious institutional breakdown, with some of the Obama administration's most important policy findings failing to make it to the Trump official charged with authoring the national security strategy of the United States. So many hard questions remained at the end of the session that the group's co-chairs decided to focus the next year's meetings on technology.

McMaster and Schadlow, faced with a chaotic administration, adroitly focused the U.S. government's attention on the most pressing strategic issue: the need to directly confront the Chinese Communist Party. Despite decades of economic integration, it was clear that Xi's China was not playing fair and had become a threat to democracies. Now was the time to reckon with this uncomfortable truth.

In the months that followed, McMaster and Schadlow went on to implement the most fundamental changes in U.S. policy toward China since Kissinger. In a shift carried out with the help of Matthew Pottinger, a Mandarin-speaking former marine officer who worked in China for the *Wall Street Journal* before serving as the NSC's senior director for China, the Trump administration pivoted from the Obama approach. Whereas previously China had been viewed as a nation whose rise could be managed without coercive measures, it would now be treated as an economic and military threat that needed to be contained. The new bipartisan consensus that formed in response to China's aggressive actions opened the door to a historic about-face. A generation of U.S. policies were designed to advance the U.S.-China economic relationship. But as China transformed from partner to adversary, those policies now needed to run in reverse, gating off China from access to advances in technology it could use against the U.S. McMaster was the architect of the beginnings of the technological containment of China that the Biden administration continued and carried still further. Had McMaster returned to Aspen the next year, it would have been a victory lap. But by then the Trump administration had devolved further into chaos; McMaster had been fired and replaced by John Bolton, who didn't bother to come to Aspen or send anyone in his place.

THE COLD WARRIOR'S WORRY

Madeleine Albright was the Strategy Group's senior member and was becoming increasingly vocal that we were again in a crisis on par with the early Cold War. She wasn't sure the "indispensable nation," as she described the U.S., would prevail when it came to artificial intelligence.

Born in Prague on the eve of World War II, Albright was a stalwart defender of democracy and human rights. Though she stood only four feet, ten inches tall, she struck fear into villains and tyrants the world over. She had faced down Saddam Hussein, used U.S. military force to remove Slobodan Milošević from power, and negotiated with Kim Jong-il over North Korea's nuclear missiles. Albright had seen the worst of the world. Now her inner sirens were blaring. She saw how, in the hands of an autocratic power like China, AI could change the course of history, undermining democracies while empowering autocrats. AI was throwing global affairs a curveball—a silicon curveball.

The ever-curious Albright was no stranger to technology. She was among the first visitors to DIU—and she arrived at our office in Mountain View with twenty former foreign ministers in tow. It was an almost all male group that jokingly referred to themselves as "Madeleine's Exes," since they'd each had a diplomatic relationship with her in the past. She wanted these grizzled diplomats from Canada, Italy, the UK, Australia, Spain, Greece, Mexico, France, Egypt, and eleven other countries to see firsthand how technology was changing war and peace.

At the DIU offices we walked through a number of our projects, showing off drones powered by artificial intelligence and our autonomous sailboat. Albright and the ministers left more than a little unnerved. It was clear that technology could change the world, and that anyone could access it.

That night we hosted a reception at the Rosewood Hotel with venture capitalists and startup CEOs. Chris and the Secretary gave a toast to DIU and its work. It struck Chris that to almost everyone else in the room, technology was a source of convenience and benefit. But Albright had seen it used in other ways.

NSCAI

It was by now apparent that the new administration needed to move faster to address the rising technological threat. In the restrained prose of a Council on Foreign Relations Task Force report, whose members included Raj, Eric Schmidt, Reid Hoffman, and the president of MIT, "the Trump White House has been slow in driving the development of AI." The task force's view was that the U.S. urgently needed a national strategy on AI. It listed two dozen countries that already had one. It then mentioned a new commission created by Congress that might help fill in the gap. Its name was the National Security Commission on Artificial Intelligence, or NSCAI.

The commission was the handiwork of alarmed members of Congress, who saw that the nation was adrift. A bipartisan coalition of lawmakers from the House and Senate ushered the commission into existence in legislative language written into the National Defense Authorization Act.

Four months after Chris started work for Eric Schmidt, Congressman Mac Thornberry—who previously saved DIU by restoring its budget—appointed Eric to the commission. News broke on the day Eric was hosting a holiday party for the Schmidt Futures team.

"Chris," Eric asked, "what do you think I should do with this AI Commission?"

"Well," Chris said, "I actually wrote my Ph.D. dissertation on national security commissions."

"You're kidding."

"Nope, I'm really that big of a super-nerd," Chris replied. "My dissertation is titled 'Fixing the National Security State: Commissions and the Politics of Disaster and Reform.'"

As the rest of the staff gathered for the holiday celebration, Chris gave Eric a quick tutorial on what makes commissions successful. "The first commission in the U.S. was empaneled in 1794 by George Washington to put an end to the Whiskey Rebellion. It failed. Washington had to get on his horse and ride with the army toward Pennsylvania. So these things don't always work.

"There are three types of commissions," Chris went on. "Crisis commissions, like the 9/11 Commission, have the highest success rate implementing their recommendations—fifty-six percent to be exact, based on a study of all fifty-five national security commissions created between 1981 and 2009. The AI Commission is an 'agenda commission.' There isn't an immediate crisis that needs to be solved, but rather a complex issue that the political system can't tackle. Agenda commissions have the second highest rate of success—thirty-one percent. What you don't want to be on is a 'damage control commission.' They're formed when a politician wants to deflect blame and needs somewhere to punt the ball."

"Can you help me with this?" Eric asked.

Days later the commission's members elected Eric its chair. The members included Oracle CEO Safra Katz, Microsoft research lead Eric Horvitz, and future Amazon CEO Andrew Jassey. Bob Work, the deputy Secretary of Defense who'd given DIU its name, was elected vice chair. Once the commission was up and running, Raj also joined, as an affiliated expert—both of us thrilled to be working together again. Chris's role was to help ensure the commission's work as a whole was a success.

On the flight home from New York, Chris's first thought was that he had to find an all-star executive director. He knew right away whom to call. Ylli Bajraktari and Chris had worked together under the Chairman of the Joint Chiefs of Staff and Ylli helped lead Deputy Secretary Bob Work to the conclusion that the Pentagon needed a Silicon Valley outpost. If anyone could work at Eric's speed, it was Ylli. Grateful that the United flight's Wi-Fi was for once working, Chris texted Ylli, who like a good national security aide was always up on comms.

"Hey, there is a job you could make a tremendous contribution by taking. Send me your résumé," Chris wrote.

"Okay. What is it?" Ylli replied.

"Executive director of the National Security Commission on AI. You'll work directly for Eric Schmidt."

Chris and Ylli had met in 2010 traveling on an Air Force C-17 plane carrying the deputy Secretary of Defense on a tour of Iraq and Afghanistan. They went on to serve together on the personal staff of the Chairman of the Joint Chiefs and then again when DIU was stood up. Chris had also been with Ylli's brother Ylber in Iraq, where they were both civilian advisors during the surge, living in the Green Zone in trailers behind Saddam's palace.

Displaced from war-torn Pristina, Kosovo, the Bajraktari brothers had an "only in America" story. Immigrating to the U.S. after the NATO military action Madeleine Albright orchestrated to stop Slobodan Milošević's ethnic cleansing, they went on to become American citizens, and eventually civil servants at the Pentagon. Ylber became Ash Carter's deputy chief of staff and Ylli went into the Trump White House as H. R. McMaster's chief of staff.

Chris sent Ylli's résumé to Eric, who replied in minutes, saying, "Looks great!!!"

By the time Chris landed in San Francisco, the commission had its executive director.

It was a chilly March day in Washington when the commissioners converged in a borrowed conference room for their first meeting. The staff was still securing office space of their own. Some commissioners flew in on private planes. Most others flew coach, the only class of service permitted by the Department of Defense. A few who lived in town took the metro.

To start the day, Chris spoke to the group about what makes commissions successful. Then a briefer from the intelligence community gave a threat overview, sharing how adversaries were planning to use AI. Because not every commissioner yet had a security clearance, the brief was unclassified, but plenty scary nonetheless for commissioners who hadn't worked before in national security.

"Think about AI in terms of three things," the briefer said. "Doing bad things with AI, doing bad things to AI, and bad things happening because of AI."

To illustrate the first—doing bad things with AI—the briefer flashed photos on the screen of a partially autonomous Russian tank that had just been deployed in Syria. The Uran-9-tracked ground-combat vehicle had a 30 mm autocannon on a turret with thermal and electrical-optical sights, a laser rangefinder, and guided anti-tank and surface-to-air missiles. It looked like something out of a *Terminator* movie and could use AI to move autonomously. It even had a "Skynet" feature where four Uran-9s could operate in tandem. It hadn't yet proved to be a Terminator on the battlefield—limitations with data links and other operational issues marred its mission effectiveness. But it was only version one. Improved models were coming.

To illustrate doing bad things to AI, the briefer talked about how even sophisticated computer vision systems can be easily fooled. Something as simple as putting a small sticker on a stop sign makes some autonomous cars blow right past them. It was easy to imagine corrupting an enemy's AI system in a similar way, or having an enemy corrupt yours. The third category, bad things happening because of AI, was the most alarming—especially the possibility that AI systems might introduce false signals that accelerate the dynamics of escalation.

It would be like an episode of the fictional sci-fi series *Black Mirror*, in which two nations that don't mean to go to war accidentally do. It's happened before, even to the U.S. The Gulf of Tonkin "incident" in August 1964 became the casus belli that led the U.S. to escalate its engagement in Vietnam. On day one, North Vietnamese forces and the destroyer USS *Maddox* got in a brief firefight. On day two, as tensions heightened, radio operators thought they heard communications intercepts about an impending attack, and three U.S. destroyers then reported being in a firefight. In response, Congress passed the Gulf of Tonkin Resolution, which gave President Johnson carte blanche to provide warfighting assistance to any Southeast Asian country whose government was threatened by "communist aggression." U.S. conventional forces entered South Vietnam shortly thereafter, even though those communications intercepts were later proved false. Not a shot was actually fired at those destroyers that had thought they were under attack.

The accidental escalation in the Gulf of Tonkin inspired the 2003 documentary *Fog of War*, in which former Secretary of Defense Robert McNamara expressed regret for overseeing a war that left over 1.3 million dead. To imagine the modern-day equivalent of that accidental escalation, simply switch out a North Vietnamese patrol boat for a Chinese destroyer, and a misinterpreted communications intercept for a false positive from an AI system. Instead of a land war in Vietnam we could have a nuclear exchange between superpowers.

By now the energy in the room had deflated into a sober realism about the task ahead. The sitting U.S. president wasn't going to solve the nation's AI crisis. Congress was a partisan hellscape. Almost half of the political leadership of the Defense Department wasn't in place. No one else was coming to the rescue.

It was up to the fifteen volunteer commissioners to chart an AI path for the world's superpower.

In the afternoon, Eric convened the commission's first executive session. He sobered the mood even further by posing what he thought were the hardest questions the commission had to answer. They included: Since most AI discoveries are open-sourced, is there even a way to control its spread? And if we could, would the costs in scientific discoveries, such as not curing cancer, outweigh the security gains? What should our grand strategy with China be—deepening our engagement so we become like Siamese twins, or attempting to decouple an economic partnership that has pulled millions of Chinese out of poverty and fueled the greatest creation of wealth ever in the United States?

A day that had begun with coffee and pastries ended with a sense of dread. This was going to be hard, and getting the answer wrong might change the course of history.

Eric convened the second and third meetings in California, out of respect for the many commissioners who lived in San Francisco or Seattle. They were as dispiriting as the first. Briefings revealed China was remarkably close to reaching parity with the U.S. in AI research, in the deployment of AI by its commercial firms in global markets, and in use of AI to fuel discoveries in other scientific fields. For every briefing on what China was doing, there was another briefing on what the U.S. was *not* doing. One analysis of Pentagon contracts revealed that, outside of DIU, the DoD was working with only three of the top 100 U.S. AI firms. Even if the Pentagon wanted to adopt AI, its cloud computing infrastructure couldn't handle the computing requirements of advanced AI applications.

BACK TO THE FUTURE AT DIU

Mike Brown, now in place as DIU's director, felt his own sense of déjà vu watching the AI commissioners wrestle in 2019 with China and the problem of how to wake up a slumbering Pentagon. China's rise was the primary reason Mike had joined DIU in 2016 as a Presidential Innovation Fellow, after stepping down as the CEO of Symantec, at the time the world's largest cybersecurity company. Having run a company that helped customers avoid being hacked by the Chinese, Brown was convinced China was a serious threat. In his first project at DIU, he explored the extent to which China had access to U.S. technology through venture investing. What he found surprised everyone.

In his research, Brown unearthed astonishing facts about how deeply Chinese investors were embedded in innovative U.S. companies. In a paper titled "China's Technology Transfer Strategy: How Chinese Investments in Emerging Technology Enable a Strategic Competitor to Access the Crown Jewels of U.S. Innovation," Brown wrote that Chinese investors participated in 15–18 percent of all venture deals—essentially, granting them significant visibility into a substantial fraction of U.S. startups. Worse, they'd peered into the technology of far more companies than they'd actually invested in—perhaps three to four times as many. Brown discovered that the U.S. government doesn't restrict venture investing or the potential transfer of early-stage technology know-how. It also lacks a holistic view of how fast technology transfer is occurring or what technologies we should be protecting. The terrible truth: our greatest potential strategic competitor had no need to actually *spy* to steal our technology—though, of course, it was doing that as well. Chinese investors could simply write checks to startups, which would do the work for them.

Brown was alarmed at what he'd uncovered and, in the draft of his report, offered aggressive recommendations to begin remedying the situation. The paper, which DIU published in early 2017, ended up triggering the largest shift in U.S. policy on foreign investment since the end of the Cold War.

Chris passed the paper through DIU's formal chain to the Secretary of Defense while discreetly sharing it with others he knew at the White House and around D.C. who'd value its conclusions. While it sat in the

Secretary's inbox waiting to be read, a classic Washington phenomenon ensued. The paper leaked, and the *New York Times* ran a prominent above-the-fold story, titled "China Bets on Sensitive U.S. Start-Ups, Worrying the Pentagon." Everyone in the Beltway, including five cabinet secretaries, immediately read every page of Brown's paper.

Predictably, Mike soon became the go-to authority, conducting a summer study for the National Security Council and briefing members of Congress. Five months later, Senator John Cornyn introduced legislation to change the process by which the U.S. government vets foreign investment.

Within a year President Trump signed into law the Foreign Investment Risk Review Modernization Act of 2018, which significantly expanded the kinds of investments and joint ventures the Committee on Foreign Investment in the United States can restrict.

Mike's paper hadn't just made a dent. It had become an asteroid that created a smoking crater reaching from the Oval Office all the way to Beijing.

Years later, when they were reminiscing, Chris remarked, "It's really rare that you get to write something that actually ends up in law."

"Or even gets read, period," Mike said.

DIU AND AI

DIU was by now starting to apply the full transformative power of AI to its projects. The results were game-changing, especially as more technical talent joined DIU's ranks.

A young AI researcher we knew named Jared Dunnmon asked us for career advice over lunch. Energetic and affable, with brown hair that matched the brown leather jacket he permanently wore, Jared was a true polymath, with a Ph.D. in Mechanical Engineering from Stanford, and an MBA from Oxford, where he studied as a Rhodes Scholar.

By the time his postdoc was coming to an end, Jared faced the by now all too familiar dilemma of top talent in the Valley. If he so much as glanced at an AI startup, a seven-figure offer would instantly appear in his inbox. But his grandfather was a Green Beret, and both his parents were air force physicians. His sense of public service ran deep. At Stanford he'd taken Hacking for Defense the same semester as Capella founder Payam Banazadeh.

Over burritos in Palo Alto, we urged Jared to explore a role at DIU. "Go talk to Mike Brown. Get a sense for what you could do with the AI portfolio. You might be able to carve out a technical role managing AI projects while also contributing to AI policy."

By the next time we met, Jared had started at DIU as technical director for the AI portfolio. It took nearly two years, but Jared's first big win came in partnership with PMS-408, the Naval office responsible for expeditionary systems. One of their missions was deploying technology for counter-mine operations.

Naval mines were first invented by Imperial China and described in a fourteenth-century treatise by a Ming Dynasty artillery officer. The technology made its appearance in almost every military conflict from then on, including in the American Revolutionary War, when colonists used it to send a British warship to the bottom of the Delaware River.

The engineers at PMS-408 wanted to use AI in autonomous de-mining vehicles in ways that could revolutionize the navy's anti-mine capabilities. The fastest path to do so was to embed the latest machine vision technology in a new generation of mine-clearing underwater vehicles, which DIU, in fact, did, prototyping two modular underwater vehicles—both from commercial manufacturers—to clear mines with more than twice the endurance of the current models in half the usual development time. The new vehicles were infinitely more advanced in the way they used AI. But there was a catch. Operators noticed that when the vehicles changed environments, the computer vision models responsible for detecting mines sometimes degraded in performance. PMS-408 called up DIU to ask if this was a problem they'd heard of.

"It was music to my ears," Jared said, excited to implement a "full life cycle" approach to AI inside DoD.

In short order, Jared and PMS-408 began solving the problem and making the UUVs even more effective as they were deployed in different locations.

"You'd put the original UUV in the water and give it a search pattern," Jared recalls, "and it would go out and search, using some combination of sensors. Then it would come back and you had to look through all the sensor data manually and identify the things you think are mines, and often then go back and re-image them in greater detail. Imagine doing that over a large swath of water. It's a very, very time- and resource-intensive mission. Why not have the UUV recognize, 'Hey, there's a mine over there, so maybe I should get a better picture of it while I'm here,' while at the same time evolving the model so it can incorporate what it has learned as it faces new environments."

It was one of the first DIU programs to continuously improve AI models inside a military platform, showing what is possible when industry-best approaches are applied with DoD operator know-how. But this singular success only made the real problem more apparent. If the military was going to exploit AI fully, it needed thousands of projects like this, not just one.

DIU IN THE WILDERNESS

Just as DIU was beginning to hit on all cylinders under Mike Brown's leadership, the unit found itself out in the wilderness, alone and out of sync with the Pentagon. Almost everything was going wrong.

Brown's selection as director had started on a high note, in the form of a fifteen-minute conversation with Secretary Mattis. "Mattis told me three things," Brown recalls. "The first was not just to focus on individual projects but to change the capability of the entire Department. The second was 'I want you to raise hell. I want you to be very disruptive and make things happen in the Department.' Which was really a head scratcher for me. How can DIU, this very small organization, bring new capability to the whole Department? But his charge stuck with me. We started selecting projects that would have broader impacts across the services."

The third thing Mattis told Brown was that "bureaucracy is going to be hell. People will try to stop you. Anytime you have trouble navigating it, I want you to pick up the phone and call me."

"I couldn't have known at the time how right he was," Mike recalls.

After Mike had been in the seat for ninety days, Mattis invited him to a meeting to highlight three DIU projects. "I was just so impressed with how he handled that meeting," Mike recalls. "He spent the first fifteen minutes talking about his own experience with technology and how it had gotten him out of jams in Afghanistan and other combat zones. Then he tells me about a meeting with the Chinese defense minister where Mattis wanted him, when thinking about conflict with the U.S., to conclude that tonight is not the night."

It was classic Mattis. Once asked what keeps him up at night, he replied, "Nothing keeps me up at night. I keep my enemies up at night." At the end of the meeting Mattis made clear that his ambitions for DIU were just as transformational as Ash Carter's had been—that he wanted DIU to help change the whole military. "The work you're doing, if we do it right, will be important not for me but for my successor's successor's successor," Mattis said.

"It just was one of those moments where you really are struck by someone's leadership and approach," Mike remembers.

Things went downhill for DIU when Mattis resigned in January 2019, over Trump's sudden withdrawal from Syria, and was replaced first, in the interim, by Deputy Secretary Patrick Shanahan, and ultimately by

Secretary of the Army Mark Esper, a West Point graduate who'd fought in the Iraq War.

"We suddenly had no help, no interest, no nothing. I call it the walking in the wilderness period," Brown recalls. The walk was lonely. It was also made unpleasant by the fact that DIU was now reporting not to the Secretary of Defense but to Michael Griffin, the former administrator of NASA who'd been named undersecretary of defense for research and engineering and then went on to ignore DIU and fire Defense Innovation Board members.

"Mattis's view was that DIU's reporting to him would mean that it basically wasn't reporting to anyone," recalls Ben FitzGerald, a technology expert who joined the Trump administration after directing the technology and national security program at the Center for a New American Security (CNAS), an influential think tank. "So the question then was, to whom should DIU report? R&E emerged as the most logical candidate."

Nearly seventy years old when he assumed office, Griffin had a long reputation, and it wasn't flattering. "He had to be the smartest person in the room and he clearly didn't care about getting along with anyone," Mike Brown remembers.

"The literal quote from Griffin when it came to how to work with his Pentagon colleagues was 'I don't share,'" FitzGerald said.

Griffin's relationship went immediately south with his most important counterpart, the undersecretary for acquisition, Ellen Lord. Within days Griffin and Lord couldn't stand to be in the same room with each other. "He even wanted Ellen's office," FitzGerald remembers, because hers had nicer views.

Even as the demand for DIU was growing within the Pentagon, Griffin refused to endorse the higher levels at which Congress was willing to fund it. Under Trump, DIU's expenditures at their high mark constituted only 0.01 percent of the DoD budget and less than .05 percent of the procurement budget.

"DIU per year costs about as much as one F-35" is how the head of DIU's Space Portfolio and its senior military officer, now Major General Steve "Bucky" Butow, put it. Rather than growing into something on par with the size of DARPA, with a $3 billion annual spend, and leading the adoption of commercial technology for the entire military, DIU's comparatively modest budget never gave it the heft Ash Carter or Jim Mattis had hoped for.

In September 2020 Griffin shocked everyone by firing members of the Defense Innovation Board, including Eric Schmidt. "He thought the DIB was kind of pointless because he was personally smarter than all the members," FitzGerald remembers. Griffin's reckless behavior eventually caught up with him and he himself was asked to resign after less than eighteen months on the job. But he'd done serious damage.

Even though circumstances were less than ideal and DIU's budget remained small, Brown continued to put points on the board. "We expanded our in-house contracting capacity, and that allowed us to do up to one hundred projects simultaneously. More than half of our projects successfully transitioned to military units who now use them every day. And we grew the number of companies willing to work with the DoD. DIU was going gangbusters," Brown remembers with pride.

NSCAI PART II

As the Trump Pentagon turned innovation into an afterthought, heading up the AI Commission became Eric Schmidt's full-time focus. Throughout the spring, summer, and fall of 2019 Eric was in constant motion, chairing meetings, keeping staff on track, running ideas by Raj and other outside experts, and beginning to build the political consensus in Washington needed to see through the commission's eventual recommendations.

Eric's shuttle diplomacy was paying dividends. The staff kept generating deeper, more concerning analysis about the competition with China. The commissioners, reacting to alarming insights they were absorbing, increasingly backed bolder policy prescriptions. Eric and Bob Work would shop them around town, in front of all-congressional staff audiences at the Capitol and through press interviews and roundtables.

The AI Commission got off to such a great start that others aspired to mimic its model. Congress chartered a Cybersecurity Commission. Uniquely, two sitting senators and two sitting representatives served on that commission, one each as the commission's co-chairs. Appointing sitting lawmakers as commissioners was a brilliant structural innovation because it created a built-in mechanism to transfer findings into law. Indeed, that is exactly what happened. An extremely high percentage of the commission's recommendations were enacted.

The Cybersecurity Commission's executive director had read the memo Chris prepared for the AI Commission and asked if Chris could deliver the same briefing to his commission. So one day Chris found himself at the Capitol, where political divisiveness had reached new heights and many Republicans and Democrats were no longer speaking to one another. Before delivering the brief, Chris hit the men's room across the hall, only to find the one open stall had a toilet caught in permanent flush. The high-pressure spray of water swirling straight down the hole seemed like an apt metaphor for the current state of American politics. That no one was rushing to fix it only made the metaphor more apt.

The mood in the briefing room—one of bipartisan cooperation—was a welcome respite from the trench warfare consuming the rest of Washington. The positive atmosphere was due to the extraordinary dedication of the four members leading the commission's work. Angus King, the independent senator from Maine, co-chaired the commission with Mike

Gallagher, a moderate Republican from Wisconsin who'd served in Iraq with H. R. McMaster. Two other remarkable men joined them: Nebraska senator Ben Sasse, who has a doctorate in American History, and Jim Langevin, the first quadriplegic to serve in Congress.

The engaging conversation led to a second one, the impetus for which was Chris's waking up the next morning to a note from Senator Sasse inviting him to lunch in the Senate dining room. Were Republican senators even *allowed* to host former Obama appointees at the height of the Trump administration? Sasse, a true patriot, was one of the few Republicans who would willingly cross the aisle if it better served the nation.

MEETING TRUMP

Ylli Bajraktari, in his role as the AI Commission's executive director, had by now amassed an exceptionally talented staff, including many of the best and brightest from the National Security Council, CIA, and Departments of State, Commerce, and Defense. It showed in their piercing briefs and reports. The commissioners too had grown more comfortable with each other and their thinking was converging. Eric had managed the commissioners—and Ylli the staff—to an important juncture in late 2019 at exactly the right moment. It was time to put pen to paper and deliver to Congress their interim report.

In Washington, interim reports are nothing-burgers. Commissions, like term-paper-writing college students, save their best work for deadline. Ylli and Eric deliberately guided the AI Commission to a different place. Strategic thinking was desperately needed, and each day that the commission *didn't* outline a strategy for AI was one more day China raced ahead. So in November the commission rented a hotel ballroom for an all-day symposium three blocks from the Capitol, and invited everyone who mattered to advancing AI policy.

The interim report, landing at 96 pages, with 239 footnotes, made 27 preliminary judgments, and advanced 7 consensus principles to shape discussion about AI policy. Its clear prose reflected the intellectual clarity the commission had achieved in eight months of furious work.

On a stage backlit with the commission logo, and in front of a standing room only crowd, thirty-five speakers held forth. Senate majority leader Chuck Schumer spoke, as did the Secretaries of Defense and Energy.

One session was particularly notable. Eric led a discussion on the partnership between government and the private sector with Lieutenant General Jack Shanahan, director of the Pentagon's Joint AI Center, and Google's general counsel Kent Walker. Those who had followed the Project Maven controversy immediately understood they were witnessing a peace committee—that Eric had brokered a truce. Kent Walker announced that Google had resumed working with the Department of Defense after pausing to develop principles for what uses it would put its AI to. Though Google landed on not deploying technologies that could directly cause harm, Walker emphasized that this was in no way indicative of a "broader unwillingness" to work with the Defense Department. "At the end of the day we are a proud American company and we are committed to the defense of the United States, our allies and the safety and security of the world," Walker said.

To back up his declaration, he noted that Google had resumed deploying AI with the Pentagon on a range of uses, from cybersecurity to health care to spotting deepfakes. Having first brokered peace with Google's own employees, Walker was asking for a détente with Washington. In so doing he joined the CEOs of Microsoft and Amazon in publicly pledging to work with the Department of Defense—a significant change in the post-Snowden years catalyzed in part by the arrival of DIU in Silicon Valley.

The always thoughtful Shanahan was gracious in return. "I view what happened with Google and Maven as a canary in a coal mine," he said. "The fact that it happened when it did as opposed to on the verge of a conflict or a crisis where we're asking for help, we've gotten some of that out of the way, and can now move on."

More remarkably, Ylli had pulled off an extraordinary coup that he kept secret until the last minute. He'd convinced President Trump's staff that the best way the President could show leadership on AI was to personally receive the interim report in the Oval Office. It would be the first time in history a sitting president gave an audience over an interim report.

"The Oval, really?" Chris exclaimed when Ylli told him.

Ylli loaded up a subset of the commissioners and staff into vans for the quick trip down Pennsylvania Avenue to the White House and back.

Trump, it turned out, already knew Eric Schmidt and wasn't bothered by the large crowd that now surrounded him on both sides of the Resolute desk. Later that day the White House released a photo of the group in the Oval with Trump holding up the interim report—signaling that he supported NSCAI's efforts. It was an incredible coup—NSCAI was now working directly with the White House to accelerate efforts to address AI. The Trump team had already hosted a White House summit and, later, issued an executive order and national strategy published by the White House Office of Science and Technology Policy.

The commissioners and staff, still not quite believing how they'd nudged the nation to a new consensus on AI policy, celebrated together that night at a nearby bar.

CHIPS ACT

With the interim report received by the President himself, it was time to be even more ambitious. The most concerning facet of the technological competition the commission had focused on was computer chips. They powered everything Americans used in their daily lives, from toasters to automobiles to smartphones and more. Almost anything plugged into an outlet or powered by battery ran on chips. Without them, modern life would stop. It wouldn't even matter if you still had electricity. There wouldn't be anything it could power. More than that, high-power chips were essential to the demanding computing requirements of AI. Whoever had the best chips had the best chance of winning the competition.

Transistors were invented at Bell Labs in 1947, and the first fabs to make semiconductors sprang up in Palo Alto in the 1950s. The fabs proliferated so quickly that they gave Silicon Valley its name. Through about 1980, the United States led both chip design and production. But in less than a generation the economics of globalization shifted the historical patterns of production beyond all recognition. Suddenly it made economic sense to relocate manufacturing lines to Japan, and then South Korea and Taiwan, where labor was less expensive. Chips continued to be designed by engineers in California, but, increasingly, the high-tech fabs moved to Asia, and Taiwan in particular.

With China no longer a friendly neighbor, basing the entire global supply of advanced chip production at three clusters of factories run by the Taiwan Semiconductor Manufacturing Company (TSMC) on the island nation's west coast suddenly posed an enormous vulnerability to the American way of life. China was by now regularly conducting mock invasions of Taiwan, flying fighter and bomber aircraft and sailing ships and submarines deep into Taiwanese territory. Were China to take over the island or sabotage the fabs on it, technological progress in the U.S. would freeze and then run in reverse. The chips that make automobiles and computers run would eventually fail, only this time there'd be no spares to replace them. The iPhone, a new version of which arrives each fall, would become a technological time capsule, its development frozen in place. As more electronics aged out, life in the U.S. would revert to what it was before the Internet. We'd all go back to talking on landlines and reading books.

It was by now dawning on the commission and other experts that offshoring chip production, once a source of economic gain, had become the nation's greatest national security vulnerability. Yet fixing it would not be easy. The problem had taken two generations to manifest and would take at least a generation to unwind. Fabs cost billions of dollars and years to build. Even if the U.S. was willing to invest the capital, it lacked the know-how to make the most advanced fabs run. TSMC not only had a monopoly on the physical means of production; the specialized labor to operate these plants was now concentrated eighty-one miles off the coast of America's potential enemy. Who knew if TSMC would even be willing to share? If they gave away their secrets, would the U.S. rush to Taiwan's defense when the Chinese finally came?

Bringing fabs home would take industrial policy on a scale not seen since the Cold War. Taiwan would have to be coaxed into sharing its secret sauce. Yet this was exactly what would now need to happen if the U.S. were to avoid being held hostage by Xi Jinping. The AI Commission staff had arrived at the national strategy its congressional sponsors asked it to craft. Its most crucial plank was to on-shore chip production with all possible speed.

Intense huddles were now occurring with strange bedfellows that foreshadowed big political shifts. The chip industry also swung into gear, building a coalition that included car and electronics manufacturers, research universities, and governors eager to strengthen the innovation hubs in their states.

Draft legislation for a "CHIPS Act" came together in Chuck Schumer's office. Shortly thereafter, Eric had the AI Commission host a dinner with Speaker of the House Nancy Pelosi and other lawmakers. The idea was to discuss the commission's work and the CHIPS act with Pelosi and have the Speaker signal her commitment in front of a bipartisan group of lawmakers and the commissioners themselves. The dinner was held on a cold night in 2019, at a restaurant a few blocks from the Capitol, with two national security stalwarts, Representatives Mike Gallagher and Mac Thornberry, in attendance.

Pelosi was late to arrive, having flown back from a summit in Europe. Her staff was in touch with Eric's staff, who tried to stall tired lawmakers to stay longer.

Pelosi, age eighty, wore a cashmere blazer, a purple dress, and heels. While taking small bites of cheesecake seated across from Eric, she thanked everyone for staying and apologized for arriving later than planned. "I want to tell everyone about the first time I met Eric," she said. "It was in San Francisco more than fifteen years ago. He'd just started working with two founders named Larry and Sergey. He told me their company, Google, was going to revolutionize how we use the Internet," she recounted. "I thought the name was a little strange. But by golly he was right." Eric, not one to easily smile, was beaming.

Pelosi went on to thank the commissioners and their staff for their service and then rattle off from memory the commission's policy ideas, including about chips. She told everyone she was committed to seeing them become law and said she was already laying the bipartisan groundwork to move the commission's recommendations through the House. It was a mesmerizing performance. And it wasn't just a show. Pelosi stayed true to her word, helping pass some of the most significant national security legislation in decades. The nation was embroiled in political and cultural turmoil not seen since the 1960s. Yet when it matters most, its institutions retained their ability to steer a sensible course.

A SHOWDOWN IN MUNICH

Two months later, Eric embarked on the most significant diplomatic contact the United States had yet had with China on AI. He was going to sit down in a live, televised conversation with China's top AI diplomat, Ambassador Fu Ying, the deputy foreign affairs minister. They were to meet at the Munich Security Conference held each February at the Hotel

Bayerischer Hof. Some 350 diplomats and heads of state from seventy countries convene for three days of meetings. It's the kind of place where motorcades dropping off heads of state create their own VIP traffic jams.

Ylli stayed in Washington, which meant Chris accompanied Eric. Ylli and his team built a schedule for Eric in Munich designed to expose him to tough questions in preparation for his live session with Fu Ying. The tough questions did indeed come, first at a dinner with the NATO intelligence chiefs, next at the session with the conference's young leader program, and lastly at a lunch hosted by the Aspen Strategy Group.

The most talked about topic at the conference was the rise of China and technology. The big takeaway was that Europe was lagging in developing its own technology strategy even as it increasingly worried about China's rise.

At the same time, another issue was brewing, quite literally, right in Munich. Reports of an atypical pneumonia in the Chinese city of Wuhan had emerged six weeks before. Chris, who had served on the White House Ebola Task Force and helped lead the military's mission to stop Ebola in West Africa, was already unnerved about traveling to an event that drew hundreds of people from around the world into a crammed hotel in winter. He and Eric only learned later that COVID-19 was spreading rapidly across Munich at the exact moment they were there. Germany's first case was confirmed just miles from the hotel. Shortly after they left, Germany closed schools and imposed curfews, and the world became a very different place.

The day before Fu Ying's session with Eric, she showed a flash of China's "wolf warrior" diplomacy by aggressively hurling accusations at Nancy Pelosi, who'd flown in from Washington to deliver a keynote. This happened in front of the entire conference, during a session on the main stage. Pelosi had already come out swinging, calling the Chinese phone maker and telecom firm Huawei's practice of hiding backdoors to Beijing in its products "the most insidious form of aggression." Pelosi explained that to the U.S., there was more to this than commercial considerations. "This is about choosing autocracy over democracy on the information highway," she said. "It is about putting the state police in the pocket of every consumer in these countries, because of the Chinese way. Why would we want to give license to the Chinese to direct the traffic on that information highway of the future? It is a big price to pay in terms of national security, in terms of economy, and in terms of our values and our governance. And that is why we have bipartisan support for this position. It is not about an economic advantage. It is about a values urgency: autocracy versus democracy. And we choose democracy."

Ambassador Fu Ying quite literally leapt to grab the mic and went on to tell Pelosi that "China, since its reform started forty years ago, has introduced all kinds of Western technologies while maintaining its political system. It is not threatened by these technologies. How, if Huawei's technology with 5G is introduced into Western countries, will it threaten the political system? Do you really think that the democratic system is so fragile that it could be threatened by this single high-tech company of Huawei?"

Chris, watching from the audience, was astonished not by the substance of the remarks, which were the usual bald-faced lies told by Chinese officials, but by the hostility with which they were delivered. What better way to push Europeans to view China as a threat than to have the Chinese ambassador on AI literally screaming at the woman who was third in line to the presidency of the United States? The session with Eric was going to be interesting indeed.

That night, Chris and Eric reviewed the Fu Ying–Pelosi exchange as they prepped in his bizarrely modern hotel room. The conversation was to be moderated by the president of Estonia, Kersti Kaljulaid, whose nation had been the first to fall victim to a massive cyberattack. In 2007 Russian cyber operations targeted everything from telephony to financial transactions and shut off the Internet in most places in Estonia. The country had ever since ensured that it was among the most digitally resilient nations. We were intrigued to see what Kaljulaid had to say about China and AI.

As Eric walked into the venue where the live event was about to begin, Fu Ying greeted him warmly, dressed in a green jacket with gilded jewelry on her left lapel, like a Chinese Madeleine Albright. Eric was in a checkered blazer. Kaljulaid sported a bright red dress. The Estonian president opened the session by noting that the Munich Conference had "attempted to discuss AI two years ago, but it quickly became obvious our understanding of artificial intelligence does not much differ from how our ancestors understood thunder," which was to say, not at all.

After the humor, Kaljulaid plunged into the most controversial issue, asking Eric about the weaponization of AI in military systems and what risks we faced with lethal technology.

Eric pushed back against the killer robot scenario.

"The simplest way to understand AI is that if you have a lot of training data, you can predict what will happen next. In national security there are plenty of examples where that would occur if we had a lot of training data," he said. "If you look at a typical kinetic conflict, which is fortunately very rare, there isn't very much training data, so the initial uses in national security will be mostly in terms of intelligence analysis and vision and monitoring."

Kaljulaid went at Eric again with the terminator scenario.

He gave an even sharper reply. "I appreciate the narrative, but what you're describing is a movie."

The first question to Fu Ying was about AI and privacy. Her response made the elephant in the room larger.

"I visited one company, and they do health management," she said. "You walk through and the mirror tells you how to improve your skin and the mattress tells you how to improve your sleep. So that sounds very good, but I didn't want to go through it because I don't know how they are going to use my data."

Fu Ying went on to maintain that "in almost every sector, the Chinese government is following very closely, looking for ways for business to protect privacy. In China, if I am a consumer, I trust the government more than the private sector. Once I went to inquire about buying a flat, and ever since I've received advertisements for flats because the person I called sold my telephone number." She went on to suggest that "countries operate in different ways, so the way they develop their rules and regulations should be within that kind of environment."

It was boilerplate Chinese rhetoric designed to paper over what was really happening. It's true that in China, privacy is a leading citizen concern. Particularly with children's access to the Internet, China has built more elaborate safeguards than Europe and the U.S. But focusing on data collection by Chinese companies while not talking about the surveillance state China has erected, and the uses to which it is put, was a way of avoiding rather than addressing the sharp differences between how China and the West employ AI. Fu Ying might not have given her data to the health company, but that type of "should I or shouldn't I?" dilemma was far easier to cope with than, say, the oppression faced by Uyghurs in concentration camps who were hunted down and reeducated by the Chinese state.

Twenty minutes in, Eric took a stab at turning the conversation to a positive topic—the potential for global cooperation in AI. "We're on the cusp of tremendous systems that help humans live better lives. Markets that are faster. Education systems that are better. We of course have to stay consistent with our laws and our principles. I accept that principles and laws in China are different. But we can learn from each other," he said. "If they invent something in health care, that helps Europe and helps America and vice-versa. There are so many areas where there is a global benefit from advances."

The conversation then veered in a different direction, leaving unaddressed what AI cooperation between the U.S. and China might look like and how we should work toward it.

The first audience question was asked by General John Allen, president of the Brookings Institute. He went right to the core issue.

"I hope that the audience recognizes that the leaders of this conversation are highly symbolic," Allen said. "We have China and the United States in a conversation being moderated by the president of [Estonia]. And I think this is really symbolic about where we need to go in the future. If we are going to have norms of behavior for AI and other emerging tech, we have got to find a way the U.S. and China can find common ground."

Allen's intervention too failed to spark the meaningful exchange the AI Commission was hoping would occur. Chris glanced at Tara, the NSCAI press secretary, who sat next to him. They locked eyes and telegraphed their mutual suspicion that this session wasn't going to produce the grand diplomatic moment they'd hoped for.

A few minutes later it briefly looked like the conversation might touch more serious issues. Kaljulaid pressed Eric on how AI will "impact how we fight with each other or how we deter each other."

"I think the good news is that there's going to be less kinetic conflict. If you look at the data since World War II, the number of deaths globally continues to decline. There's every reason to think that as a society, things are getting better. Globalization is working. People want to work together and not kill each other as a general rule. The numbers are getting better."

He continued: "What's also true is that countries are spending an awful lot of time in non-kinetic conflict, whether it's election interference, monitoring each other, and so forth. Most of that activity today is not being done using AI."

It was a valiant attempt by Eric to bring a real issue up for discussion—what happens when countries start using AI to interfere with the internal affairs of one another?

Kaljulaid didn't pick up the thread Eric laid down. The remaining twenty minutes were swallowed whole by one-off audience questions.

In the end, the meeting between China's AI diplomat and American's de facto AI diplomat was a missed opportunity. Perhaps too much had been expected from the format. Perhaps a different moderator could have coaxed the conversation closer to the fault lines that exist. Or perhaps Fu Ying had been told by higher headquarters to hold off after her swipe at Pelosi was panned in the global press. For whatever reason, this wouldn't be the day when China and the U.S. made progress toward understanding each other or beginning to sort through what AI had introduced into their already complex relationship.

Those who crowded around the bar at the evening festivities didn't know it then, but COVID was about to make the tensions between China and the U.S. dramatically worse. China's withholding of data about the virus and refusal to cooperate with the World Health Organization, followed by President Trump's rhetoric about the "Wuhan virus" and open hostility to Chinese leaders, made further cooperation on AI impossible. Eric and his team had tried to crack open the window of AI diplomacy. Now a virus was about to nail it shut.

ELECTION 2020

Soon after the team returned from Munich, the NSCAI office in Washington came to resemble a set from *The Walking Dead*. With shelter in place orders shuttering businesses and schools, the work of the AI Commission continued from home, where it was harder to recreate the "let's do this" vibe Ylli had fostered.

As spring turned to summer, the campaign for president dominated the airwaves alongside news about COVID. Chris was invited by the Biden transition team to author a paper on restructuring the National Security Council (NSC) for technology. It was easy to do, as he'd already laid out his recommendation in the NSC–Office of Science and Technology Policy review.

In the middle of summer, he received a cryptic phone call from a former boss who was deep inside the Biden transition team. After pleasantries were exchanged, the caller posed a question: "Would you be interested in returning to Washington to work again on the technology issues you handled before? If so, there's a role available." Chris let out a deep sigh, remembering how brutal his last stints had been at the Pentagon, White House, and DIU. *It's just too soon*, he immediately thought. After a long pause, he said, "Gosh, I hate to say this, but I really am settled here in San Francisco. I've started a new life, met someone new. We've moved in together. I want to help the new team in any way. But I don't think now is the time for me to come back into government."

Chris didn't ask which position was on the table. He didn't want to know.

That same week the transition team asked Eric Schmidt if he could gather a group of technologists to provide an independent assessment of asymmetric ways to outcompete China. The many threads of Eric's life were beginning to twine together.

The thirteen people tapped by Eric to join this latest adventure made for a fascinating crew. They included Avichal Garg, one of the smartest minds in crypto and Web 3; Marissa Giustina, an expert in quantum computing at Google; Gary Rieschel, a venture capitalist with deep knowledge of the Chinese tech sector; and Alexandr Wang, CEO of Scale AI and the youngest self-made billionaire in American history.

For three months they met weekly, assessing the competition dynamics playing out in America's rivalry with China. With COVID raging, the meetings were all virtual. The gatherings built a new community to replace those lost in the pandemic.

The study group handed over a thirty-four-page report in October, yet another attempt to document the challenges a rising China presented to America. Biden won the election one week later.

The election set in motion a chain of policy events that built on McMaster's earlier actions. At the White House, the National Security Council established a deputy national security advisor for cyber and emerging technology, just as Chris had recommended. President Biden went on to inhibit China's access to advanced microprocessors and curtail foreign investments in sensitive U.S. technology, tightening the screws even further than Mike Brown's paper originally recommended.

The Pentagon created a Chief Digital and Artificial Intelligence Office and named the former head of machine intelligence at Lyft to lead it. Following the recommendations in Mike Brown's 2017 paper, in late 2022 the Pentagon established the Office of Strategic Capital to liaise with private markets.

With the renewed focus on technology competition, Chris second-guessed his decision to stay out of the administration. Ron Klain was named Biden's first chief of staff. Chris had worked directly for Ron during the Ebola crisis, and the Ebola czar had been a mentor. Klain's team reached out to inquire if Chris was ready to put cleats back on and work in the Biden White House.

Chris called his longtime mentor, communications strategist Ricki Seidman, for advice. She asked three simple but piercing questions. "What do you remember about the last time you worked in the White House?" Answer: "Trying hard not to crash my car on Rock Creek Parkway driving home at 2 a.m. in the morning." "How long has your divorce been finalized?" Answer: "Just over a year." "Are you really ready to leave San Francisco?" Answer: "No."

It was a quick resolution to a difficult dilemma.

The farther away you get from national security jobs, the more glamorous they look. Government jets. Meetings in the Situation Room. Walking into the Oval Office. But in reality the positions are traumatizing—extreme stress, life-and-death decisions, and seeing things that cannot be unseen. "You know, I used to be in the loop for every U.S. drone strike," Chris told Ricki, letting out another long sigh. "Target, weapons platform, strike window. I don't want to do that anymore."

Each time Chris was asked why he didn't go back in, he told the story of his exchange with Ricki.

MIKE BROWN'S NOMINATION

While Chris stayed put in San Francisco along with Raj, DIU director Michael Brown put in an offer on a condo in D.C. President Biden had nominated Brown to serve as the undersecretary of defense for acquisition and sustainment. Brown would be the first person in decades with a Silicon Valley background to oversee the Pentagon's $200 billion procurement spend, the last being Secretary of Defense William Perry, who stepped down in 1997, and earlier, David Packard, cofounder of Hewlett-Packard. Brown's job would essentially be to remake the entire Pentagon acquisition apparatus to work at DIU speed. The emphasis would be on open architectures and rapid iteration, and helping Silicon Valley startups compete on an equal footing with the defense primes.

"When I was tapped for the assignment, I was over the moon," Brown recalls. "The vetting process was ridiculous. Everything about your background, your character, your finances, whether my classic rock band had played songs with lyrics that could be embarrassing to the president. They went through everything I'd ever done with a fine-tooth comb."

Between being nominated and awaiting Senate confirmation, Brown turned to preparing for the new role.

"I was actively trying to supplement my knowledge because I was nervous about how much I didn't know about the job," he remembers. "Knowing that you're going to be co-chairing with the Department of

Energy the refurbishment of the nuclear triad, what the heck do I know about that?"

We both swung into action, starting conversations with former officials and organizing a dinner in Georgetown with Bill Lynn, the former deputy Secretary of Defense, who knew the role inside and out. Raj called around and assembled a roster of staff willing to serve in Mike's front office, right down to his military assistant. Ash Carter and H. R. McMaster were also actively advising Mike.

Weeks before his confirmation hearings were to begin, a former DIU employee leaked to the press a whistleblower complaint that had been previously adjudicated. The complaint was about whether DIU, under Brown's leadership, had misused hiring authority. The accusation had been tendered by that employee on his last day on the job. After an exhaustive internal investigation, DIU's general counsel in an eighty-page report had found the complaint's claims to be spurious. Case closed. But now a vague accusation in the press made it appear as if the matter hadn't been investigated.

One of DIU's core missions was to attract the best in Silicon Valley to work in national security. DIU didn't even administer its own hiring—that authority sat with offices back at the Pentagon. So it was an odd complaint. It alleged other petty irregularities, including that junior officers overseeing the office snack fund used an insufficiently robust system of cash accounting to buy Cheetos and coffee for the office Keurig. Suddenly, the Inspector General's Office, which had initially declined to investigate, said they would do so and that—unbelievably—the investigation might take a year or more.

The Secretary, Deputy Secretary, or the White House could have asked the IG to expedite its investigation. An investigation had already been done by DIU's general counsel, so ascertaining the facts could be done quickly. Yet they took no steps at all, leading Brown's nomination to collapse. In a cruel twist, the IG fully exonerated Brown eighteen months later, one week after he stepped down as DIU director in the fall of 2022.

The IG report ended up praising the approach Brown took to hiring top talent. Watching Biden's team not push Brown's nomination through was a huge blow to advocates of innovation, who know that "personnel is policy" especially in an administration's opening months.

Reflecting on it years later, Brown says, "The overall lesson is the system is broken when you can weaponize the IG and have, for whatever reason, the President's choice for a position denied. And it's not because the Senate decided not to confirm them. Why should there ever be that situation? I'm happy to be investigated, but as we all know, there's no reason for something like this to take over a year to adjudicate."

For Brown it was a sour note on which to conclude his public service. Given the innovation agenda he would have brought into the Pentagon, it also made him wonder if the complaint's sudden resurfacing had more complex origins than a single disgruntled individual sending old news to reporters. He couldn't help but notice that the whistleblower was working for a consultancy that exclusively did business with the major defense primes. No one will ever know exactly what happened, but Brown does know that the primes opposed his nomination in private even as they talked positively about it in public.

Eventually he put the episode behind him and decided to continue DIU's mission in the same way Raj had. He joined as a partner in Raj's venture firm, Shield Capital.

NSCAI FINAL REPORT AND CHIPS ACT

On July 13, 2021, more than five hundred people flooded a ballroom to standing room only capacity at the Mayflower Hotel, two blocks north of the White House. Thousands more joined the livestream online. The NSCAI's Global Emerging Technology Summit was one of Washington's biggest events that summer.

The commission's final report, at 746 pages, weighed in at 5.5 pounds. The report first examined defending America in the age of AI, and then how to win the technology competition. Following was an equally lengthy section entitled "blueprints for action," which spelled out in detail the implementing steps for each recommendation. It was as close to color by numbers as you could get in government.

Equally impressive was the crowd of senior officials who turned out to endorse the report and the strategy it advanced. The secretaries of commerce, state, and defense each spoke, as did the President's national security and science advisors. Senator Schumer, minority leader Kevin McCarthy, and Elise Stefanik from congressional leadership spoke by video, as did Jacinda Ardern, the prime minister of New Zealand, and a dozen other foreign and digital ministers and science advisors from U.S. allies. Sam Altman, the cofounder of OpenAI, spoke from the stage alongside one of the cofounders of Ginkgo Bioworks. To a person, they celebrated the commission's work.

Madeleine Albright spoke in an afternoon session moderated by CNN's Fareed Zakaria. She appeared by video from the study of her house on 34th Street in Georgetown, a trademark broach on her lapel. No one in the audience knew then, but she had only months to live. At age eighty-four she'd been diagnosed with cancer. This would be her last extended set of remarks on technology.

Fareed turned straight to Albright, asking her about the new crises in international cooperation on technology. He noted how she had "tried mightily" as secretary of state "at the beginning of the postwar efforts to create a new alliance and greater degree of cooperation among the world's democracies."

"Many people worried at the time," Albright said, "that the world's democracies really wouldn't come together, that what brought them together was the Soviet threat, and that without that just the idea of values was not a strategic glue that was strong enough. When I became secretary of state," she went on, "we talked even more about how to get democracies together, and how NATO, in fact, could be expanded, because it's not only a military alliance, but an alliance of democracies. And this is something that has to be considered now. The twenty-first century had some megatrends and their downside." Among them, she said, "was technology, which obviously did incredible things to unite people. But the downside was that the information was de-aggregated, social media entered in, people didn't know where they were getting their information, and that divided people."

Former NATO secretary general Anders Fogh Rasmussen spoke next about how technology had returned them to the fault lines of an earlier era, with stark differences between free and un-free societies. These veteran diplomats, who grew up in the shadow of the Second World War and themselves lived through the Cold War and its aftermath, found technology—and especially AI—taking them back to an earlier, bleaker time.

Albright said in conclusion, "This is the moment. Time is of the essence. The organizational aspect of this is very complicated. I am an optimist who worries a lot. I am worried that we are going to lose time on this. . . . That we are admiring the problem rather than really dealing with some of the very specific aspects."

Earlier, while preparing to deliver her remarks, she'd told her team, who weren't aware she was so ill, that "This AI stuff—I'll be long gone before we figure it out. It will be up to your generation to sort this out."

The woman who had spent her life fighting fascism was passing the baton.

The commission had actually fashioned a national AI strategy, 746 pages long. The team celebrated their success at the Hamilton, a popular restaurant a few blocks away from the White House. The group walked there together down Connecticut Avenue, Eric at the front. The last staffer standing was a stalwart Foggy Bottom hand who'd go on to write the executive order restricting advanced chips from export to China—an act one analyst called "technological asphyxiation."

There was one coda still to come, and that was the passage of the CHIPS Act, which the commission had been so instrumental in drafting. A larger constellation of legislative politics stalled its passage for reasons unrelated to the bipartisan support it had garnered. It was signed into law by President Biden on August 9, 2022. The bill unlocked $80 billion in public funds to rebuild the U.S. semiconductor industry. The act underwrote the on-shoring of microprocessor production as well as government-sponsored research for future chip generations and AI.

It was a stunning acceleration of the decoupling with China and the first major act of industrial policy in decades. The moves, which constituted one of few policy decisions with broad bipartisan support, deepened a kind of U.S.-China cold war while at the same time making the geopolitical dimensions of commercial technology more visible.

The United States was in new territory, but at least now it had a plan.

Raj Shah flying in an F-16C over Afghanistan. The lack of a simple "moving map" to tell Raj if he was wandering into Iranian airspace was a sign that the Pentagon hadn't yet fully embraced the software revolution led by Silicon Valley.

1

Chris Kirchhoff, visible just over Secretary of State John Kerry's left shoulder in the White House Situation Room, would draw heavily on what he learned in those high-level strategy sessions when he took a lead role at DIUx.

2

Ashton B. "Ash" Carter, the defense secretary (2015–17) whose vision of a partnership between the Pentagon and Silicon Valley drove DIUx forward, leans over to consult with Senator John McCain, then head of the Senate Armed Services Committee and a key supporter of DIUx.

3

When Raj visited the Combined Air Operations Center (CAOC), which coordinates all aerial combat missions across the Middle East, he immediately spotted a way for DIUx to save the military countless hours and millions of dollars.

4

During the war against ISIS, a U.S. airman in the CAOC would manually schedule the refueling of thousands of fighter aircraft. It was a laborious and expensive process that DIUx automated with a modern app.

5

A rendering of the first-of-its-kind synthetic aperture radar developed by Capella Space. DIUx pushed hard for Capella's microsatellites to monitor mobile missile launchers in North Korea, but their potential wouldn't be fully utilized until after the Russian invasion of Ukraine in 2022.

6

A tiny autonomous drone funded by DIUx. With it, a U.S. Special Operations soldier could map the interior of a building in advance of a raid.

DIUx's Rogue Squadron was the U.S. military's first commercial drone unit. It specialized in deploying friendly drones to support U.S. troops and in building systems to defeat enemy drones in combat.

Counter-drone jammers, some developed with the help of DIU, are now widely used on the battlefield, including in Ukraine.

Joby Aviation's autonomous VTOL (vertical takeoff and landing) aircraft, DIU's first "flying car," is shown here on a military test range.

James Mattis, an enthusiastic supporter of DIU who succeeded Ash Carter as Secretary of Defense, walks with Raj outside the unit's headquarters.

DIU advocated for expanded use of autonomous sea drones that could remain at sea for years. These drones could provide many of the surveillance capabilities of a Navy destroyer for a fraction of the cost.

Project Maven, which used machine learning to identify people and objects in drone videos, was incorrectly viewed by some in Silicon Valley as a kind of weapon, igniting a firestorm of protest. In 2018 three thousand Google employees signed a letter demanding that the company end its participation, kicking off a season of activism that also included anger over alleged sexual harassment and gender inequality.

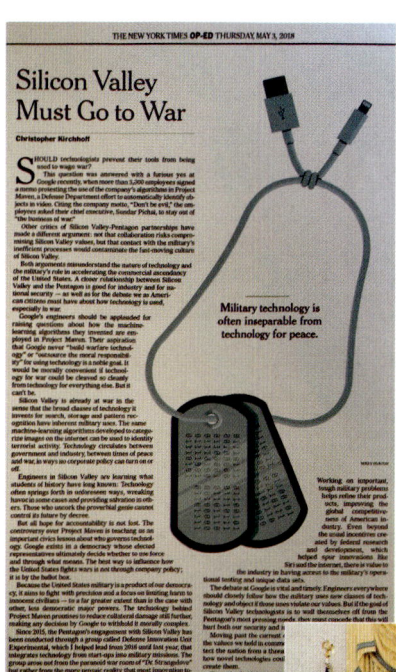

In 2018, Chris wrote a *New York Times* op-ed, "Silicon Valley Must Go to War," to make the point that protecting our nation's security requires integrating the newest technology into the Pentagon's systems—and that the process need not involve any type of ethical compromise.

Former Google CEO Eric Schmidt and members of the National Security Commission on Artificial Intelligence delivered their report to President Trump in the Oval Office; the report helped form the basis for a national strategy on AI.

The Remus 300 autonomous minesweeping underwater vehicle was an advanced implementation of AI led by DIU.

Raj speaking at the inaugural Tech Track 2 (2019), an initiative he cofounded to bring together senior Pentagon and Silicon Valley leaders for off-the-record conversations about how the two communities can collaborate more closely. Former national security adviser H. R. McMaster is seated at Raj's right; Stanford scholar Amy Zegart is to his left.

17

Of growing concern is how "siloed" the military has become from the general population, with only a small minority of citizens serving. The chart shows that Congress, too, has increasingly few members who are veterans of the armed services.

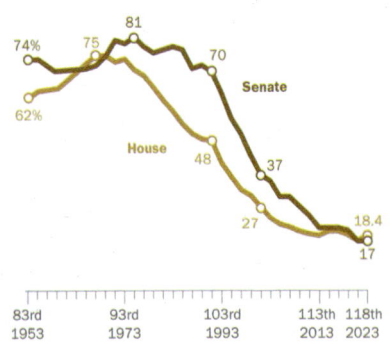

Share of members in Congress who are veterans has fallen in recent decades

% of members with previous military service

74% 75 81 70 Senate
62% House 48 37 27 18.4 17

83rd 1953   93rd 1973   103rd 1993   113th 2013   118th 2023

Note: Data does not include nonvoting delegates or commissioners.
Source: Pew Research Center analysis of data from Military Times, Congressional Research Service, Brookings Institution and House Committee on Veterans' Affairs.

PEW RESEARCH CENTER

DIU teammate Lauren Dailey forged a faster and more flexible way to accelerate technology into the military through a new acquisition pathway, which so far has resulted in $70 billion of technology procurements. Here she is in the West Wing, about to meet President Trump as part of a roundtable on American innovation.

Chris Kirchhoff at far right with, from left to right, all three current and past DIU directors—Mike Brown, Doug Beck, and Raj Shah—celebrating DIU's attaining over $1 billion in contracts.

In the years following DIU's creation in 2015, venture capital interest in national security has grown exponentially. Shield Capital, founded by former DIU members, military veterans, and entrepreneurs, is helping to lead this shift.

Eric Schmidt emerged as one of the Valley technologists most supportive of the military's needs—and one of its key advisers. He is shown here (on right, with hands extended) in Kyiv meeting with Andriy Yermak, head of the office of the president, and Oleksiy Reznikov, Ukraine's defense minister.

In Ukraine, combat often boils down to drones fighting drones. Here, Raj and Chris fly a long-range surveillance drone at a test range outside of Lviv in October 2023.

CHAPTER SEVEN
VENTURE CAPITAL GOES TO WAR

The turnabout in U.S.-China relations that propelled much of the work of the National Security Commission on Artificial Intelligence (NSCAI) was also driving changes in capital markets. Raj, sensing opportunity, took an entrepreneurial approach that ultimately led to the founding of Shield Capital, a venture capital firm with a focus on national security.

Raj believed the U.S. needed to match the "civil-military fusion" strategy of the Chinese Communist Party (CCP) by creating our own version of that civil-military partnership but with a uniquely American twist. The CCP's civil-military fusion strategy seeks to integrate the Chinese defense sector with their commercial sector to boost military capability. It's their answer to DIU but with authoritarian powers: the CCP can force private companies to support the military and even take over production if they desire. The CCP has even embedded party apparatchiks into the leadership ranks at promising technology startups.

The U.S. answer to the CCP's civil-military fusion is not to copy it but to leverage our unique advantages. First, the U.S. is a great place to live. Our embassies overseas have lines wrapping around the block with people aspiring to become Americans; that's not the case with China. Second, we have a vibrant technology and innovation ecosystem. Eight of the world's ten largest tech companies are based in the U.S., with one in Taiwan (TSMC) and another in China (Tencent). In the U.S. we can't force companies to build products for the military, but we can create strong incentives for them. Private companies and investors are driven by a profit motive. The government just needs to harness that profit motive to encourage the behavior it desires. For example, if the government buys advanced technology from nontraditional suppliers, companies and investors will follow in droves. When this happens, U.S. companies typically outperform their state-owned and state-backed competitors in China.

That said, as the U.S. entered the 2020s, its entrepreneurs and the Pentagon had only begun talking. Despite DIU's great successes, cultural divides persisted between Washington and Silicon Valley. To keep both sides focused on the importance of the opportunity before them, after leaving DIU Raj founded an initiative called Tech Track 2 that is housed at the Hoover Institution, a public policy think tank at Stanford University. "Track 2" is what the State Department calls "backchannel diplomacy." "It's usually used for countries like Russia and China," Condoleezza Rice said at the first Track 2 meeting, "but now we need it for government and industry."

Raj cofounded Tech Track 2 with Lieutenant General H. R. McMaster, the former national security advisor; Amy Zegart, senior fellow at Stanford's Hoover Institution; and Mike Brown, then head of DIU. They organized a conference and invited forty people—twenty from the Pentagon, twenty from the Valley—for a full day of private conversations. At the foot of the tower at the center of Stanford's campus, they gathered in the Annenberg Auditorium, a small, circular room with a round center table surrounded by an outer ring of chairs. Raj kept it off the record so that people would feel free to express their true thoughts and be more open than they might be in public. Neither the names of the attendees nor the items on the agenda were published. But had you been walking on the campus that day, you might have noticed a fleet of black Suburbans pull up outside and deliver a group of generals, including General David Goldfein, then chief of staff of the U.S. Air Force, plus several former secretaries of state and secretaries of defense, as well as Doug Beck, DIU's future head, and Philip Bilden, Raj's future Shield Capital cofounder. Ash Carter joined by video.

By day's end, Beck and Goldfein had agreed to a talent swap: Apple would send five engineers to spend time with the air force, and the air force would send five service members to spend time with Apple. The idea was to help infuse each side with the culture of the other. To be sure, ten people weren't going to magically transform the culture of enormous organizations. But it was a start.

Raj also had been named a visiting fellow at the Hoover Institution and started teaching a class at Stanford called "Technology, Innovation, and Great Power Competition," with Steve Blank, who, as we mentioned previously, was a successful tech entrepreneur, and Joe Felter, a West Point graduate and former Army Ranger who had served as U.S. deputy assistant Secretary of Defense for South Asia, Southeast Asia, and Oceania. This class on how technology fuels the rise of nations and military power was an evolution of "Hacking for Defense," which had spawned several successful companies. The goal was to nurture interest in defense technology strategy among the bright undergraduate and graduate students at Stanford. As with the Tech Track 2 conference, Raj hoped to build connections between the military and civilian worlds. Tech Track 2 dealt with high-level policymakers and influential investors, but this class took a grassroots approach, reaching out to young students who perhaps could be inspired to apply their talents to national security if they learned about the military's culture and purpose. Guest speakers included Jim Mattis, Ash Carter, and Michael McFaul, the former U.S. ambassador to Russia. McFaul had sat across a table from Vladimir Putin. He gave students a firsthand assessment of the Russian president's beliefs, resentments, and view of the world—and prompted them to think about how the U.S. might counter the threat that Putin and Russia represented.

While the efforts to connect people were important, Raj believed the biggest impact would come from helping tech entrepreneurs build products at the intersection of national security and commercial use cases. He was interested in funding companies that solved important problems for both private and military customers. Fortunately, there was no shortage of interested entrepreneurs. Pretty much anyone with an idea for a startup that had some defense application found a way to connect with Raj—many even made their pitches around Raj's dining table in San Francisco's Noe Valley. In their minds, contributing to the defense of democracy felt more fulfilling than creating the next photo-sharing or food delivery app. They wanted to solicit Raj's advice—and his investment.

Together with Philip Bilden and a small coalition of other investors, Raj began making angel investments—writing small checks, $100,000 on average, to help startups get going before they were ready to raise a proper Series A round of venture capital. Philip was a cofounder of HarbourVest Partners, a global private equity investment manager with over $100 billion under management. He'd built and led the firm's Asia Pacific business while based in Hong Kong, where he had a front row seat watching China's rise. He and Raj had talked about the idea of a national security-focused VC firm before Raj took the helm of DIUx. Now that Raj had stepped down, they swung into action.

In the Valley ecosystem, angel investors play a critical role for the earliest of companies. These individual investors take on risks that large firms won't. And they mentor and prepare fledgling startups to scale up once institutional investors get involved. One rule Raj made for himself was that he wouldn't invest in companies that he had worked with while at DIU—he felt that would be a conflict of interest. This meant passing on some of DIU's success stories, such as Anduril and Capella. Over the course of three years, he met with leaders of more than two hundred companies, listened to numerous pitches, and sat through countless PowerPoint presentations, and in most cases he passed on the opportunity. In the end he made two dozen small investments in early stage startups, many of which blossomed into successful companies building vital solutions for national security.

There was Vannevar Labs, named after Vannevar Bush, an engineer who during World War II had led the U.S. Office of Scientific Research and Development, which oversaw the Manhattan Project and its creation of the atomic bomb. His 1945 report "Science, the Endless Frontier" spurred Congress to create the National Science Foundation.

Over coffee in Raj's kitchen, Vannevar's two cofounders shared their vision for using natural language processing, a form of AI, to support U.S. counterterrorism efforts by enabling analysts to sift through huge amounts of data and find significant details. The pair were Nini Moorhead, a former counterterrorism officer in the U.S. intelligence community, and Brett Granberg, a veteran of In-Q-Tel, the CIA's venture capital arm. Another of Raj's early investments was HawkEye 360, which operates a constellation of satellites that can detect radio frequency (RF) signals for geolocation purposes—something that in the past only the U.S. and Soviet spy birds could do. The satellites can manage everything from finding survivors of natural disasters to spotting drug smugglers by locating signals from their push-to-talk radios. HawkEye 360's founder John Serafini would later join Shield Capital as a venture partner.

A third investment was Nexla, whose founders were building high-speed software "pipes" that soup up the performance of AI systems. All three of these companies have thrived in the ensuing years, becoming leaders in their respective fields. They also share a few similar characteristics that made them appealing investments. They were inventing advanced technology that would be difficult for others to copy; their customers would include both government and commercial buyers; and most important, they were led by passionate, almost maniacally focused founders.

The investment with the most conspicuous sci-fi cool factor might have been Elroy Air, whose founder, David Merrill, had the audacious goal of building small autonomous aircraft that could enable same-day shipping to every person on the planet. Merrill designed an electric-powered vertical takeoff and landing aircraft (eVTOL) called the Chaparral that can operate on its own, without a pilot, and carry up to three hundred pounds of cargo with a three-hundred-mile range. The company is named after Elroy Jetson, a character from the early 1960s television show *The Jetsons* about a space-age family who zip around Orbit City in flying cars.

Merrill is a youthful-looking guy in his thirties with a pedigree and track record that made him stand out. With a background in computer science at Stanford and a Ph.D. from MIT, he'd already, by the time he met Raj, built and sold one startup. Merrill, his cofounder Clint Cope, and their small team were building a prototype aircraft in an old warehouse in an unglamorous industrial neighborhood in Bayshore, ten miles south of San Francisco. Raj was impressed by the prototype but even more impressed with Merrill's passion.

Merrill's original plan was to build an air taxi similar to what Joby was building. But early on, he and Cope realized there were potential military uses. The two of them attended an autonomous aviation conference and heard a representative from the DoD describing a problem the army needed to solve. The military needed a way to deliver heavy cargo in "contested environments." They were using helicopters to do that work, but helicopters are expensive. And often there weren't enough to keep up with demand in a high-tempo resupply operation. But most important, flying choppers into dangerous areas meant putting lives at risk. "If anybody out there is thinking about autonomous aerial systems and would focus their attention on cargo and military resupply, please come talk to me," the DoD representative said.

For Merrill and Cope, this was a lightbulb moment. They spent the afternoon talking to the army officer and quickly decided that this would become the company's first mission. "We believed there was a huge global need," Merrill recalls. That belief was reinforced in the coming months as they met with people from FedEx, as well as from the World Food

Programme, which supplies humanitarian aid by air. "We heard from everybody that they needed new aerial cargo options and we realized that there was an opportunity to build a business that had military resupply as one of the important pillars."

In this case, Elroy already had a customer and just needed to build the product. "From an entrepreneurial point of view it was really exciting to hear from a customer who so clearly needs the product that you have the capability to build. And that got us fired up to do it," Merrill recalls.

Designing a workable aircraft was a huge challenge. It would require a great deal of capital investment, a lot more than, say, creating a software company. But an even bigger challenge would be figuring out how to sell that aircraft to the Pentagon. The fact that Raj knew the ins and outs of dealing with the military had spurred Merrill to seek him out.

Elroy soon landed a contract with Air Force Special Operations Command (AFSOC) after its founders met an air force major who quickly recognized the military value of the aircraft and acted to help fund development. While employees at some tech companies have balked at the idea of working with the military, Merrill says that hasn't been the case at Elroy, partly because new employees come in understanding that they're building for the military as well as commercial customers, but also because they know the aircraft will be used for cargo—not kinetic operations. "There are some folks on our team who feel very strongly that they wouldn't want the vehicle directly weaponized. They don't want to build a system for strike. But the military has given us a clear signal that they want Chaparral for resupply and logistics, so they can avoid using big manned assets like C-130s and Black Hawk helicopters," Merrill says.

By the time Elroy unveiled the finished version of the Chaparral in January 2022, the company had already secured agreements to provide five hundred units to commercial, military, and humanitarian aid customers. Those include AYR Logistics, which works with the United Nations and the World Food Programme (WFP), and Mesa Airlines, which will use them for parcel delivery. Military contracts helped Elroy get initial traction, but Merrill believes the bulk of Elroy's business will ultimately be with commercial customers.

RAJ'S NEW DIRECTION

A conversation with Eric Schmidt at his apartment proved to be a turning point for Raj. Gathered on couches were a number of those who'd worked on technology and national security issues, including Avril Haines, the former deputy director of the CIA, and and Chesley "Sully" Sullenberger, the pilot who became famous after his emergency landing of a US Airways flight on the Hudson River in 2009.

Over an informal dinner, Raj sought Eric's advice about what he should do next professionally. His experience at DIU had given him unique insights that would be valuable to Silicon Valley investors, and he was being courted by several firms. He was still helping lead his second startup, a cybersecurity insurance company named Resilience, that he and DIU partner and air force veteran Vishaal "V8" Hariprasad had founded. But Raj wanted to do more—to continue the mission of bringing Silicon Valley technology to the military but in a way that could scale.

Thanks in part to DIU's impact, defense investing was getting hot. Some of the top Valley VC firms wanted to build a defense practice and were seeking a partner who possessed the technological savvy to spot promising startups, but also understood how to navigate the Pentagon's thickets of bureaucracy and obstructionism—in other words, a guy who could help portfolio companies close contacts with the military. That rare combination of talents made Raj a unique commodity. A Silicon Valley venture capital firm had just offered him a lucrative partner-level job to scout for defense-related investment opportunities. But what Raj most wanted to do was found his own VC firm that would focus on companies at the nexus of commercial and national security technology. Such a firm would help preserve democracy and the American way through private enterprise and markets. Raj and Philip Bilden had resurrected their idea to build a firm together. But both had to weigh the significant—probably twenty-year—commitment it would take. The time for a decision was looming. Raj sought counsel from friends and mentors. Chris believed Raj had no choice but to start a firm, because, as Chris put it, "You're a terrible employee. You need to do your own thing." Ash Carter loved the idea. H. R. McMaster and former NATO supreme allied commander Admiral James "Jim" Stavridis were both encouraging. All three statesmen offered to lend their support by joining as advisors.

The not so small problem Raj and Philip needed to surmount was how to raise capital for a first-time fund. Venture capital firms raise money from investors called "limited partners," like pension funds, college endowments, and wealthy private families, and invest those funds on their behalf. These investors expect extraordinary performance. Investing in early-stage startups is a high-risk business. Why take the risk unless you can reap a better return than you could by investing in the stock market? So those potential institutional investors are wary of new funds and for good reason: the majority of VCs do not beat public stock market returns in the long run. However, the top 25 percent tend to exceed them by a wide margin. Most investors would rather wait and see how you do with your first fund. If you hit a few home runs, maybe they'll participate in the second fund or the third.

Raising a first-time fund would be a challenge, but there was the even bigger challenge of spotting winners and making smart bets. That talent is an art as much as a science, requiring gut instinct and, in every deal, a big leap of faith. Sometimes even the best venture capitalists, veterans with long track records of reaping windfalls, can run into a bad patch, make too many losing bets, and end up shutting down. However, when venture capital works, it can create tremendous results, helping build iconic companies and generating long-term returns for investors such as pensions, endowments, and foundations.

Eric had done something similar. In 2001, he took the CEO job at a startup founded by a pair of Stanford graduate students, Larry Page and Sergey Brin, who had started a company with a kooky name—Google—and had a crazy idea of building something called a "search engine" that could find anything on the Internet. When he became CEO, Eric put some skin in the game by investing $1 million in the fledgling startup, despite the fact that it had barely begun generating revenue by selling ads. By the time he and Raj were talking at the kitchen table, Eric was one of the world's wealthiest people.

It was perhaps no surprise then that, to Eric, it was clear: Raj should forget about the lucrative position that a VC firm was offering and instead shoot for the moon—aim to found a firm rather than join an existing one. Besides, this wasn't just about the money; it was the mission. With a defense-focused fund, Raj could fund dozens of new startups that would potentially transform the U.S. military and protect our way of life. It was the best way for him to carry on the work he'd started at DIU.

"You've only got one life," Eric said. "You need to put yourself out there and build your own venture firm."

Inspired by Eric's enthusiasm, Raj glanced outside at the twinkling lights of the Manhattan skyline. The world seemed alive with possibilities. "Okay," he said. "I'm going to go for it."

SHIELD CAPITAL: BUILD IT AND THEY WILL COME

As the new year began in 2020, Raj found himself on the oceanfront veranda of Philip Bilden's home in Palm Beach, overlooking the Atlantic Ocean, which was glistening blue. In charting a course for their inaugural fund and making plans to build the team that could execute their vision, they had locked onto the name "Shield Capital" to align the firm's mission of advancing national security.

The two founders had complementary interests and strengths. Raj was a company founder with his fingers on the pulse of Silicon Valley, with deep connections to entrepreneurs interested in building companies supporting national security. Philip's experience as a pioneer in private equity provided access to institutional capital around the globe. They both had served as officers in the military. Most important, they and their families had become close through their time angel investing together.

Raj and Philip understood that founding a venture capital firm and the responsibility of investing other people's money would require a decades-long commitment. There was no guarantee of success, and the barriers to entry of raising the first fund were daunting, even for a seasoned investor like Philip, who'd previously managed billions of dollars of institutional capital.

Philip was now in his mid-fifties and recently retired from HarbourVest Partners, the global firm he helped build. Raj knew he wasn't the kind of guy who'd be happy playing golf and pickleball in Palm Beach. Although Philip had withdrawn his name from consideration to be secretary of the navy in the Trump administration, he was active in a number of national security causes, including serving on the Chief of Naval Operations Executive Panel and on the board of directors of the navy's largest shipbuilder, Huntington Ingalls Industries. His two sons, both Naval Academy graduates, were serving on active duty as officers in the navy. Private innovation was what our nation's warfighters, his sons and their shipmates, needed.

Raj and Philip recognized that technology was rapidly evolving beyond the ability of the defense industrial base and the Department of Defense to adopt and adapt. The U.S. aerospace and defense industry had consolidated from hundreds of firms into five massive, bureaucratic defense contractors whose corporate incentives were aligned to build what Congress budgeted rather than what warfighters really needed to win. These publicly traded defense conglomerates were spending more on stock buybacks than on research and development. In contrast, the CCP was forcing large and small Chinese companies to unite and support military development. Further, in the multitrillion-dollar U.S. venture capital market, very few firms were focusing on national security technology—some declined because of philosophy, most because of their lack of understanding of how government buys technology. A highly specialized venture firm, with the right team and strategy, could bridge the gap.

Now was the time to move out, and lead before others would inevitably follow. With a handshake and a toast, a new venture firm was founded. Philip said to his new cofounder, "Raj, Shield Capital will be our highest and best purpose for the next two decades of our lives. If we build it, they will come: the team, the investors, the entrepreneurs, and of course the returns."

CALLING THE A TEAM

Raj and Philip got down to the business of building Shield Capital from the ground up, which meant long hours, limited staff, funding expenses out of pocket, and fundraising with hats in hand to ask friends, family, and former business partners for their trust. Most important, they had to build a team of rock stars, motivated by the mission and experienced enough to make great investments. Looking for ways to even further support their prospective investments, Raj and Philip surveyed the aerospace and defense industry for a strategic partner open to a novel collaboration. While many defense primes had dabbled with venture capital, their track records were poor. They needed a company willing to try innovative approaches, which led them to L3Harris Technologies, whose CEO, Chris Kubasik, had scaled up through over thirty-five acquisitions.

On a frigid and rainy Veterans Day in 2020, Raj and Philip met with Sean Stackley, the senior vice president of L3Harris and former acting secretary of the navy, to pitch their idea. The L3Harris offices were eerily empty due to the COVID pandemic. After listening to their brief, Stackley nodded his head approvingly and said, "I think my boss would find this of interest." A few months later, at a seaside restaurant in Melbourne, Florida, Raj and Philip met Chris Kubasik, the L3Harris CEO. Kubasik lived up to his reputation. Ten minutes into the pitch, he said, "I get it, guys. Shield Capital could be part of my Trusted Disrupter strategy for L3Harris. Let's do this. I'll anchor your fund. Just make it work."

Securing an "anchor" investment from L3Harris, the fifth-largest prime defense contractor, with $17 billion in annual revenues, created great tailwinds. On its face the deal might seem counterintuitive. The primes were the companies that Silicon Valley startups were supposed to disrupt, right? But Kubasik understood the Silicon Valley maxim that it's better to disrupt yourself than to let others do it for you. Investing funds into Shield Capital gave L3Harris a way to reap a return from the defense tech boom. But more important, it would help L3Harris stay on top of the latest innovations from the Valley and spot promising ways to collaborate with startups. "Innovation and technology from startups are critical to providing L3Harris's customers the very best capability," Kubasik says. "Partnering with Raj, Philip, and the Shield team gives us unique access to companies in Silicon Valley and beyond."

Landing an anchor investor made it easier for them to recruit an A+ team. Raj and Philip likened it to the Blues Brothers' "getting the band back together." Their advisory board included Ash Carter, Jim Stavridis, H. R. McMaster, Letitia "Tish" Long, the former director of the National Geospatial-Intelligence Agency, and David Goldfein, former chief of staff of the air force and early supporter of both DIUx and Tech Track 2.

From Hawkeye 360, they brought in John Serafini, a West Point–trained Army Ranger, venture capitalist, and company founder. Goldman

Sachs veteran Dan Holland joined as COO. Raj recruited DIU alumni, including Mike Brown and U.S. air force acquisition "ninja" David Rothzeid, who'd led all contracting there. Akhil Iyer, a Marine Corps Special Operations officer who'd once been Ash Carter's teaching assistant, joined while still completing his graduate studies at Harvard.

Lisa Hill, who'd worked with us at DIU and then joined Raj at Resilience, signed on to run investor relations. Her husband, Nick, is a distinguished Navy SEAL and career officer. In Lisa's view, Shield Capital lets her continue to serve her country in a new way. "It feels like my work matters," she says. "This is about impact, about transformation." Lisa was especially motivated to maintain her own career after an incident in 2011 in which thirty-eight service members, including seventeen of Nick's fellow Navy SEALs, were lost when a helicopter was shot down in Afghanistan. She and Nick went to Ramstein Air Base in Germany and watched the coffins coming off the plane. "For weeks, I was haunted," she says. "Every time I closed my eyes, all I saw was that line of widows. I swore to myself that I would never be in a position where I didn't have the means to take care of my kids if something happened to Nick."

Shield Capital's biggest investment to date was Albedo, a startup whose satellites boast exponentially higher resolution than what is typical today. To get a sense of the difference, each pixel of the satellites that deliver images for Google Earth resolves one square meter of the earth. Albedo's eagle-eyed cameras create images where each pixel represents ten centimeters. It's the difference between being able to identify that an object is a car and being able to tell what kind of car it is and whether it has a bumper sticker.

Shield Capital's timing turned out to be prescient. The firm closed its first fund in the fall of 2021 and announced its official opening in March 2022, just weeks after Russia invaded Ukraine. The invasion of Ukraine set in motion a new gold rush in Silicon Valley, where venture capitalists who had once balked at investing in defense technology startups suddenly couldn't fund companies fast enough. In 2022, VCs pumped $33 billion into defense technology companies, compared to $16 billion in 2019. A new set of defense unicorns was minted, including Anduril and Shield AI. Venture funds often exhibit herd behavior, and these success stories generated significant followership.

Silicon Valley was finally doing its part and cranking out new products for the military. The burden now fell to the Pentagon to figure out how to buy them—and to do it fast enough to prevent the pendulum in the Valley from swinging away due to a lack of customer action.

Four years after Philip and Raj's handshake in Palm Beach, their firm was becoming a driving force in Silicon Valley. Shield Capital was in business with a close-knit team, a unique strategic partnership with a prime, and an oversubscribed fund that closed at $186 million. Build it, and they will come.

BRIDGING THE CULTURAL DIVIDE

Investing alone will not solve the challenges our nation is facing from new adversaries abroad. Creating an American version of civil-military fusion involves more than just developing cool new technologies and connecting startups to customers in the DoD. There are also significant cultural issues that have built up over the years, paradoxically because America has mostly been at peace. For years, we have been pounding the table about the fact that instead of having civil-military fusion, the U.S. has created a civil-military *unfusion*, a cultural divide. Especially in the years after Vietnam, the civilian and military worlds have grown apart from one another. Graduates from top universities are no longer serving in the armed forces, State Department, or intelligence agencies in meaningful numbers. In 1960, Stanford and MIT each graduated more than one hundred ROTC members, but today those two institutions graduate a dozen or fewer. In 1980, 64 percent of Congress and 59 percent of Fortune 500 CEOs were military veterans—a legacy of World War II, Korea, and Vietnam. Today, those numbers have fallen to 19 percent and 6 percent respectively. Members of Congress have become disconnected from the military—yet they control the DoD's budget and make decisions about how money should be allocated.

Another troubling trend is that military service has become hereditary. Nearly one-third of new recruits have parents who served, and 60 percent have a close family member who served. That's a problem, because it perpetuates a small class of Americans who serve and a larger class who don't. This insularity causes military families to experience a life of deployments and a culture not found in the families of their civilian peers. History has shown, starting with ancient Rome, that the loss of deep bonds between warfighters and civilians is not conducive to a healthy democracy. Further, all branches of the military are finding it more difficult to find new recruits. Fewer than 1 percent of the U.S. population has ever served in the armed forces.

For the past few years Raj has been proposing policy changes that could improve U.S. military readiness. Here are a few:

Mandatory national service. Conscription is a controversial idea, yet countries like South Korea, Singapore, Austria, Sweden, and Taiwan each mandate military service. It's a terrible idea to have a tiny group of Americans fighting wars while the vast majority are doing everything else. There must be shared sacrifice. For one thing, this would expose more civilians to the military. But also, when more of us have our children in uniform, we reduce the likelihood of going to war. If every senator had had a kid who'd have to go to war in Iraq, would we have invaded? Perhaps not. People like Raj, who've gone to war, are the most reluctant to support more of it. Indeed, the biggest reason for us to develop better defense tech is not to be able to defeat enemies in war, but to prevent wars from starting.

Put a rich kid from New York in a foxhole with a poor kid from Alabama and you start to erode the cultural divide and polarization tearing apart our country. Walking in each other's shoes builds empathy and makes possible the national solidarity we now lack. Nothing gets done when we have powerful people on both sides who are less interested in fixing our government than in screaming at each other in front of TV cameras. Forcing Americans to serve beside one another is the very basis of shared sacrifice in service of citizenship. A short stint of mandatory national service could help mend this divide. While it would be difficult to create opportunities for all young Americans to serve in the military, national service could include stints with the intelligence agencies and other civil government departments. Further career paths for service beyond ROTC or a multiple-year enlistment would certainly help. The professionalized, all-volunteer force America has today is a tremendous achievement, yet it has come at the cost of lost bonds between soldiers and citizens. For national service to achieve the broad goals of bringing our nation together, there can be no exemptions or deferments.

Reopen shuttered military bases. Over the past few decades, the DoD has closed bases in affluent areas like San Francisco, Los Angeles, New York, and Boston and moved service members to less expensive places in Arizona, Texas, and Georgia. In the Bay Area, where we live, there are no active-duty bases left at all. Moving away from high cost-of-living areas saves the DoD money but reinforces the civil-military divide. We should begin by reopening major military installations in San Francisco and Boston, our two leading centers of technology innovation.

Consider that a generation ago, no matter where you grew up, it was common to see people in uniform walking around. There were kids in your class whose dads or moms had served. You were less likely to think of service members as perpetrators of violence. Rather, you saw them simply as normal people doing a job they believed in, who viewed war as a last resort option. Today, there's a gap. Our neighbors in San Francisco for the most part get their understanding of the military from Hollywood movies. It's safe to say they're not perceiving anything close to reality. They've seen Tom Cruise pulling Mach 10 in a fighter jet and Special Forces operators torturing terrorists in black sites. They don't consider serving in uniform themselves or realize that a person can make important contributions by working as a civilian in the Pentagon, even if just for a few years.

Expand ROTC, National Guard, and Reserves. Students graduating from top engineering schools can go anywhere they want after graduation. We should make it easier for them to choose military service. The Reserve Officers' Training Corps (ROTC) program gives students of most universities a path into service. However, many leading universities have closed their ROTC programs. We should reopen those that were closed in the Vietnam era, including the one at Stanford. Currently, Stanford ROTC students must drive to Berkeley, a trip that can take up to two hours each way in traffic. Service in the Reserves can be attractive to people who are interested in donning the uniform but who also want to work in the private sector. To encourage participation, we should stop the practice of training all Reserve units to be combat-ready and able to be immediately deployed, and instead treat a portion as a strategic reserve, stocked with people and capabilities the active force doesn't have. Reservists could be especially helpful in areas like software development and cybersecurity. Raj's entry into the military was through the Air National Guard unit closest to Princeton, enabling him to prepare for service while still an undergraduate.

Create better career paths for active-duty service members. Offering servicemen and -women the flexibility to join the private sector or a Reserve unit for a few years and then return to the military would markedly improve retention as well as broaden skill sets. Further, the Pentagon should create programs to hold security clearances active for a few years after an active-duty member separates, enabling them to more easily return in a Reserve or civilian capacity. Essentially, in a world where top talent no longer spends thirty years at places like IBM or GE, the military must reform its human capital and assignment systems to create greater flexibility and make it easier for service members to transition to and from the private sector.

Fix our immigration system. Our current immigration policies drive away top engineering talent from other countries, hindering Silicon Valley's ability to develop defense-related technology for the Pentagon. Virtually every one of Raj's portfolio companies has encountered hassles relating to obtaining H-1B visas for critical engineers. We need to make it easier for non-citizens to obtain an H-1B visa and work in the United States, and, relatedly, we need to lift caps on immigration. In the field of cybersecurity alone, there are nearly half a million open positions that companies can't fill owing to the lack of candidates. The new AI boom is producing a similar gap. The U.S. could hire ten thousand top AI scientists from around the world and we'd still need more. More proactively, if the U.S. offered visas to the top twenty AI scientists, and their families, to settle in America, we could appreciably shift the global AI race in favor of democracies.

We also should create policies that encourage foreign students to remain in the United States after earning degrees in STEM fields. In 2009, Representative Jeff Flake proposed the STAPLE Act (Stop Trained in America Ph.D.s from Leaving the Economy), which would have enabled foreign students to obtain a green card when they obtained a Ph.D. (The name was intended to promote the idea—figuratively if not literally—that when someone got their Ph.D. we'd "staple" a green card to their diploma.) The bill fizzled out, and Flake left Congress. But we should resurrect the idea.

Immigrants are more likely to become entrepreneurs. In the U.S., 25 percent of startups are created by immigrants. If you look just at "unicorns," companies with valuations above $1 billion, 55 percent were founded or cofounded by immigrants. Google, eBay, Stripe, Uber, Yahoo, SpaceX,

Zoom, Nvidia—the list goes on. Why are we making it more difficult for the founders of the next batch of unicorns to come live here? If the U.S. could attract the top 1 percent of the smartest people in the world, we'd be unstoppable.

Don't give orders—*place* orders. The Pentagon doesn't need to put money into Silicon Valley VC funds or, worse yet, try to start their own funds. A common DoD approach has been to organize conferences and dinners and try to direct the way VCs invest their money. That's going at things backwards, reflecting the way the Pentagon engages with the primes. The DoD needs to let the free markets optimize the flow of capital and then influence that flow as a buyer. A venture capitalist's job is to invest in great companies. What's a great company? A company that has customers. All the Pentagon needs to do is be a great customer. Buy products, and trust that good venture capitalists will pour money into the companies building those products. This sounds obvious, but for the Pentagon this represents a huge shift in mind-set. The DoD is used to working with primes, and in those relationships, the DoD plays the role of VC, putting up the money to develop products. As the DoD shifts more spending to Silicon Valley, it needs to learn how to be a new kind of customer.

Finding ways to counter the Chinese model of civil-military fusion has as much or even more to do with culture than with technology or venture capital. The U.S. can't adopt the Chinese approach. Nor should we. It's easy to imagine that China's autocratic system is more functional than our own, because its top-down, highly controlled system is more effective at producing technology and adapting technology to military purposes. But our system is superior in the long run; it just needs a few tweaks. The U.S. has the most vibrant innovation ecosystem in the world, a history of welcoming immigrants and providing strong support for science funding, and strong alliances with free nations in Europe and Asia. Unlike China, we have a system where information flows freely and where competition ensures that the best ideas and products rise to the top. It's messy, but across the decades it's proved to be a winning approach.

Western democracies, from India to Japan to the U.S., will prevail by betting on their entrepreneurs, their risk-takers. Building a business from scratch is hard—a startup always begins as an underdog. On three occasions Raj's two startups came within weeks of shutting down. After putting his life savings into his first company, Raj found himself with only a week of payroll remaining and no easy path forward. At that point, strapping into an F-16 and going back to war felt much easier than the prospect of having to fire all the employees who'd put their trust in him. But through a lucky break and a last-minute contract with a Fortune 500 customer, Raj and the company made it through—the kind of near-death experience that virtually all startups have on the way to succeeding. Supporting these risk-takers is what venture firms do. Today, Shield Capital helps innovative companies survive these existential crises—as a way to make money, yes, but also to preserve democracy. It's absolutely possible to do well by doing good. And the trend is catching on, with more and more senior officials from the Pentagon helping startups work with the Department. Market forces pushing the DoD toward innovation are gaining steam.

The Pentagon has an equally critical role to play by ingesting the technology being created for it. Its procurement dollars, if deployed to buy the products of VC-backed startups, will make the flywheel of capital-driven defense innovation spin ever faster.

CHAPTER EIGHT
UKRAINE AND THE BATTLEFIELD OF THE FUTURE

The conflict in Ukraine became the war DIU had envisioned, fought with drones, satellites, and artificial intelligence, hackers on both sides launching cyberattacks, and Ukrainian citizens using smartphone apps to alert their military to enemy positions. It's a hybrid war, with legacy technology like tanks and artillery used in combination with a digital overlay.

Capella Space, the satellite company we had wanted to surveil North Korea, now was flying a constellation of satellites and observed the Russian invasion as it began to unfold. Payam Banazadeh, Capella's founder, had been busy since we'd seen him last. His company had almost gone bankrupt after we couldn't deliver the full $50 million in Pentagon funds we'd promised. Despite that setback, Payam had persevered, as the best entrepreneurs do. By 2022 he'd built a thriving business, launching a constellation of seven synthetic aperture radar (SAR) satellites and selling satellite data to commercial and government customers. Capella's next-generation birds had mesh antennas eleven feet wide. They sent signals bouncing off earth's surface that, once returned, resolved details smaller than twenty inches. That's like seeing a basketball from 350 miles up, through any kind of weather, day or night.

Now, with war looming, DoD needed Capella more than ever. For weeks Vladimir Putin had been amassing forces along Ukraine's border. Tanks, infantry, missile batteries, and air assault units were arrayed in a thousand-mile arc from Southern Belarus to the Black Sea. To many, it looked like the world's most foolhardy bluff. Putin, already a pariah, was riding Russia's economy into oblivion. Yet buoyed by rising oil prices and a new alliance with China, and with nationalist sentiments stoked at home, he threatened to invade Ukraine.

Putin started the job in 2014. Forces without military insignia flooded Crimea, which Russia then annexed. The conflict had smoldered ever since, and now Putin wanted more. There was a prolonged period during which he was thinking about it. And while that was going on, there was intense debate inside the national security community among people who followed Russia. Most believed that an invasion was a far-fetched possibility, but others thought Putin was so driven by his desire to reclaim old Soviet states that he might actually take the risk.

Capella satellites saw it happening in real time, and they suddenly became a powerful instrument in the U.S. campaign against Russian disinformation. "Putin kept saying, 'I'm not going to invade,'" Mike Brown remembers. "He put out video of tanks being loaded on railcars, portraying them being sent back to Russia. But we knew he was actually amassing forces." When Putin denied that Russia intended to invade, the Pentagon released a Capella image to CNN, and President Joe Biden cited that image as proof that Putin was lying. "We were the first unclassified, open-source satellite imagery that showed the imminent invasion," Payam recalls.

On February 24, 2022, columns of Russian armor rolled across the border toward Kyiv. Cruise missiles slammed into Ukraine's communication nodes, including the data center that powered Ukraine's government operations. A massive cyberattack unfolded. Computer viruses targeted forty-eight Ukrainian agencies and enterprises. Airborne assault forces landed on airfields on the edges of Kyiv. Spetsnaz troops infiltrated the capital and almost succeeded in their mission to assassinate President Volodymyr Zelensky. Russia's military, which wields 5,889 nuclear warheads, was rolling west toward the NATO block, and Europe's largest land war since World War II was playing out in real life. "It reminds me of NSC gallows humor," Chris told Raj in a phone call. "Just when you think things can't get worse, you realize how much of an idiot you are for thinking that."

But then something extraordinary happened. What was supposed to have been a cakewalk by Russian forces quickly turned into a rout of those same forces. Troops that had planned to march in a Kyiv victory parade were now in retreat, taking heavy casualties as Ukraine forces pushed them back east. Part of the reason was that Ukraine was skillfully wielding commercial technology. In conventional weaponry, the Ukrainians were vastly outgunned. But their tech-savvy military had obtained an advantage by anticipating Russian moves and devising workarounds. When Russians jammed Ukrainian radios, Ukrainians switched to SpaceX Starlink Internet terminals provided by Elon Musk and Android phones to keep orders flowing from the Defense Ministry. On WhatsApp and Signal, citizens reported Russian troop movements. Ukrainian soldiers zipped cheap Chinese-made DJI drones over enemy lines to scout positions and direct artillery fire. They armed quadcopters with grenades, turning them into kamikazes. One DJI drone destroyed a Russian T-90 tank while another filmed the attack.

Soon uncrewed small boats attacked Russian navy warships in the Black Sea. Ukraine's Soviet-era surveillance drones, modified with explosives, shredded strategic bombers deep in Russia's territory. Spotter teams in pickup trucks streaming video via Starlink racked up kills by the hour. Turkish Bayraktar TB2 rear-propeller drones slammed missiles into Russian convoys. "Welcome to hell," the TB2's forty-two-year-old designer, an MIT graduate, captioned a social media post showing the slaughter. Russia replied by blasting Ukrainian power stations with $20,000 Iranian-made kamikaze drones. Those drones gave Russia an asymmetrical advantage, as the only way for Ukraine to defeat them was to use Western-provided missiles that cost anywhere from $140,000 to $500,000 each. Illustrating how commercial technology levels the playing field for all, 82 percent of the Iranian drones' components were made in the U.S. It was all part of the "flatter world" that Chris had written about in 2016.

Silicon Valley tech companies leapt into the fray to support Ukraine. Planet Labs' electro-optical satellites were surveilling the battlefield. HawkEye 360, a company Raj had invested in, intercepted Russian radio messages. Skydio, the first U.S. drone maker to become a unicorn, rushed its autonomous quadcopters to Ukraine infantry units. BlueHalo, mobilized by a $24 million Pentagon contract, delivered its Titan counter-drone systems to the battlefield, with antennas powered by machine learning algorithms. Palantir, developer of AI-powered data analytics software, sent engineers to Ukraine to help the Defense Ministry sift through huge amounts of intelligence information and draw conclusions from the data. Anduril deployed hardware and software systems, including its Ghost drone, a near-silent autonomous helicopter loaded with sensors. A DIU-backed company called Somewear Labs provided communications and mesh networking technology.

The big firms were in the thick of it as well. "I mean, they put the entire government on a Snowball," Amazon's suitcase-sized petabyte-hard drive, "and got it out of the country and into the cloud," one DIU engineer said. Some 10 million gigabytes of tax, property records, banking, and other data were backed up. Microsoft's rapid response team went on war footing too, working in tandem with U.S. Cyber Command to push patches that caused Russian malicious code to bounce back, like bullets off a tank.

Bay Area venture capitalists started getting requests for help buying drones, night-vision goggles, Kevlar vests, and other equipment for Ukrainian troops. Many wrote personal checks, organized shipments of gear, and shipped it by FedEx to the battlefield. People in the Valley who'd once pushed back against the idea of working with the military were now "thinking different," to quote Apple's famous mantra. Two weeks into the invasion, Chris was invited to a dinner hosted by Matthew Stepka, an early Google employee who lived in the Russian Hill neighborhood of San Francisco. Years before this, in the early days of DIUx, Chris had attended a similar dinner party at Stepka's place and received a chilly reception—the wealthy technorati sitting around the table weren't thrilled that the DoD was setting up a shop in Silicon Valley and luring entrepreneurs into collaborating with the military. This time, however, the mood had changed. A person who years before had peppered Chris with hostile questions now wanted to understand the difference between U.S. and British anti-tank missiles. The Project Maven controversy had turned some tech people away from the military, but now Ukraine had brought them back.

DIU SPRINGS INTO ACTION

The U.S. government turned out to be less nimble than the private sector in getting commercial tech to the front. Two months into the fighting, the U.S. and forty of its allies met in Germany to plan how to provide military and economic assistance to Ukraine. The Pentagon created a new command, the Security Assistance Group–Ukraine, whose mission was to push supplies into the country. The Biden administration and Congress committed $16 billion in funds in the war's initial months, some of that money to be spent on immediate shipments from stockpiles and the rest on contracts for new production. At DIU, leaders sprang into action. Jared Dunnmon, who led DIU's artificial intelligence portfolio, became the DIU rep on a crucial Pentagon body, the Senior Integration Group-Ukraine (SIG-Ukraine), tasked with blasting through Pentagon bureaucratic blockers that could slow down the delivery of aid. It was a job tailor-made for DIU. Ukraine needed small drones to help aim artillery;

DIU maintained a list of drone-makers that could supply them. Ukrainians were relying on noisy generators to power their Starlink terminals—the noise betraying their positions. DIU had a portfolio of energy companies that made long-duration batteries.

Even in a time of crisis, the Pentagon couldn't get out of its own way, and the Ukraine conflict laid bare the cost of an acquisition apparatus built for the weapons systems of the Cold War. In an episode worthy of the novel *Catch-22*, SIG-Ukraine tried to buy and ship technology products using the Presidential Drawdown Authority (PDA), which enables the DoD to deliver equipment in days or even hours during emergencies. But the rules said you could only ship equipment that had already been purchased and stockpiled. So even though the DoD had standing contracts with the right technology companies, there was no ready mechanism to ship over the arsenal of new weapons and capabilities DIU had developed over its seven-year existence.

Other absurdities involved data. When commercial satellite companies like Capella transmitted images to the DoD through military networks, they technically became classified "NOFORN," meaning they couldn't be released to foreign nations. Even though these images were completely open source—some were playing on CNN—from the DoD's point of view, the images couldn't be automatically released to Ukraine. "Our team couldn't share the data," Dunnmon says. "It was ridiculous." Pentagon lawyers exacerbated the absurdity by claiming that commercial satellite images might contain "personally identifiable information," in which case sharing them with the Ukrainian military might violate U.S. privacy laws.

"Where is that coming from?" Chris asked a DIU official.

"In this case it's coming from the privacy and civil liberties people."

"Well, they should try living in Ukraine," Chris replied.

It was a problem of system misalignment. The actual capabilities driving the future of war had eclipsed what the Pentagon's system of security assistance could deliver. In the first eighteen months of the invasion the

U.S. provided $41 billion in military aid, with others contributing another $13 billion. But Ukraine's requests for advanced commercial technology often slipped through the gaps. One of the first tranches of aid contained an order for communication units made by Somewear Labs. These were little backpack-sized devices that the National Guard uses to set up networks when responding to a crisis. For reasons no one could explain, the order got lost in the system. Dunnmon spent days pestering people at the Pentagon and at U.S. European Command in Stuttgart, Germany, which was managing shipments. They had no idea what he was talking about. After days of back-and-forth, Dunnmon flew to Stuttgart and spent five hours in the EUCOM headquarters digging out the line item for the Somewear units from where it was buried in a budget spreadsheet.

"The acquisition system is built for supplying Patriot missile batteries in five years. It's not built for supplying a drone tomorrow," Dunnmon says. "The amount of effort that had to go into just getting routine things done was disheartening in a lot of ways." Given the context, it wasn't just frustrating—it was terrifying. Soldiers and civilians were dying. While many things went right in arming the Ukrainians, we couldn't get some of the most important commercial equipment to the front. Worse, we were getting a glimpse of how our military might perform if the U.S. were to go to war, and it didn't inspire confidence.

TECHNO-GUERRILLAS

The day after the invasion, Andrey Liscovich, a Ukrainian-born tech executive, flew from San Francisco to the Warsaw airport then made his way overland to his hometown of Zaporizhzhia, twenty-five miles from the border, where his parents still lived. After evacuating his parents, Liscovich walked into an army recruiting office and volunteered to fight. When recruiters learned Liscovich had been CEO of Uber Works, a former subsidiary of Uber, they suggested that instead of carrying a rifle Liscovich might be more valuable if he could help use his connections in Silicon Valley to get technology to the front. He began visiting frontline units and asking what they needed. Generators, Starlinks, and small drones, they told him. His key insight came when he learned the difference between "corrected" and "uncorrected" artillery fire. The latter often takes sixty rounds to strike the target. But add in a commercial drone—a pair of flying binoculars—and the same fire team can kill the target in five rounds or less. Andrey realized the best way he could help was by liaising between Ukraine military units and the Western technology companies that could aid them.

Liscovich created the Ukraine Defense Fund, a nonprofit that supplies nonlethal aid. On a fundraising swing through Silicon Valley, Liscovich brought Chris a Russian infantry shell that he'd picked up not far from his parents' house. The exploded steel casing sat uneasily on Chris's kitchen table between plates of quiche he'd served for breakfast.

Raising money, buying products, and shipping them to Europe was relatively straightforward. The big challenge was the "last-mile gap," getting gear out to the battlefield. Liscovich and his team devised a way to ship equipment from the U.S. through Amsterdam to Warsaw, and then on trucks to Ukraine, in less than ninety hours. Their fastest delivery took only forty-eight.

This kind of thinking was prevailing across the front. Ukrainian President Volodymyr Zelensky had called up military-aged males, from sixteen to sixty, many of whom had technical skills. "Techno-guerrillas," they were called. Ukrainians just needed the West to put weapons and commercial technology into their hands, and they could do the rest. "Ukraine's military is, at its heart, a grassroots fighting force with a significant number of software engineers distributed through its ranks," said a brief from the Special Competitive Studies Project (SCSP), a think tank Eric Schmidt founded to carry on the AI Commission's work. Another observer described Ukraine's military as "a partisan army with a Silicon Valley arm attached." "Ukraine was learning what happens when you conscript three hundred thousand of the world's most capable software engineers and send them into battle," the chief technology officer of Palantir, Shyam Shankar, said, referring to the large number of programmers in Ukraine, many of whom joined the war effort.

Ukraine possessed a modern technological infrastructure, with a level of sophistication that surpassed most of its European neighbors and even the U.S., where government online services remain embarrassingly out of date. In 2019, Zelensky had campaigned on a platform of moving the country into "a smartphone state." Zelensky's Ministry for Digital Transformation created an app called Diia, for "action," which was a secure one-stop shop for eighty public services that could be accessed from the web or a smartphone. Users were able to verify their identity via a government biometric database. On the app you can do everything from pay taxes to renew passports, register a vehicle, or create an LLC.

After the invasion, programmers in the digital ministry quickly added features for citizens to report Russian forces. A system of crowd-sourced intelligence was thus built out of an app every Ukrainian already used daily. Diia used an encrypted messaging service to transmit pictures taken by citizens to servers in the Ministry of Defense, which scanned the images to locate and identify targets. The result was known as Ukraine's "Uber for Artillery," with citizens effectively calling in requests for strikes and the Ministry of Defense carrying them out in near real time. Programmers in the Ministry of Defense next created a real-time battle command application called Delta that blends information from citizen reports with data from NATO systems, fusing the eyes, ears, and smartphone cameras of the Ukrainian people with commercial and classified intelligence. Ukraine's own tech sector mobilized as well, hardening the digital backbone of Ukrainian government operations so effectively that Russian state cyberspace attackers never severed government services or web access. Though the Internet in Ukraine today is sometimes slow due to denial-of-service attacks, citizens can still access it at home or through the 4G LTE cell networks that have continued to operate during the war.

ANDURIL AND THE DRONE WAR

Palmer Luckey's wife tried to talk him out of going to Ukraine. "There are people in the military whose job it is to do that," she said. But as the twenty-nine-year old founder of Anduril explained to us, he felt compelled to go. "How stupid will I feel if Russia wins, and I spend the rest of my life feeling that I could have had an impact on this conflict?" he told her. "It's not something I could ever live with. Right before I left, she said, 'You better not die or I'm going to kill you.'" We nodded in understanding. We'd each been there too, telling a loved one we were heading off to war. "I responded to her with a quote from the movie *Team America: World Police*, that my friends and I use to my wife's chagrin all the time. I said, 'I promise I will never die.' I just love that line."

Luckey crossed into Ukraine in August 2022, six months into the war, becoming the first CEO of a major U.S. defense company to do so. He wanted to see his company's drones in action and ask soldiers what problems they were having so that he could try to fix them in the field. Luckey brought along three software engineers to train soldiers on how to operate Anduril's Ghost drone and its ALTIUS loitering munition drone.

As mentioned earlier, Luckey founded Anduril in 2017 with Trae Stephens. They aimed to build a new prime with a product-oriented approach. "The current incentive structure rewarded companies that foisted as much risk as possible onto the taxpayer, that were slower, that had more process, that were very good at writing proposals and lobbying, not necessarily building technology. It was literally the inversion of what you do when you want to run an efficient product company," Luckey said.

Luckey's connections to Ukraine reached back to several years before the war. In 2019 he'd met Zelensky after the Ukrainian president read a *Wired* magazine article about Anduril's border security technology. Zelensky asked for a meeting to explore whether Anduril's Lattice surveillance towers could be deployed along the Russian border. "His position from the very beginning was Russia was going to invade Ukraine, that it was going to happen, and we needed to prepare now," Luckey recalls.

When war broke out, Ukraine started placing orders for Anduril products, including its Ghost drone, which is small enough to be carried by a single person and can be set up in three minutes. Ghost drones use AI software and can operate autonomously. Ukraine employs them for surveillance and intelligence gathering and to help target artillery fire.

Drones were playing a huge role in the war, more so than in any previous conflict—it's fair to say Ukraine was the first full-scale drone war. Infantry and artillery spotters on both sides of the conflict were using inexpensive DJI quadcopters. The Russians were using larger, weaponized Iranian drones; the Ukrainians were countering with Turkish Bayraktar TB2s. Across any given stretch of the front, between twenty-five and fifty UAVs from both sides were flying. Even the most lethal weapons system in Ukraine, the U.S.-provided High Mobility Artillery Rocket Systems (HIMARS), was having its fire directed by drones that could be bought on Amazon.

Ukraine trained ten thousand of its citizens in the essentials of operating drones and formed sixty drone strike units. Ukrainian companies also swung into action. Dozens of new startups—more than sixty by one early count—began building custom models less reliant on GPS to navigate. Among the innovations being tested were inertial navigation technology—in which onboard accelerometers allow a drone to deduce where it is—and software that can use cheap cameras to follow terrain visually. A British trainer described Ukrainian artillery operators as having a "cyberpunk" approach to targeting Russian positions. The killer robots crowd finally had something to worry about. Swarms of killer drones were in the air, hunting down individual soldiers who ran from their units during attacks. Russian bloggers posted videos to teach troops what to do when being hunted by a drone.

During a visit to Ukraine, Eric Schmidt marveled at the small kamikaze drones that cost $400 and carried three pounds of explosives. These were "nearly impossible to shoot down," Eric wrote in the *Wall Street Journal*. Even more terrifying is what comes next, when drones are allowed to make decisions and work together in packs. In the future, like flocks of starlings, "ruthless swarms of AI-empowered kamikaze drones will track mobile targets and algorithmically collaborate to strike past an enemy's electronic countermeasures," Schmidt wrote.

DIU Rogue Squadron leader Mark Jacobsen recognized years before how important drones would become on a future battlefield. "Ukraine is the war that we were preparing for," he said. "Both sides are operating combat support labs with hackers working on DJI drones, and both sides are racing to exploit the technology faster." He added that technology Rogue Squadron developed has found its way onto the battlefield in Ukraine, including an early donation to the Ukrainian Army by Edgesource, a company Rogue Squadron partnered with, of $2 million of counter-UAS capabilities.

Perhaps even more significant is that drones are changing the very nature of war. "What we're really witnessing is the democratization of precision-guided munitions. Every actor, every individual in the battlefield can have a precision-guided munition," Jacobsen says. "For me, as an air force officer, this is a big deal. Because in the past the way we projected power was by putting a bunch of $200 million airplanes on a parking ramp behind a fence in the combat zone. That's what we did in Afghanistan and Iraq. But now those airplanes are big juicy targets. One drone can come in and take them out. So this leads us to rethink how we deploy power."

The Russian military, startled by Ukraine's sophistication in using drones, stationed powerful electronic warfare systems every six miles along the front. The systems jammed radio signals and spoofed GPS. Ukraine's drones would fly only a few hundred yards and then lose communication links, rendering them useless. A British think tank estimated Ukraine was losing five thousand drones a month. Russia's powerful jammers were felt miles from the front. "You can't order an Uber above the third floor of any hotel in Kyiv," Andrey Liscovich said. "If you try, your location will come up somewhere in the Indian Ocean." The Russians also rolled out a secretive new electronic warfare system, Tobol, to attack SpaceX's Starlink satellite network. Tobol was originally devised as a defensive weapon to protect Russian satellites, but now the Russians were deploying it as an offensive weapon. Tobol works by blending a spoof signal on the satellites' own frequency to try to jam the communication.

Russia and Ukraine were engaged in the same kind of cat-and-mouse game that goes on between cybersecurity professionals and hackers—the kind of battle that DIU's Rogue Squadron drone team had waged years before in their hangar on Moffett Field, reverse-engineering the software in DJI drones to prevent them from sending data back to China. One side writes software that defends against a certain kind of drone; on the other side hackers furiously crank out fresh code that enables drones to skirt the defenses.

This was the hacker battle that Luckey and his Anduril engineers wanted to see firsthand. They flew to Warsaw and drove to Kyiv, where Luckey and Zelensky had "the obligatory handshake photo," and Zelensky griped about the hassles Ukraine was encountering in dealing with the Pentagon, whose bureaucracy was delaying the shipment of weapons. From Kyiv, the Anduril team traveled to the front. Luckey and his engineers ran training exercises showing Ukrainian soldiers how to install the latest hardware modules on the Ghost. They also wanted to figure out how the Russians were jamming the communication and navigation systems in Anduril drones, so they could update their operating system software to evade Russian electronic warfare technology. One day Luckey and his engineers were coding on laptops on a former Soviet airfield when Luckey was shaken by a distressing realization: "We're at this airfield and there was a pretty significant military presence there. If I'm Russia, I'm thinking, 'Okay, we've got an airfield with a whole bunch of people who are learning to use the latest, most cutting-edge drone technology that's just been shipped in from the United States. This is a site that's full of high-value American hardware and some high-value American people who maybe aren't really supposed to even be there,'" Luckey recalls. "It was a non-zero chance that this would be a pretty great target for Russia."

He made sure not to mention this to his wife when he got home.

THE WAR OVER LESSONS

At the Pentagon, war was brewing over what lessons to draw from the war. The fault lines were familiar. Innovators at DIU and the Defense Innovation Board, which had since been reconstituted, saw the future they'd been preparing for on full display in Ukraine, a real-life test of the silicon kill chain they'd envisioned. "For me," Eric Schmidt wrote after a visit to Ukraine, "the war answers a central question: what can technology people do to help their government, and the answer is a lot. Ten programmers can change the way thousands of soldiers operate. . . . I departed Ukraine with an unexpected sense of optimism," he wrote in his trip report.

For Lieutenant General Jack Shanahan, who led Project Maven and was the first leader of the Pentagon's Joint Artificial Intelligence Center (JAIC), Ukraine represented vindication. The AI-enabled image-tagging that DIU pioneered in Project Maven now runs inside the National Geospatial Agency supporting Ukrainian operations. Shanahan believes we're in a critical "bridge period" where the most creative and innovative warfighters must figure out how to mate legacy equipment with emerging technologies and come up with new ways to wage war. "What I'm seeing in Ukraine tells me we were right," Shanahan says. "It's this weird mix of legacy or traditional weapon systems with commercial and leading-edge technologies. The side that gains the advantage is the side that figures out how to use that combination of technologies in new and different and creative ways."

Alex Karp, CEO of Palantir, traveled to Ukraine as well and came back convinced that AI would soon define the outcome of wars. "If you go into battle with old school technology," Karp said at an event on AI in warfare, "and you have an adversary that knows how to install and implement digitized targeting in AI, you obviously are at a massive disadvantage."

While technologists in Silicon Valley saw one thing, the old-guard standard bearers in Washington saw something else altogether. Defensive trenches, tank-on-tank, missile system–on–missile system—there was strong continuity with the past, even if it wasn't exactly the past that was becoming the present. The war over what lessons to learn was thus fought all around the Pentagon's E-ring. It broke out into the open after the Pentagon's chief weapons buyer dismissed the importance of Silicon Valley technology. Eight months into the conflict, Pentagon acquisition chief Bill LaPlante—the man most responsible for future U.S. armaments—said this in an interview:

> We're not fighting in Ukraine with Silicon Valley right now, even though they're going to try to take credit for it. The tech bros aren't helping us too much in Ukraine. . . . It's hardcore production of really serious weaponry. That's what matters. If somebody gives you a really cool liquored up story about a DIU project or OTA contract, ask them when it's going into production, ask them how many numbers, ask them what the unit cost is going to be, ask them how it will work against China. Ask them all those questions because that's what matters. And don't tell me it's got AI and quantum in it. I don't care.

LaPlante's belief that commercial technology is not a significant driver of battlefield outcomes in Ukraine and has few use cases against DoD's pacing adversaries—the ones who are closing in on the U.S.—is not altogether wrong. Indeed, the conflict in Ukraine has affirmed the importance of major weapons platforms such as tanks and howitzers and the companies that manufacture them. But to adopt LaPlante's assessment misses the wider view. There is no doubt in innovation circles that Ukraine is indebted to the heroic leadership LaPlante and his colleagues in the Pentagon's Acquisition and Sustainment Office provided—for getting traditional weapons platforms and munitions to the battle space, mobilizing the defense industrial base when our stores of advanced munitions proved woefully inadequate, setting up 24/7 callback centers to help Ukrainian personnel master new weapons systems, and restarting production of key armaments despite factory lines having been idled for fifteen years or more.

But it would be wrong and even tragic to read the dynamics in Ukraine as a reassertion of old warfighting paradigms, or as justification for preserving the industrial base in its current form. To do this would be to miss the beguiling hybridity and asymmetry of the battlefield that has evolved in Ukraine, as well as parallel developments in other battle spaces, such as what is occurring in Armenia-Azerbaijan, the North Korean drone incursions into Seoul, and the People's Liberation Army's experimentation with commercial technologies under Xi's doctrine of civil-military fusion in China.

From our point of view, the lesson is that commercial technologies are being deployed by both Russia and Ukraine in tandem with traditional, exquisite weapons systems, both to enhance their effectiveness and enable their defeat. At a Stanford symposium, Chris argued that "one of the most significant lessons emerging from Ukraine may be the difference commercial technology makes in great power conflict—its ability to attrit superior enemy weapons systems, supplant legacy command, control, intelligence, and reconnaissance, and multiply the combat effectiveness of stock armaments from Ukraine, Russian, NATO, and the United States." As Raj told the conference participants, "From a scale standpoint, we need more mass." The goal is to make our current systems more effective by leveraging commercial technology. "There's $600 billion in private capital going to technology every year. Ukraine has completely changed attitudes in the technology world and in Silicon Valley. There are so many young, mission-oriented entrepreneurs who now want to work in defense and, promisingly, venture firms willing to back them."

The DIU ecosystem is having real impact. By one count, thirty new products created by startups, mostly in California, were being used on the Ukraine front lines. Capella Space, the maker of SAR satellites, saw its revenues triple in 2022, and it looked as if they might triple again in 2023. Startups were nevertheless only modest players in the war compared with the primes. In December 2022, the primes threw a kind of appreciation party at the Ukrainian Embassy in Washington. Invitations were embossed with the logos of Raytheon, Northrup Grumman, Lockheed Martin, and Pratt & Whitney. Chairman of the Joint Chiefs Mark Milley showed up, as did most members of the House and Senate Armed Services Committee. There was a lot to celebrate. Lockheed Martin had booked several billion in orders supplying Ukraine. Raytheon had won $2 billion in contracts from the army alone.

As the Pentagon's policy agenda took greater shape toward the midpoint of President Biden's term, any assessment of defense innovation would necessarily reach mixed conclusions. Individual services and the Office of the Secretary of Defense have more innovation entities than ever before. More acquisitions are being made through streamlined Commercial Solutions Opening processes, with $70 billion in purchases to date. But a composite military vision or approach that fully leverages commercial technology into a new construct for joint warfighting has proved elusive. And resources are still not flowing to innovation at anywhere near the scale needed for the department to realize Ash Carter's "fast-follower" vision.

To the extent present military and civilian leadership were articulating a strategy when Putin's forces crossed into Ukraine, it was built for the most part on a continuation of previous programmatic and budgetary trend lines with a few significant departures from historical baselines, with the exception of the Marine Corps retiring tanks that would never see battle and replacing them with long-range missiles and electronic warfare systems. If there is a strategy for losing a future war with China, this is it. Shortly after Bill LaPlante made his remarks about Silicon Valley tech, Northrop Grumman publicly revealed the new B-21 strategic bomber, which LaPlante oversaw as head of acquisition for the air force. With a reported unit cost of $692 million, the total program cost to develop and operate one hundred B-21s will exceed $200 billion. In comparison, each Anduril ALTIUS loitering munition drone costs about $250,000. Certain essential missions require stealth bombers, yet their cost compared with other approaches cannot be ignored.

Contrary to LaPlante's assertion, the "tech bros" are in Ukraine and they matter to the fight. The next question is what they might do for other wars in other places.

TODAY IN UKRAINE, TOMORROW IN TAIWAN

Ukraine has become a laboratory not only for DIU operational concepts that pair commercial tech with traditional weapon systems, but also for how a Chinese invasion of Taiwan would likely unfold. "Arguably the most important task DoD faces today is deterring China from invading Taiwan, thus avoiding a war that would be devastating for both countries and risk nuclear escalation," says Mark Jacobsen. The war in Ukraine is already being viewed by Chinese strategists as a struggle between superpowers. In the first year of the conflict Chinese researchers wrote over one hundred papers assessing the war and its implications. Though Chinese analysts hadn't expected Russia to fare so badly, they noted that China's military budget, at $225 billion, was three times the size of Russia's and that China has a vast manufacturing capacity to build the drones and other weapons that Russia lacks. Chinese analysts are readying for what might be the next battle, with military rocket scientists noting that "faced with the threat of Starlink, we must develop and build our own low-orbiting satellites." "Not a moment can be spared in developing 'soft-kill' and 'hard kill' measures," one said. As a Western analyst observed, "China is close to this in a way that wasn't true of Iraq or even Afghanistan. They see themselves potentially in Russia's shoes, in more or less going to war against America."

Anduril's Palmer Luckey is already anticipating the potential conflict. "Our entire internal road map has been around how do you deter China, not just in Taiwan, but Taiwan and beyond," Luckey says. Anduril is losing money selling drones to Ukraine but is gaining valuable know-how from the opportunity to test its technology in actual combat. "The Ukraine war has been a financially detrimental but necessary detour for Anduril. There's a lot of things that we're doing that are relevant in Ukraine that are also relevant to a potential fight in the Pacific," he says.

Taiwan would be infinitely more difficult to defend than Ukraine. Kyiv sits only 428 miles from a major NATO base, while there are 7,000 miles of ocean between Taipei and permanent U.S. military forces. Ukraine avoided power interruptions in part because its over-engineered power grid boasts twice the capacity that the country needs—ironically, the system was originally designed by the Soviets to withstand a NATO attack. In the first days of a conflict with Taiwan, China would likely knock out its energy grid, communications infrastructure, and Internet and blockade the island, choking off a country dependent on food and fuel imports from the rest of the world. The war's opening moves could unfold so quickly it would be effectively over before the U.S. could stop it. In December 2023, Chris met in Taipei with former national security advisor Linwu Guo and former member of Parliament Jason Hsu. The latter spoke urgently about the need for Taiwan to create its own DIU and turn itself into a "porcupine" that can defend against an invasion by a foe that outnumbers its population 58 to 1.

To us there is an even darker lesson. Putin's attempt to grab Ukraine was against all of Russia's long-term interests. "Yet Putin did it. It's a reminder that if the leader captures the state, like Xi has done in China and Putin in Russia, they can do as they please," Chris said to Raj. "It's the most dangerous possible situation. We are so far from *The End of History and the Last Man*," Chris lamented, referring to Francis Fukuyama's 1992 political science book that predicted the triumph of free markets and democracy would lead to a forever peace.

"It's time to bring back Thucydides," Raj said. The chronicler of the Peloponnesian Wars theorized that states act toward each other out of fear, honor, and self-interest.

"And Hobbes," Chris rejoined. The seventeenth-century English philosopher believed that without maintaining a monopoly of the means of violence, humans would devolve into a state of nature, where all fear violent death.

CHAPTER NINE
FROM STEEL TO SILICON

The email arrived at 6:04 a.m. on a Tuesday in October 2022, sent from Ash Carter's personal account: "It is with deep and profound sadness that the family of former Secretary of Defense Ashton B. Carter shares that Secretary Carter passed away Monday evening in Boston after a sudden cardiac event."

The grief was immediate and overwhelming. Carter was only sixty-eight years old, seemingly in good health. Raj had spoken with Carter early the day he died, about a potential startup investment. Ylli Bajraktari had a call scheduled with Carter to discuss a fellowship program on technology and geopolitics just hours after we all got the same terrible note. Chris was to have seen Carter four days later at Harvard, where Carter was teaching. Still reeling from the news, Chris walked up alone to Carter's office on the third floor of the Kennedy School. Instead of hearing his trademark "Hey there brother," there was silence. The lights were off. Tribute notes and flowers were piled on either side of the door.

On a cold January day ten weeks later, official Washington gathered to lay him to rest. The service was held in the cavernous National Cathedral. Carter would have liked that the sun was shining through a stained-glass window holding a moon rock, enshrined there by the crew of Apollo 11. The service was a time and a place where everyone who believed in the future Ash had envisioned came together once again. President Biden gave the eulogy. The Secretaries of State and Defense also spoke. The entire Joint Chiefs of Staff sat in a pew.

Carter was the second of two giants to fall. Madeleine Albright's funeral at the cathedral had happened nine months before.

With so many of Washington's leaders gathering to pay their respects, the Secret Service established a perimeter and attendees were advised to arrive two hours beforehand. After clearing security, Chris was handed a green card, one of seven colors the Protocol Office had printed. This being Washington, seating was carefully choreographed. Green was the section for Carter's personal staff. It was the section closest to the pulpit, in the cathedral's north eave. Chris sat with Ylli and Eric Schmidt. Doug Beck sat two rows away. Eric Rosenbach was also there, Carter's chief of staff who'd negotiated our terms when we were signing on to DIU back in 2016.

There were a few "only in Washington" moments as everyone milled about before the service. Chris ran into the President of the Council on Foreign Relations in the men's bathroom. One former Pentagon staffer who'd gone on to lobby for a defense prime stood near the entrance glad-handing people and passing out business cards. As if to say, "I'm more patriotic than you," he wore an American flag pin on his lapel—only it was askew, a full ninety degrees sideways.

Todd Park, the former U.S. chief technology officer who in 2016 had told Carter that version 1.0 of DIUx was screwed and needed new leadership, was crying profusely. "Chris," he said, "what would Ash Carter want us to be doing right now? He would want us to carry on the mission he gave us. There's more work to do." Todd had watched DIU's struggle to win attention in the Pentagon, and he now wanted to help reboot it again.

With the United States Marine Orchestra joining the cathedral's organist and choir, Bach's "Jesu, Joy of Man's Desiring" rang out along with "America the Beautiful." A full military honor guard stood at the ready. With spit-shined shoes and immaculate precision, they carried the urn containing Carter's cremated remains down the aisle. The blue battle flag of the Secretary of Defense followed.

Biden stepped up to the pulpit and gave a stirring eulogy. No stranger to grief, his words helped explain why Ash's loss was especially piercing. "I have some idea how hard this is, how unreal and unfair it seems," Biden said. "To lose someone you love so suddenly, someone who should have had so many years ahead of them. The suddenness, in my view, magnifies the grief. It makes it just inescapable."

He went on to talk about his relationship with Carter, and to sum up the man's life. "Over the course of four decades, working in and out of the Pentagon, walking miles and miles of laps, Ash made an impact felt far into the future."

For Biden, it was personal. In 2007 he'd led the fight on the Senate floor to fund the production of mine-resistant, ambush-protected vehicles—the MRAPs so badly needed by our troops facing improvised explosive devices in Iraq and Afghanistan. MRAPs had protected Biden's own son Beau, who'd deployed to Iraq. It was Ash who'd accelerated their production, ultimately helping to deploy twenty-four thousand of them. Biden recalled a photo Ash had sent him: "Four feet long and maybe a foot high, the photograph was of MRAPs lined up side by side. The picture had a note saying, 'Thanks. Ash Carter.' I have it hanging in my office at home. His integrity—it was indomitable. Never had to wonder whether there was an edge to it, whether there was a secondary motive I didn't see. And he literally saved, I think, in consequence of it, hundreds and hundreds, thousands of lives and limbs."

There was one lighthearted moment when Biden referenced Carter's legendary impatience. Biden turned to deliver the line to the green card section, where Carter's staff sat. "He believed not just in getting things done but getting things done in record time, which I'm sure those who worked for him found very interesting sometimes." The green section erupted with chuckles, and Biden nodded at the reaction. "I got a lot of laughter on this side," he told the rest of the cathedral. It was Biden's way of saluting those who'd helped make Carter's many visions real.

"Each of us here today, and generations of national security leaders, decades of eager and brilliant students, the entire Armed Forces of the United States of America—we all will forever bear the imprint of Ash Carter, thank God," Biden said.

RESURRECTING DIU

Two weeks after the funeral, Chris delivered a blistering paper at a private conference at Stanford. The Hoover Institution spent considerable resources commissioning research and flying in key players. Raj spoke, along with Secretaries of Defense Jim Mattis and Leon Panetta; Mike Mullen, former Chairman of the Joint Chiefs; and Congressman Mac Thornberry, who'd led the House Armed Services Committee. Chris's paper was a lament, dedicated to Carter and written in anger. It was titled "A Requiem for Defense Innovation? Ukraine, the Pentagon's Innovator's Dilemma, and Why the U.S. Risks Strategic Surprise."

The conference organizer had asked him to tone it down.

Chris did not.

Instead, he called out the Secretary and Deputy Secretary of Defense for their lack of leadership, noting how Deputy Secretary Kathleen Hicks hadn't even visited DIU during her first trip to Silicon Valley. The pointed critique was the kind of thing you only do knowing you're never going back into government. "Despite notable progress in specific areas and on small scales," Chris declared, "the organs of innovation Ash Carter set in motion have not meaningfully transformed how the Pentagon as a whole adopts emerging technologies or procures large systems for the future of war."

In the latest absurdity, which Chris highlighted in his paper, Heidi Shyu, the undersecretary for research and engineering who followed

Griffin, was administering a new fund intended to expeditiously transition emerging technologies—it was the signature innovation initiative of Secretary of Defense Lloyd Austin. Of the fourteen critical areas identified, the commercial sector had leapt ahead of the primes in eleven. But out of ten contracts that Shyu announced, only one was made to a venture-backed business.

Mac Thornberry delivered a paper at the Stanford event that backed Chris's view to the hilt. He opened his own paper with fighting words as well, quoting from Matthew 6:21—"For where your treasure is, there your heart will be also"—and then from *Jerry Maguire*: "Show me the money." It was Thornberry's way of saying that while a lot of people were saying the right things about innovation and technology, we continued spending the defense budget on the wrong things.

Among the tributes that poured in for Carter in the days after his death, one said, "DIU is a true gift Secretary Carter gave to the world." Yet in January 2023, after Carter was buried, DIU was once again rudderless and adrift, lacking a leader. Mike Brown, whose appointment wasn't renewed by Heidi Shyu, had departed, and a junior official was serving as DIU's acting lead. Shyu's office, charged with the search for Brown's successor, had let the ball drop. It seemed as if the whole Biden team had forgotten about DIU and Silicon Valley, even as Ukraine was aggressively deploying DIU technologies on the battlefield. To be sure, these were honorable people working on the E-ring. But it was their duty to come to the right answer, and they were blowing the call. The National Security Council staff knew it, and those in its technology directorate were livid at the state of affairs. They had put on as much pressure for different outcomes as they could, but the Pentagon was like a supertanker, not easy to turn.

Meanwhile, worries continued to mount, and not just about Ukraine. China had launched the world's first nuclear-capable hypersonic weapon—which flies at ten times the speed of sound and evades all known defenses. Its titanium sheath could sink any navy ship at sea. "As I assess our level of deterrence against China, the ship is slowly sinking," chief of naval operations Admiral John Richardson said in public. It was a rare airing of alarm that members of the Joint Chiefs customarily reserve for civilian leadership in private. "They are putting capability in the field faster than we are. This Ukraine crisis that we're in right now, this is just the warm-up. The big one is coming. It isn't going to be very long before we're going to get tested in ways that we haven't been tested in a long time."

After Speaker of the House Nancy Pelosi visited Taiwan to signal U.S. support in August 2022, China literally went ballistic. During the next two months the People's Liberation Army flew twelve hundred mock invasion sorties, 40 percent of them entering Taiwan's air defense identification zone, a clear provocation. There were also flashes of jamming, with drops in communication and GPS over the island. Russia's sophisticated electronic warfare capabilities in Ukraine were downing drones by the thousand—yet that was nothing compared to what the Chinese possessed and would use against the U.S. in a conflict.

China's sorties over Taiwan were followed by an astonishing provocation of the U.S. itself. In early 2023, China flew from Alaska to South Carolina a spy balloon that loitered over U.S. nuclear weapons sites and military bases. NORAD's billion-dollar sensors didn't initially see it floating across the U.S. The balloon itself seemed to have used the DIU playbook, crammed as it was full of commercially available U.S. gear connected to more specialized Chinese sensors.

Across every military domain, commercial technology continued to change the game. SpaceX had by now launched forty-five hundred Starlink satellites—more than half of all satellites in orbit. Some thirty-seven thousand more were on the way. Elon Musk now had more control over satellite communications than the world's superpowers. In one instance he refused to extend Starlink's capabilities to Ukrainian military units aspiring to attack Russian warships in the Crimean Peninsula with unmanned explosive sea drones. The war in Ukraine now turned on what one man said rather than what the U.S. and Ukraine decided. Given his extraordinary intervention in the Ukraine-Russia conflict, would Elon decide to sell his services to Taiwan even though his other business interests, especially Tesla, involved China? The geopolitical complexity was deepening, with the U.S. government behind. To catch up with SpaceX, China was racing to build out its "Guo Wang" constellation of thirteen thousand satellites. *Interstellar*, Christopher Nolan's 2014 space thriller, was set in 2067, yet the on-orbit adventures the movie depicted now felt much closer at hand.

Though Putin was bogged down in Ukraine, his military was still devising hair-raising new weapons, the kind Nolan wouldn't in his worst nightmares have imagined—from nuclear-armed cruise missiles that could skim below radar range and annihilate U.S. cities with no warning, to super-cavitating nuclear torpedoes able to take out entire aircraft carrier groups. Putin even readied the potential launch of a space-based neutron bomb that, when detonated, would wipe out global communications. These technologies could defeat many of the U.S.'s deployed platforms. Then there was quantum technology—miniature sensors that can defeat stealth, power inertial navigation systems, and, when developed into quantum computers, break all known forms of encryption.

The U.S. military needed a technology overhaul, and quickly.

Then a ray of hope appeared.

DOUG BECK AND DIU 3.0

In April 2023, Secretary of Defense Lloyd Austin made a bold decision and named Doug Beck to be the new director of DIU. Doug was a vice president at Apple and a navy vet who'd commanded DIU's Reserve Unit.

Over the years Doug had quietly cultivated relationships in defense circles. He'd advised three chiefs of naval operations, lectured at the Naval

Postgraduate School, and served in various defense-related advisory roles in Washington. Ash Carter had pushed Doug hard to succeed Mike at DIU, telling him there is one reason to give up his beloved role at Apple: "Duty." Doug also served as an unpaid innovation advisor to Deputy Secretary of Defense Kathleen Hicks. Hicks had chartered an Innovation Steering Group and asked it to identify groups in the DoD that were advancing the innovation mission. The group discovered a large and diverse ecosystem, with more than fifty separate organizations, as commands in each service set up their own miniature DIUs. To illustrate the reporting relationship between them, the DoD printed one of its "horse-blanket" charts—Pentagon vernacular for a diagram so large it could keep a horse warm.

It was one thing to make a chart that enumerates organizations flying the banner of innovation, and quite another to prosecute a strategy to bring innovation into the Department at scale. Indeed, for some senior leaders, the existence of an innovation office under their ambit provided cover to give change lip service and hide from making hard trade-offs.

If anyone could do that scaling up, it was Doug. His appointment demonstrated that the Secretary of Defense meant business, especially when Austin insisted that DIU would now report directly to him, as it had under Ash Carter. Doug would also serve as Austin's advisor on innovation, spotting technologies that had strategic impact.

Behind the scenes, as Doug was discussing the offer from Austin, we'd helped him develop a list of demands and conditions, the sort we'd made before we signed on in 2016. When Doug was appointed, he asked us to join the DIU team again. Chris became an unpaid special government employee and took an advisory role. Doug asked Raj to take the job Doug once had: commanding DIU's Reserve Unit, which meant leading one hundred technologists who served within it. These were the people who worked in technology companies but also wore the uniform—the connective tissue between leading edge commercial technology and the projects DIU was scoping.

Shortly after Doug's appointment, we met him at a classic San Francisco diner, Mama's on Washington Square. Doug walked in expecting frank thoughts on how to succeed in his new mission, but wasn't expecting just how frank they would be. Truth was, we were worried Doug wasn't ready for what was about to hit him when he made his first trip to Washington as the director of DIU.

To be sure, Doug had relationships in every corner of the Pentagon and Congress, built in large part by serving on multiple advisory boards and even in combat with many of its leaders. His network was part of the reason Austin had selected him. But we warned him—those relationships were about to change.

"You keep referring to these people as your friends," Chris said. "They aren't. They are people you know. You like them, and they like you. But you're no longer an advisor. You'll be making real decisions. For the first time, you'll be threatening their turf, asking them to do things that are hard."

"Remember," Raj said, "in Washington it's a zero-sum game. It's not like Silicon Valley, where folks can expand the pie by working together. In D.C., power is budget and people. The only way to expand is to take something from someone else. This leads to monumental infighting."

"You're reporting directly to the Secretary. That's great," Chris said. "But for every hour you spend with Lloyd Austin, someone else is getting left out."

"So be careful," Raj concluded. "Watch your back. You've seen us get stuck by cloaked daggers, including by 'friends.'"

A NEW FOCUS

Doug and Secretary Austin made a smart opening move by narrowing DIU's focus. During our tenure, and that of our successor, Mike Brown, DIU had worked with a broad spectrum of commercial technology applicable to many kinds of military missions. Under Doug, DIU would zero in on the most strategically consequential technologies to U.S. war plans on China, Taiwan, Ukraine, and Russia. Other innovation entities across various branches of the military could work on the rest.

Austin was changing the metric by which DIU was judged. Instead of counting the number and size of contracts DIU negotiated each year, Austin wanted DIU to drive changes in key Operational Plans—O-Plans, in military speak—to prepare how we'd fight in every imaginable war scenario, especially in the Indo-Pacific. DIU would work closely with the combatant commanders and their war-planning staffs, developing new joint operational concepts powered by novel technological approaches. The insights Doug and DIU gleaned would ultimately roll up to the Secretary himself, helping him change what would get bought across the "Future Years Defense Program," the elaborate DoD budgets that run five years into the future.

Ash Carter would have been amazed to see this happening—this was his vision, at last operating at scale.

THE ASH CARTER EXCHANGE

Four months after Ash Carter's funeral many of the same people who'd been at the cathedral gathered in Washington for an all-day event to advance the mission Carter had asked us to pursue.

There were lots of great panels—Raj spoke onstage with the DARPA director and with Doug, who was making his first remarks as DIU director. But the best indicator of the change occurring in D.C. were remarks made by secretary of the air force Frank Kendall and Chairman of the Joint Chiefs of Staff Mark Milley.

Onstage, Kendall shared his plans to buy one thousand to two thousand supersonic drones that would fly as autonomous wingmen alongside fighter aircraft—a project that had started under our tenure at DIU. Driven by AI, able to operate on their own or in tandem with manned aircraft, and with a range equal to the width of China, the drones would carry out a variety of missions, from striking targets, to gathering intelligence, to conducting surveillance, to engaging in reconnaissance. The "Collaborative Combat Aircraft" program was the boldest change to the air force's doctrine ever. At $3 million per unit, compared to $70 million for an F-35 fighter, these wingman drones would give the air force what its strategists called "affordable mass" in any fight in the Pacific.

The most transformational vision came at the end of the day when Milley brought down the house with rousing closing remarks. He first honored Carter by saying "his action saved American lives on the battlefield, including my own." Ash understood that "technology is driving the largest fundamental change in the character of war in human history—that the stakes were enormously high." Our top priority, Milley said, is to prevent the outbreak of a great power war. "No one in this room and in fact none of us in uniform in any nation on earth has lived through a great power war." Members of Milley's family were on the front lines of World War I and World War II, and over that thirty-year period, 150 million people were slaughtered. "We are in the midst of one of those fundamental changes," Milley said. "Nations that are able to successfully combine new technologies are able to create potentially decisive military advantages."

Milley then made a remarkable statement about technology: "In the next fifteen years we are going to see a pilot-less or at least partially pilot-less air force, a sailor-less or partially sailor-less navy, and a crew-less or partially crew-less tank force on the ground." His speech captured just how swiftly the uniformed military had come around to the vision that led Ash Carter to create DIU. Milley's remarks served as a bookend to what Carter had said eight years before, when he made the first trip to Silicon Valley by a Secretary of Defense in over a generation, asking technologists for their help.

Shortly after the gathering, President Biden announced his choice for the next Chairman of the Joint Chiefs of Staff, nominating General Charles Brown, the forward-leaning air force chief of staff whom Raj had escorted at Tech Track 2 events.

Then, in an even more astounding development, Congress swung into action and gave DIU's budget an eye-watering boost—to $1 billion a year. Additional funds from other parts of the military will likely push DIU's annual outlay for new technologies to $2 billion or more. The 2024 National Defense Authorization Act dedicated an entire section to DIU, granting it new powers in law and stipulating other guidelines that further bolstered its authority. The House and Senate ultimately codified the practice of DIU direct reporting to the Secretary of Defense, established in law the director's ability to "communicate views . . . directly to the Secretary without obtaining the approval or concurrence of any other official within the Department of Defense," and upped DIU's ability to unilaterally enter into contracts up to half a billion dollars. The new authorities ran a whopping four pages in the final bill, 1,392 words carving in granite what had previously been scrawled with erasable pencil. Five days later the Senate confirmed Steve "Bucky" Butow's promotion to major general, awarding a second star to DIU's space maverick who'd been willing to ruffle feathers to deliver for the warfighter.

We were a long way from the days of battling Evelyn and Ed, the two small-minded appropriations staffers who'd "zeroized" DIUx's tiny $30 million budget the day after Carter traveled to Mountain View and announced our appointment. When Austin made his next trip to Europe, Doug Beck flew on the plane with him to meet with the coalition supplying weapons and aid to Ukraine.

A VISIT TO UKRAINE

Chris crossed into Ukraine in the middle of the night in the front seat of a Volkswagen sedan whose driver had spent the early months of the war ferrying Starlink Internet terminals to the front. We had been invited by the Ukrainian General Staff and Andrey Liscovich, CEO of the Ukraine Defense Fund. Except for those living within a few miles of the front, Ukrainians went about their lives unpreoccupied by the war—dining out, enjoying warm afternoons in outside cafes, mindful that a cruise missile strike was a real possibility but determined not to be cowed by it. Ukraine was infinitely safer than Iraq or Afghanistan, where violence engulfed every city.

The war the Ukrainians were fighting was everything those at DIUx had imagined—innovators working side by side with soldiers at the front, new kinds of weapons made in garage shops rushed into battle, software being updated on a daily basis, all focused on defeating an authoritarian enemy.

Chris's first meeting with the General Staff was surreal. A cell of programmers and engineers drafted into military service had taken over the headquarters of a cosmetics company in Kyiv. Andrey guided Chris past armed guards and up a courtyard elevator. Sliding glass doors emblazoned with images of cosmetics models opened to reveal hulking Ukrainian Special Forces troops checking IDs. It was a scene straight out of James Bond. Behind the doors several hundred Ukrainians were writing military software. Created in the mold of Carter's Defense Digital Service, the unit streamlined the military's internal processes, turning its paper-intensive reporting system—every battalion command along the front lugged along a laser printer and extra toner—into a paperless future. Officers who'd previously found themselves spending hours filling out routine forms rather than leading combat missions could complete their tasks on a tablet in minutes, thanks to the new apps being coded behind the cosmetic company's doors.

The second meeting took place inside a public facility commandeered by the Ministry of Defense. There Chris met with the intelligence chief responsible for targeting Russian forces through commercial imagery and signals intelligence. His team used Capella SAR images overlaid with signals intercepts plotted by Hawkeye 360 to attack Russian positions. While U.S. spy satellites provided better targeting information to a select few in the Ukrainian chain of command, the commercial data could be widely shared with front-line troops without fear of compromising classified sources. It was a glimmer of the future, in which anyone with a credit card could buy imagery and signals intercepts that only superpowers once had.

Outside formal Ministry of Defense structures, tinkerers of all kinds worked around the capital in secret workshops hidden in alleyways and unmarked office spaces. A year and a half into the war two hundred scrappy companies designed drones and counter-drone systems, self-driving vehicles, autonomous de-mining robots, even remotely controlled machine guns. Drones by this point in the war had become akin to shells or bombs or bullets—a commodity used by militaries fighting one another. One of the larger drone factories in Kyiv was set up in the storefront of a former electronics retailer—the Ukrainian equivalent of Best Buy—whose vacant showroom still had wall signs advertising big screen TVs. An assembly line would, in minutes, deliver a four-rotor kamikaze drone ready to be mated with a 1.75-kilogram shell—with either a brass-colored ballistic cap to penetrate armor or one with a ball of steel needles to attack dismounted soldiers. These munitions had been used to repel Russian attempts to take the city of Avdiivka and its railway junctures and coal-rich districts. Ukrainian drone operators—piloting quadcopters from behind the front—stopped infantry assaults before they started, by killing entire platoons of Russian soldiers as they exited armored personnel carriers, and used armor-piercing rounds to disable over two hundred tanks and tracked vehicles.

Homegrown Ukrainian drones were so effective Russia began targeting drone factories with cruise missiles, leading many companies to move their facilities to the city of Lviv, which was located in Western Ukraine, only an hour from the Polish border, mostly out of range. Raj and two investors from NATO's new venture capital fund met Chris there. They'd arrived by overnight train, looking to identify companies they could invest in directly or start a joint venture with. What we found was at once astonishing and disappointing, and yet at the same time an enormous opportunity.

Our first stop that morning in Lviv was at one of Ukraine's most advanced robotics manufacturers. As we arrived, we could hear in the distance the rumblings of a cruise missile strike—a reminder that we were in a country at war. Our second stop took us to a company whose drones functioned as miniature U-2s. Their digital cameras flew in a lawnmower-like pattern over the battlefield. They returned priceless imagery that was quickly turned into real-time maps and images of potential targets. Attack drones would then utilize artificial intelligence to home in on Russian positions, killing the "picture" their targeting algorithm was programmed to see. Our third stop was at a test range where drones battled against counter-drone electronic warfare systems in a game of mock combat using software that teams had updated just the night before. There, we watched as a Ukrainian drone pilot latched a bottle of Diet Coke to his drone's weapons bay—simulating an actual kinetic payload—and, using artificial-reality piloting glasses, proceeded to drop it directly in the target ring.

We also controlled a long-range surveillance drone, using a joystick to swivel and zoom thermal and optical sensors back at the test range from ten kilometers away. Despite costing one-hundredth of a similar Western system's price, the optics were so good that we could easily identify ourselves among the crowd assembled at the test site. The auto-lock function precisely tracked a person as they walked away. None of the jamming equipment at the range that day succeeded in disabling the drones that were flying—not the quarter-million-dollar truck-mounted system deployed by a Western defense contractor or the rifle-style electronic warfare guns made by Ukrainian firms. Raj, of course, had used such technology in his F-16, but marveled at how cheaply and quickly the technology was evolving.

Impressive as all this tech was, it was apparent that it would be an error to think of the two hundred Ukrainian entities experimenting with UAS and C-UAS as traditional early-stage companies. Most were small teams supported with private capital from wealthy Ukrainians with only a loose goal of creating a long-term business. Their primary aim was to kill Russians. Almost all lacked managerial robustness, the ability to navigate supply chain bottlenecks, or the skill to market to either the Ukrainian Ministry of Defense or international investors. Personal relationships with the military units determined which units actually deployed new technology and weapons at the front. All of this complicated the ability to scale local battlefield success through ordinary market mechanisms or the pull of defense requirements.

This is not to say the technology we saw wasn't ingenious. Quite the contrary. We saw controllable balloons called aerostats and "mothership drones" that had launched smaller attack drones hundreds of miles beyond the front and deep inside Russia. We met the firms that helped carry out the war's most successful attacks, devastating Russian naval assets in the Black Sea and even striking buildings in the Kremlin. We held in our hands a drone whose original use was smuggling cigarettes into the European Union, only to be repurposed as a bomber after war broke out. These systems cost pennies on the dollar compared with what Western firms could deploy, but none could yet scale in a way that would alter the course of the war.

How to address the scaling challenge was the topic of two days of meetings in Warsaw convened by DIU. We got to the conference hotel at 2 a.m., after a thirteen-hour journey out of Ukraine by car. After a short sleep we joined two hundred U.S. and Ukrainian officials, representatives from Ukrainian drone companies, venture capitalists, and business development staff from Western defense contractors. DIU director Doug Beck flew straight from the Pentagon to deliver opening remarks. The idea was to bring together in one place the buyers, the sellers, the tactical users, and the subject matter experts.

"The war is in the spectrum," one Ukrainian military official noted, speaking to the intense jamming, spoofing, and electronic warfare by each side. Another theme was that the drone threat wasn't uniquely Ukrainian. "Over the long term, every nation will face a 'drone nightmare' similar to the current crisis in Ukraine," one Ukrainian minister said. "What we learn is relevant to all democracies," noted a member of Ukraine's parliament. Dissatisfaction with the battlefield performance of Western drones was another motif. "I faced a big wave of disappointment" was what one Ukrainian soldier said about the first time he used a U.S. drone in combat. "The challenges of UAS in Ukraine aren't something we prepared Blue UAS companies for," a DIU official said, acknowledging the shortcomings of U.S. manufacturers who produced drones that for the most part were defeated by Russian EW systems within minutes of being launched. The harsh reality was that U.S. drones were the emperor without clothes—seemingly superior in specifications but dismal in actual battlefield performance. Were the U.S. in a drone fight with Russia, it could lose.

Raj led a breakout session titled "The Business of the UAS Industry" that zeroed in on barriers to scale and how to overcome them. He aimed to lay the groundwork for advanced Ukrainian companies to scale with Western partners. In a session on technology transfer, Chris and a Ukrainian lawmaker diagrammed how DIU might be able to operate faster than the current complex way in which the Pentagon provides security assistance. It was a remarkable gathering, the kind of get-together where an unarmed kamikaze drone left sitting on the sink in the men's room wasn't out of place. It was also a highly personal one, where the grief of the war borne by every Ukrainian in the room became real to those who hadn't experienced it firsthand.

At a NATO dinner the first night of the conference, held in the oldest restaurant in Warsaw, Chris sat across from a woman named Nataliia Kushnerska, the COO of Ukraine's military innovation unit, Brave 1. Her husband served as a sniper even as she tried to raise their two children, age four and seven, in an atmosphere of normalcy in Kyiv. Much of her family had been trapped behind Russian lines during the initial invasion. They were farmers and shopkeepers. Many didn't survive. The humanitarian toll was a subtext to every conversation. That feeling of acute loss continued after the conference. On the flight home Chris was seated next to a Ukrainian refugee family from Chernobyl who were emigrating to Canada. Their three English-speaking children, Denis, fifteen, Sophie, seven, and Alexander, five, were terribly nervous. Chris tried to keep them smiling but had little luck reinforcing their parents' efforts to calm them. War is a horrible thing. Chris would go on to accept an offer from the Ukrainian General Staff to become one of their international military advisors. Yet that wouldn't do anything for Denis, Sophie, and Alexander, who would now depend on the compassion of Canadian schoolmates and the suburb their parents settled them in. Raj and his wife had an equally solemn experience the day after the conference concluded, visiting Auschwitz. They flew back to the U.S. thinking about the world their four-year-old son would eventually inherit.

There was a historical echo as well. Warsaw had been leveled in the last months of 1944 by the Nazis after the Polish resistance attacked German positions as Soviet troops approached. A city of 1.2 million people was reduced to less than a thousand living amid smoking rubble. The DIU conference took place in a city built anew, yet the hotel everyone gathered in was only a mile away from the Warsaw Ghetto, in which the Nazis had imprisoned half a million Jews before sending them to their deaths at Treblinka and Auschwitz. Soviet liberators, who entered the city in January 1945, quickly turned into oppressors. Poland wouldn't win freedom until the fall of the Berlin Wall. Now its neighbor was in the grips of Russian forces whose pretext for invading was protecting ethnic Russians who lived in Crimea from alleged "neo-Nazi groups" terrorizing them.

That Putin's transparent propaganda had seemingly energized the

Russian populace was hard to fathom. We were indeed a long way from *The End of History*, where capitalist markets reinforce democracy for all.

FROM STEEL TO SILICON

The year 2024 was shaping up to be pivotal with make-or-break decisions in industrial policy and military modernization that would determine the next generation of military capability, the success or failure of the new wave of defense startups and venture funds that back them, and ultimately the geometry of Silicon Valley–Pentagon relations.

For Raj, it was particularly striking how quickly modern technology, especially low-cost drones, was changing the calculus of fighter aviation. Nearly two decades before, in Iraq, his F-16 fighter jet lacked a moving map. It was a critical capability that should have been there to help pilots from accidently crossing into Iran and coming in range of its anti-aircraft batteries. The Compaq tablet computer that Raj strapped to his knee was his personal hack to bring a moving map into the cockpit. It worked well enough to tide things over until the F-16 finally upgraded to a moving map several years later. But put Raj back in an F-16 today and there is no hack he could devise to protect himself from the omnipresent drone threat along the Ukrainian front.

The F-16 was built to shoot down MIGs. If a MIG threatened the U.S. in 2024 and Raj was in the cockpit, odds are good that he could down his adversary and return safely. But today's fighter pilots face a different enemy: before their jets even get off the runway they can be destroyed by cheap kamikaze drones. This is exactly what the Ukrainians did to the Russian air base in Pskov in September 2023. An enemy could hide hundreds of drones in the back of a passing truck just miles from our fixed bases. Not only do most U.S. air bases lack sophisticated counter-UAS systems to keep jets safe on the ground from such a swarm attack, but the F-16 and all modern fighters have no weapon capable of shooting down small drones. If drones attacked, Raj could try to quickly fly away when the alarm sounded, but he'd likely die trying. This isn't a position those whom we ask to protect us should ever be in. Nor is it even remotely acceptable that the defense of our country could fail because so many capability gaps like this compromise U.S. battle systems.

We are in a crisis unlike any our generation has faced before. Shockingly, most Americans don't even know that our military's might has been largely eclipsed by the commercial systems our adversaries are bringing to battle. Innovating is our only way out.

Ylli Bajraktari described the stakes in his classic blunt style: "We should try hard to suck less," he said. "The CHIPS Act took three years even though we had a broad coalition, with no antibodies in Congress or the administration. Why is everything so hard in our system? We're talking about getting capabilities online in 2035? Who cares? The maximum danger to our country is 2025 to 2030. That's the next budget cycle."

Ylli echoed what General Douglas MacArthur noted on the eve of America's entry into World War II, saying in 1940 that "The history of failure in war can almost be summed up in two words: 'too late.'" "A typhoon of steel" is how Japanese soldiers described World War II. Would America be ready for a typhoon of silicon?

Yet there was *some* promising news. In 2023 the army rolled out Google collaboration suites to 180,000 personnel, continuing the trend DIUx started of using commercial IT solutions instead of maintaining bespoke networks. General Milley's last major act as chairman was to propose a Joint Futures organization, whose mission would be to help the innovation centers in various branches of the military collaborate, so that the different technology platforms they sponsor can connect to each other seamlessly. The Department also expanded further the scope of OTA contracts, allowing them to be used for operations and maintenance funding—a major and previously off-limits category of expenditure—and blazing a path for follow-on production contracts to become even more frictionless.

U.S. allies were also getting in the game. Australia, the U.S., and the UK announced a series of measures to jointly develop more advanced technology, including quantum sensors and nuclear submarines, and to link their manufacturing bases tightly together, so they'd be better arrayed against China's massive industrial capability. Japan took greater steps to ready its military for the competition with China, and to link its efforts with South Korea and other Asian allies. Biden held the first Camp David summit of his presidency with the prime minister of Japan and the president of Korea, to discuss the China threat.

Other wins included the Pentagon's embrace of the generative AI revolution. The DoD launched "Task Force Lima" to speed experimentation with large language models like ChatGPT across the military. Also, Scale AI, the Silicon Valley startup whose CEO Alex Wang joined Chris to advise the White House on China, became the first company to provide generative AI capabilities to the Pentagon. Scale AI's software platform, called Donovan, uses generative AI models for military planning and battlefield monitoring. U.S. Central Command hired Andrew Moore, the former director of Google's Cloud AI, who served on the AI Commission. DIU went even further, establishing AI battle labs within the military's European and Pacific commands. A new defense venture fellowship program also placed Pentagon personnel for short immersion experiences at forty leading defense tech companies and VCs, including Joby Aviation, Shield Capital, and Beacon AI.

Then in a surprise move, at the annual conference of the Defense Industry Association, with all the primes in attendance, Deputy Secretary Kathleen Hicks announced the "Replicator Initiative," a multibillion-dollar bet on autonomous AI-driven aerial, seaborne, and undersea drones. DIU helped conceive how the initiative could integrate technology from startups with exquisite systems from the primes. It was a remarkable bet on the future and a sign of how much the conflict in Ukraine was shaping how those in the E-ring thought about which capabilities needed to be fast-tracked. Not long after, Hicks and Secretary of Defense Lloyd Austin visited DIU to see tech demos associated with Replicator and meet with the startup CEOs who will build it. Austin even hosted a meeting of AUKUS at DIU, bringing together the ministers of defense from Australia and the United Kingdom to collaborate on emerging China-deterring technologies.

Austin and Hick's pivot happened so fast it left some primes grumbling that their plans should have been more concrete and come with already passed budgets, as they're accustomed to getting before starting new work. Some startups selling to the Pentagon pushed back, apocalyptically angry at the primes' attack on the Department's new direction. "For years, defense technology companies have urged Defense leaders to move faster and buy new capabilities at larger scales," Anduril's chief strategy officer Christian Brose posted on LinkedIn. "The Deputy Secretary of Defense launched the Replicator initiative to buy and field thousands of autonomous systems in 18–24 months. Pretty good, right? Apparently not. 'Disorganized and confusing?' Compared to what? All of those multi-decade zombie programs everyone always complains about?"

Russia, meanwhile, was already a year down the road on its own version of Replicator, paying Iran a billion dollars to stand up a factory capable of producing six thousand advanced kamikaze drones a year. Russian strategists saw these swarming, autonomous, and low-cost drones as the weapon that could win the war for them.

Unbeknownst to U.S. or Israeli intelligence, Hamas also had its own miniature Replicator Initiative underway, using quadcopters to drop explosives on the generators that powered Israeli security towers on the Gaza Strip border. Those strikes enabled fourteen hundred fighters to pour undetected into Israel and massacre more than one thousand civilians, precipitating an Israeli ground invasion of Gaza and the most violent conflict in the region since the 1973 Arab-Israeli war. That same week drones launched by Hezbollah injured over twenty U.S. service members and contractors working in Syria and Iraq, leaving several U.S. personnel with traumatic brain injuries. In retaliation, the U.S. military executed multiple airstrikes on drone factories in Syria. Yet the attacks continued, numbering over one hundred by the end of 2023 and injuring forty-six additional U.S. personnel. Houthi rebels, based in Yemen but supported by Iran, then began attacking ships in the Red Sea. With the help of Iranian spy ships that pinpointed targets, the Houthis launched cruise missiles and drones at oil tankers, forcing the U.S. and allied navy destroyers to use $2 million missiles to knock $2,000 kamikaze drones out of the sky. Oil prices rose overnight as traders grew concerned that the twelve percent of global shipping that passes through the Red Sea might be disrupted. Three U.S. service members were killed in January 2024 when a drone struck their base in Jordan, leading the U.S. and U.K. to launch multiple retaliatory strikes.

Yet even as the new way of war becomes more visible, hard choices lie ahead. For the cost of a single aircraft carrier, the navy can purchase 18,000 unmanned Saildrones—more than 350 for each of the United States' fifty-plus treaty allies we're obligated to defend if attacked. Those at DIU know which *they'd* choose to buy, though, admittedly, an American admiral ordered to carry out airstrikes against a foreign country would think differently.

These are the trade-offs the military now faces. It can't be one or the other—all new or all old—when it comes to how the U.S. military will fight in the future. The Pentagon must now strike a careful balance, recapitalizing older systems with new technology while also building entirely new platforms around novel operational concepts. But at least now everyone grasps that the Pentagon will not win a future war without embracing emerging technology in equal or greater measure than its adversaries.

We think the greatest accomplishment of DIU is proving to the Pentagon that innovation is possible—at speed and at scale. "Died in the Valley of Death" is written on the tombstone of most attempts to move from experimentation to the battlefield. Countless policy wonks have imagined how to leap this chasm since the consumer technology explosion began around 1990. What DIU did is finally hit on a winning formula. That formula has seven key elements and is relevant to other large institutions seeking to innovate from the inside. The Pentagon, after all, is not the first entity that experienced success only to be hindered, as times changed, by the very processes and culture that led it to be dominant.

The first key element is to work on critical warfighter problems. While back-office improvements can help servicemen and -women, focusing on problems closer to the front of the spear makes initiatives more difficult for detractors to block. No one wants to be publicly exposed as impeding proven solutions that directly impact life-and-death situations.

The second element is to use *real* tech. In the defense world, entrenched contractors, responding to incentives, often repackage aging technology and market it as new. They take statistical techniques and with a straight face sell them as artificial intelligence to officials who are none the wiser. As disruptors, we learned to select problems and solutions where modern technology could provide a 10x improvement. That stark difference in performance significantly improves the odds of ousting a defense prime that's had the contract for a decade or more.

Having strong top-cover is our formula's third ingredient. Change is hard, especially so in the world's largest bureaucracy. Change agents need protection, the higher the better. For us it was Secretaries Carter and Mattis. We've seen other defense innovation organizations launch across the military services. Those with support at the highest levels (air force) flourished and those without (army) suffered.

Keeping a healthy irreverence is our approach's fourth plank. Pentagon processes are so tangled that outsiders must approach them like British archaeologists uncovering the Ziggurat of Ur—only with painstaking interpretation does one come to understand the impenetrable, archaic methods of operation. At times you simply have to ignore processes entirely and find a way to blast through, seeking forgiveness rather than asking permission.

Having the right fuel in your tank is the fifth element. For DIU that meant access to modest amounts of flexible money. As startups that run on shoestring budgets demonstrate day in and day out, innovation, counterintuitively, usually requires far less capital than big, bloated processes. But that capital must be flexible enough to support the twists and turns—and sometimes pivots—that occur while innovating.

The sixth element in DIU's winning formula is to battle, while at the same time co-opting, entrenched interests. Ultimately, for our work to scale, we needed the entrenched interests to come to our side, or at least cease their siege warfare. Those groups include Congress, mid-level officials, and old defense incumbents. In our most successful projects we eventually won over each through different means. It's impossible to scale as a lone ranger.

Building a team with conviction and the resolve to see it through is the seventh and most crucial element. Our fellow partners Vishaal and Isaac, COO Ernie Bio, and the other nearly one hundred uniformed and civilian members of the DIUx team each brought different skills to our fight. Yet they were all united in the cause and willing to work in service of it, whether that meant taking lower pay, risking a military promotion, or simply burning the midnight oil to notch another project success. We succeeded because our team delivered on the mission.

We also learned that innovating will not alone guarantee geopolitical stability. Deterring future war will require more than just military prowess. It will require influencing global trade, which is underpinned by the same revolutions in technology. In this way, China's strategy of civil-military fusion, and more broadly connecting the power and resources of the state to Chinese companies competing in global markets, is a pacing threat to our own economy as well as to our allies'.

China's tactics have shown some signs of success. Over the last few years, China has spent over $240 billion bailing out countries that were recipients of the CCP's Belt and Road global infrastructure initiative, causing them to be financially and politically indebted. Those among China's neighbors that are predisposed to lean toward America, such as the Philippines, Vietnam, and Singapore, are limited in doing so due to having China as their largest trading partner. And China's co-option has sometimes taken the form of brazen physical seizures. In just the last decade massive Chinese military air bases have been built on disputed lands in the South China Sea. In his 2024 New Year's address, President Xi used stronger words than ever before, calling Taiwanese "reunification" inevitable, an escalation that worried defense analysts. China has moved into the western hemisphere and signed significant military and intelligence cooperation agreements with Cuba, just sixty miles from Florida's coast. Xi has also purged senior military leadership, "disappearing" his former defense minister and appointing more compliant officials in their place. Yet cracks are emerging in the façade. Longtime China watchers believe Xi's crackdown will be fatal to China's longer-term ambitions. Leading businessmen and technologists are fleeing the country and transferring their capital assets abroad, potentially starting a death spiral in China's economy that will be difficult to reverse.

We have the tools, the people, the capital markets, and the goodwill to prevail and ensure that the American experiment of self-determination flourishes along with that of our allies, but we must rise above our internal squabbles. The changes required will be monumental, on the E-ring, at the White House, and in Congress. Fortunately, glimmers of hope have begun to emerge. The 118th Congress launched a new Select Committee on the Chinese Communist Party, chaired by Representative Mike Gallagher (R-WI), a stalwart supporter of DIU. His committee has spotlighted the challenge of delinking China's campaign of civil-military fusion from the Western capital that currently fuels it. In his words, "If American capital continues to flow to Chinese military companies, we are at risk of funding our own destruction." In 2021 the total level of venture funding invested in Chinese companies exceeded the amount invested in U.S. companies. Yet by the first half of 2023, U.S. investment in China had dropped by 30 percent, with U.S. venture investing in Chinese startups down a staggering 80 percent. The Biden administration has enacted further restrictions on U.S. investments in advanced industries in China, all but stopping outbound financial flows for AI, quantum, and advanced semiconductors. The decoupling from China boosted Mexico to become the United States's largest trading partner for the first time in twenty years.

In 2023, NATO jumped on the commercial technology bandwagon, announcing a €1 billion Innovation Fund that will make its first tech startup investments this year. Raj was appointed to its board of directors. The trilateral security pact between the U.S., UK, and Australia, known as AUKUS, will bolster technology sharing to include nuclear submarines. Other allies too have launched their own DIUs, including Singapore, the United Kingdom, France, India, Ukraine, Australia, Taiwan, Japan, and Korea. Congress has even turned the reforms lens on itself and the Pentagon by launching the Commission on Planning, Programming, Budgeting, and Execution Reform, an attempt to reform the budgeting system of the Pentagon, which has remained unchanged since Robert McNamara was running the department in the 1960s. Congress intends to make the budgeting process more flexible so the military can more quickly capitalize on technological opportunities. Raj is one of the commissioners—an appointment for which he's received an equal measure of congratulations and condolences. In March 2024, he and his fellow commissioners recommended that Congress replace the existing budget process with an agile, flexible system that can fully harness modern technology development, moving away from the three thousand line items that place money into immovable silos in the thousand-section-long National Defense Authorization Act.

The biggest challenge beyond politics will be the inherent conservatism of the military. Scholars of security policy have long noted the preeminence of politics and organizational interests in shaping what capacities defense institutions develop. The literature on this point is voluminous and depressing, with self-interest and established ways of warfighting almost always trumping new notions of prevailing threats. The British Navy at first rejected steamships. Cavalry units thought the tank would never succeed. The army was so opposed to the introduction of airplanes to the modern battlefield that the air force, an entirely new military service, had to be created. The pilots running the air force then opposed the introduction of ballistic and cruise missiles, believing manned bombers were the only answer. The same service at first opposed drones, naming them "remotely piloted vehicles" in an attempt to keep the service's culture internally coherent.

The greatest kind of patriots, we believe, are those who so cherish our country's ideals that they're not afraid to challenge the institutions that guard them. Members of Congress must show sustained leadership, taking votes that will ultimately keep their constituents safer even if this means giving up legacy defense jobs in their districts. The Secretary of Defense must drive the Pentagon to change more quickly than ever before. The Joint Chiefs must follow suit, honoring the tradition of their military services by remaking them. Stasis is even more likely in the present political environment, with its stark divides across and within the parties. *Profiles in Courage*, the title of John F. Kennedy's 1956 chronicle of political bravery, are now what we need most.

The ultimate goal is not to win wars but to deter them. Innovation is our asymmetric means to achieve and maintain peace. The question now is whether the Pentagon will develop at scale the battlefield innovations it has incubated.

Advocates of innovation must keep pressing despite the seemingly Sisyphean task of reform. Leadership must back them to the hilt.

If DIUx has taught us anything, it's that the sound of glass breaking is the melody of progress.

ACKNOWLEDGMENTS

We are deeply indebted to all those who shaped our professional and personal lives, as well as this manuscript more directly.

Dan Lyons helped craft the manuscript's every page. We're grateful for his Jedi sense of narrative and for teaching us how to pen pages that turn. Likewise, our agent, Christy Fletcher at United Talent Agency, deftly steered us right. Then came a break writers can only hope for: Rick Horgan, the legendary editor behind one hundred bestsellers, took on our project. More than that, he came to truly understand the cause we fought for. Rick's dedicated assistant, Sophie Guimaraes, and the entire team at Simon & Schuster helped on so many fronts.

In the book's gestational phase, David Litt, John Markoff, and Sarah Fuentes provided essential feedback, while Gautam Makunda and Jonathan Reiber—who helped conjure the book's title—provided unending moral support. Lirijon Kadriu helped us imagine evocative cover art. The enthusiasm of others who have written on technology buoyed our spirits along the way, including Nicholas Thompson, Tripp Mickle, Josh Cohen, David E. Sanger, Kate Conger, Ori Brafman, and Walter Isaacson.

Philip Bilden, Richard Danzig, Ylli Bajraktari, Johanna Spangenberg Jones, Lisa Hill, Lieutenant General Jack Shanahan, Mike Brown, and John Tsou were early readers of the manuscript. We're especially indebted to Philip, Richard, and Ylli for crucial steers on tone and substance.

Andrey Liscovich, CEO of the Ukrainian Defense Fund, kindly hosted us and colleagues from the NATO Innovation Fund in Ukraine. We met so many fierce and scrappy innovators whose bravery typifies that of the Ukrainian people. A highlight was Brave 1, Ukraine's own Defense Innovation Unit, especially its steely COO Nataliia Kushnerska.

Those we formally interviewed and corresponded with include Payam Banazadeh, Ryan Beall, JoeBen Bevirt, Christian Brose, Mike Brown, Major General Steve "Bucky" Butow, Lauren Dailey, Jared Dunnmon, Ryan Farris, Ben Fitzgerald, General Dave Goldfein, Lieutenant Colonel Vishaal "V8" Hariprasad, General Jeffrey Harrigian, Lisa Hill, Colonel Mark Jacobsen, Richard Jenkins, Andrey Liscovich, Palmer Luckey, Brendan McCord, David Merrill, David Rothzied, Lieutenant General Jack Shanahan, Reuben Sorensen, Lieutenant Wayne Starr, Trae Stephens, Admiral Sandy Winnefeld, and Deputy Secretary of Defense Bob Work.

We'd also like to thank Paul Jacobsmeyer and Doug McComb at the Pentagon's Office of Pre-Publication and Security Review and the official historians at the Office of the Secretary of Defense, Glen Asner and Erin Mahan, who preserve the Department's past so its leaders can better chart its future.

We're further grateful to Michael Boskin, Kiran Sridar, and the Hoover Institution's Working Group on Defense Budget Reform for commissioning Chris's paper "A Requiem for Defense Innovation?: Ukraine, the Pentagon's Innovator's Dilemma, and Why the United States Risks Strategic Surprise," which helped frame this book. Earlier work commissioned by the Aspen Strategy Group, especially Chris's papers "An Even Flatter World: How Technology Is Remaking the World Order" and "Reshaping National Security Institutions for Emerging Technology," were also seminal. We thank Joe Nye, Condoleezza Rice, Nick Burns, and Anja Manuel for including Chris in strategy group meetings, and also the Special Competitive Studies Project, where Chris worked while we wrote the proposal for this book. Similarly, the teams at Resilience and

Shield Capital were supportive of Raj even as he frequently disappeared to work on *Unit X*.

Then, of course, there is the cabal who spotted the tsunami of commercial technology on the horizon and banded together to ready the Pentagon for it: the late Secretary of Defense Ashton B. "Ash" Carter; Chairman of the Joint Chiefs of Staff Marty Dempsey, who told us to "go slay the Silicon Dragon"; Deputy Secretary Bob Work and his indefatigable team of Ylli Bajraktari (our true brother in arms), Ryan Farris, and Reuben Sorensen; Vice Chairmen of the Joint Chiefs Sandy Winnefeld and Paul Selva; NSA Directors General Keith Alexander, General Paul Nakasone, and Admiral Mike Rogers; Rear Admiral and former Naval Special Warfare commander Wyman Howard; General David Goldfein, Jim Baker, Sam Neill, and Matt Cordova on the Joint Staff; Josh Marcuse, the inaugural executive director of the Defense Innovation Board, his able deputy Mike Gable, and all the board's original members (Chair Eric Schmidt, Jeff Bezos, Adam Grant, Danny Hillis, Reid Hoffman, Walter Isaacson, Eric Lander, Marne Levine, Michael McQuade, Admiral William McRaven, Milo Medin, Richard Murray, Jennifer Pahlka, Cass Sunstain, and Neil deGrasse Tyson); Chris Lynch, inaugural head of the Defense Digital Service; and so many others, including Ylber Bajraktari, Wyn Elder, Snake Clarke, Jeremy Bash, Bill Greenwalt, Jason Matheny, and Will Roper. On the Hill, the late Senator John McCain, Senators Jack Reed and Ben Sasse, and Representatives Mac Thornberry, Mike Gallagher, Seth Moulton, and Elissa Slotkin were unrelenting advocates.

At the White House, National Security Advisor Susan Rice, Deputy National Security Advisor Avril Haines, Senior Director for Strategic Planning Salman Ahmed, U.S. CTO Megan Smith, and Presidential Science Advisor John Holdren were vital supporters, as were John Podesta, Denis McDonough, the late Secretary of State Madeleine Albright, and DARPA Directors Regina Dugan and Arati Prabhakar. Key supporters in the administration that followed include National Security Advisor H. R.

McMaster, Deputy National Security Advisor Nadia Shadlow, Secretary of Defense Jim Mattis, Deputy Secretary of Defense Patrick Shanahan, Undersecretary of Defense Ellen Lord, and Deputy Assistant Secretary Joe Felter.

When it came time to reboot DIU, former U.S. CTO Todd Park and Deputy U.S. Chief Data Scientist DJ Patil engineered the turnabout with the skill and finesse that have made them fixtures in Silicon Valley, together with Eric Rosenbach and Sasha Baker on the E-ring. The founders and investors who took the risk to work with us in our earliest days and especially DIUx 2.0's first contracts also merit a mention. Beyond those named in the book they include Marc Andreesen, Sam Altman, Brendon Tseng, Eric Demarco, Dan Gwak, Bandal Carano, and Gaurav Garg.

Finally, it should be said that this book is the product of our own journeys through the public and private sectors. We would like to thank the many people who inspired us. For Raj, these include Norm Augustine and Fred Hitz, both professionals, professors, and public servants; Bill Craven, Paul Madera, Philip Bilden, John Hurley, and Steve Blank, career consiglieres; Amy Zegart, H. R. McMaster, and Mike Brown, Stanford Tech Track 2 leaders; and John "Grinn" Barrett, Ernie "Rico" Bio, Brian "Spyder" Bradke, Dan "Razin" Caine, Mike "Cos" Cosby, Vyas "V" Deshpande, John "Ma" DiDonna, Brad "Francis" Everman, Jason "Gyro" Halvorsen, Tim "Sonic" Hassel, Thor "Thoro" Himley, Jed "Klepto" Humbert, Kevin "Grace" Kelly, Paul Pawluk, Jeff "Motown" Rouse, Neal "Drifter" Snetsky, Yarema "Yarko" Sos, and the late Brian "Spyder" Webster, who taught Raj the importance of mission and camaraderie.

For Chris, these include Professor Sheila Jasanoff for his academic training and all those he served under in government, Admiral Hal Gehman and the late Sally Ride, Stuart Bowen, Bill Lynn, Marty Dempsey, Sandy Winnefeld, John Podesta, Gayle Smith, Salman Ahmed, and Ron Klain. Additionally, Chris's former partner Karthik supported him while he was in Iraq and at the Pentagon and White House, as did Ricky

ACKNOWLEDGMENTS

Seidman. Brian Secesmeky and Paul Fierro also merit special mention, as does Ruku, Chris's golden retriever and DIU's first official dog, now retired from public service at age sixteen. Eric Schmidt has been a pivotal figure for us both—as a boss in Chris's case and investor in Raj's, and as a teacher and change-maker without parallel. Ultimately, none are more deserving of credit than the original DIUx 2.0 team, including our fellow founding partners Vishaal "V8" Hariprasad and Isaac Taylor, COO Ernie Bio, CTO Bernadette Johnson, Commander of the Reserve Unit and future DIU Director Doug Beck, Presidential Innovation Fellow and future DIU Director Mike Brown, as well as Jafer Ahmad, Ajay Amlani, Tammer Barkouki, Ryan Beall, Tim Booher, Steve Butow, Lauren Schmidt Dailey, Zac Dannelly, Jameson Darby, Leif Erikson, Harrison Ford, Chris Forshey, Matt "Doc" Goldman, Bryce Goodman, Sean Heritage, Lisa Hill, Orin Hoffman, Mark Jacobson, Brandon Johns, Johanna Spangenberg Jones, Mike Kaul, Linda Laurie, John Marburger, Brendan McCord, Mike McGinley, Kevin McGinnis, Greg Oslan, Enrique Oti, Ben Parish, Angela Ponmakha, Trek Potter, Ben Renda, David Rothzeid, Tony Schumacher, Dan Sheets, Taj Mackeuy Shittu, Sean Singleton, Wayne Starr, Rob Trejo, Zach Walker, Tom Wester, David Willard, Nyssa Wratschko, and Annaliese Yoder. Paul Milenkowic and his team at the Picatinny Arsenal were the contract ninjas supporting DIUx, including Denise Scott, John Eilenberger, Dave Banashefski, Tom Dougherty, Al Rinaldi, Dan Witt, Patrick Hamilton, Trisha Fitton, Chris Fotiadis, Norm Bonano, Michael Klein, and Bill Coolbaugh.

Finally, we count Ash Carter's wife Stephanie as an honorary member of our inaugural team and salute the tremendous efforts she has made to continue Ash's legacy through the Carter Exchange, a yearly forum discussing innovation and national security.

ACRONYMS

AT&L Undersecretary for Acquisition, Technology & Logistics

A&S Undersecretary for Acquisition & Sustainment

CAOC Combined Air Operations Center

CCP Chinese Communist Party

CENTCOM U.S. Central Command

CFIUS Committee on Foreign Investments in the United States

CSO Commercial Solutions Opening

DARPA Defense Advanced Research Projects Agency

DEPSECDEF Deputy Secretary of Defense

DEVGRU Naval Special Warfare Development Group (SEAL Team Six)

DIB Defense Innovation Board

DIU Defense Innovation Unit (x for experimental removed 2018)

DIUx Defense Innovation Unit Experimental

DoD Department of Defense

EUCOM U.S. European Command

FAR Federal Acquisition Regulations

I&W Indications and Warning

INDOPACOM U.S. Indo-Pacific Command

IQT In-Q-Tel

JAIC Joint Artificial Intelligence Center

NETCOM Army Network Enterprise Technology Command

NDAA National Defense Authorization Act

NSA National Security Agency

NSCAI National Security Commission on Artificial Intelligence

OSD Office of the Secretary of Defense

OTA Other Transactions Authority

R&E Undersecretary for Research & Engineering

SAR Synthetic Aperture Radar

SCSP Special Competitive Studies Project

SECDEF Secretary of Defense

BIBLIOGRAPHY

PRIMARY SOURCES

38th Commandant of the Marine Corps. "Commandant's Planning Guidance." July 16, 2019.

Beck, Douglas. "DIU 3.0: Scaling Innovation for Strategic Impact." Center for New American Security, February 2024.

Brown, Michael Pavneet Singh. "China's Technology Transfer Strategy: How Chinese Investments in Emerging Technology Enable a Strategic Competitor to Access the Crown Jewels of U.S. Innovation." Defense Innovation Unit Experimental, January 2018.

Carter, Secretary of Defense Ash. "Remarks Announcing DIUx 2.0," May 11, 2016, Mountain View, CA.

———. "Memorandum to Chair of the House Armed Services Committee Rep. Mac Thornberry re: DIUx Budget." October 19, 2016.

———. Memorandum to the Department of Defense, "Expansion of Defense Innovation Unit Experimental." July 5, 2016.

Defense Innovation Board. "AI Principles: Recommendations of the Ethical Use of Artificial Intelligence by the Department of Defense." October 31, 2019.

———. "Software Is Never Done: Refactoring the Acquisition Code for Competitive Advantage." May 3, 2019.

Defense Innovation Unit. "DIUx Commercial Solutions Opening How-to Guide." November 30, 2016.

———. "DIUx Dog Friendly Policy." August 31, 2016.

"Defense Innovation Unit Experimental Organizational Procedures." May 16, 2016. Signed by Chief of Staff to the Secretary of Defense Eric Rosenbach and Raj M. Shah.

Department of the Navy. "Force Design 2030." US Marine Corps, March 2020.

DIUx official charter, "DoD Directive 5105.85 Defense Innovation Unit Experimental (DIOx)." Office of the Deputy Chief Management Officer of the Department of Defense, July 5, 2016. Federal Register.

"Enabling DIUx to Work at Silicon Valley Speed." DIUx memorandum to Secretary Ash Carter requesting additional authorities, May 22, 2017.

Federal Register. "Defense Federal Acquisition Regulation Supplement: Modification of Authority of the Department of Defense to Carry Out Certain Prototype Projects." DFARS Case 2023-D006, May 25, 2023.

Kirchhoff, Christopher et al. Working group report to Secretary of Defense Ash Carter on DoD Silicon Valley Outpost, "Point of Partnership—Silicon Valley Whitepaper," v. 2.0, April 9, 2015.

National Defense Authorization Act, H.R. 2670, pp. 230–33.

Office of the Deputy Assistant Secretary of the Air Force for Operational Energy. "Optimizing Aerial Refueling Operations with Jigsaw." *Planning Tools: Developing at the Speed of Relevance*. 2022.

Office of the Undersecretary of Defense for Acquisition. "Other Transactions Guide for Prototype Projects." January 2017.

Office of the Under Secretary of Defense for Acquisition and Sustainment. "State of Competition within the Defense Industrial Base." February 2022.

"Readout of Deputy Secretary of Defense Kathleen Hicks' Visit to Silicon Valley, California." Press release. December 12, 2023.

Schmidt (nee Schmidt, now Dailey), Lauren. "Ideas on Acquisition." Internal DIUx working paper. May 2016.

"SecDef Visits Defense Innovation Unit X and Hosts AUKUS Ministers." Photo album. Secretary of Defense photo stream, December 1, 2023.

"Secretary of Defense Lloyd J. Austin III Announces New Director of the Defense Innovation Unit." Press release. April 4, 2023.

Shah, Raj M. "Memorandum for Department of Defense Senior Information Security Officer Re Commercial Service Provider Policy Waiver for Defense Innovation Unit Experimental (DIUx)." July 2016.

Shanahan, Deputy Secretary of Defense Patrick. "Redesignation of the Defense Innovation Unit." Memorandum. August 3, 2018.

United States Congress. Sec. 815, "Amendments to Other Transaction Authority," 2016 National Defense Authorization Act, Public Law 114–92, passed November 25, 2015.

United States Congress, Sec. 913, "Codification of The Defense Innovation Unit." 2024. Work, Deputy Secretary of Defense. "Establishment of an Algorithmic Warfare Cross-Functional Team (Project Maven)." April 26, 2017.

———. Memorandum to the Department of Defense, "Creation of New 'Point of Presence' Defense Innovation Unit Experimental." July 2, 2015.

KEY ARTICLES AND APPEARANCES ABOUT DIUX

"Bridging the Gap Between the Military and Silicon Valley." A conversation with David E. Sanger, national security correspondent, *New York Times*; Eric Schmidt, executive chairman, Alphabet; Norton Schwartz, president and CEO, Business Executives for National Security (BENS), former chief of staff, United States Air Force; Raj M. Shah, managing director, Defense Innovation Unit (DIUx). Milken Conference, June 26, 2017.

Cerre, Michael. "How the Pentagon joins forces with Silicon Valley startups." "The Leading Edge" segment, *PBS Frontline*, August 15, 2018.

"Chris Kirchhoff, formerly of the Pentagon's Silicon Valley office, on Recode Decode." Podcast with Kara Swisher, March 2018.

"Chris Kirchhoff, Laying the Foundation for DIUx." *The DIU-ex Podcast*, July 16, 2020, https://www.youtube.com/watch?v=7aI2lJ-ztu8.

Council on Foreign Relations. "National Security and Silicon Valley." A conversation with David E. Sanger, Eleonore Pauwels, Mary Wareham, and Christopher Kirchhoff. January 15, 2019.

Kaplan, Fred. "The Pentagon's Innovation Experiment." *MIT Tech Review*, December 19, 2016.

Shah, Raj M., and Enrique Oti. "A Story of Change." Presentation, Code for America Annual Conference, May 2018.

"Spurring Innovation Between the Pentagon and Private Sector: A Conversation with David E. Sanger and Raj M. Shah." Modern War Institute at West Point, November 2018.

Sullivan, Mark. "Silicon Valley Wants to Power the U.S. War Machine: Amid Rising Tensions With China, A Cadre of Defense Insiders and Tech Players Want to Remake the Pentagon in Silicon Valley's Image." *Fast Company*, November 1, 2021.

SECONDARY SOURCES

Ackerman, Elliot, and James Stavridies. *2034: A Novel of the Next World War*. Penguin Press, 2021.

———. *2054: A Novel*. Penguin Press, 2024.

Biddle, Stephen. "Back in the Trenches: Why New Technology Hasn't Revolutionized Warfare in Ukraine." *Foreign Affairs*, September/October 2023.

Bird, Kai, and Martin J. Sherwin. *American Prometheus: The Triumph and Tragedy of J. Robert Oppenheimer*. Alfred A. Knopf, 2005.

Blank, Steve. *Four Steps to the Epiphany*. K&S Ranch, 2nd ed., July 2013.

———. "Hidden in Plain Sight: The Secret History of Silicon Valley." Lecture, November 2008, and slide deck. See https://steveblank.com/secret-history/.

———. "Why the Lean Start-Up Changes Everything." *Harvard Business Review* (May 2013).

Boot, Max. *War Made New: Weapons, Warriors, and the Making of the Modern World*. Gotham Books, 2006.

Boskin, Michael J., John N. Rader, and Kiran Sridhar, eds. *Defense Budgeting for a Safer World: The Experts Speak*. Stanford, CA: Hoover Institution Press, 2023.

Brose, Christian. *The Kill Chain Defending America in the Future of High-Tech Warfare*. Hachette, 2020.

Brown, Michael. "Department of Defense Budgeting: The Unrecognized National Security Threat." In Michael J. Boskin, John N. Rader, and Kiran Sridhar, eds., *Defense Budgeting for a Safer World: The Experts Speak*. Stanford, CA: Hoover Institution Press, 2023, pp. 249–64.

Carter, Ash. *Inside the Five Sided Box: Lessons from a Lifetime of Leadership in the Pentagon*. Penguin Random House, 2020.

Carter, Ashton B., Marcel Lettre, and Shane Smith. "Keeping the Technological Edge." In *Keeping the Edge: Managing Defense for the Future*, ed. Ashton B. Carter and John P. White. MIT Press, 2001, pp. 129–64.

Casteau, Jeff, and Michael Levin. *The Complete Idiot's Guide to the Pentagon*. Alpha, 2002.

Christensen, Clayton. *The Innovator's Dilemma: When New Technologies Cause Great Firms to Fail*. Harvard Business Review Press, 1997.

Cockburn, Andrew. *Kill Chain: The Rise of the High-Tech Assassins*. Henry Holt, 2015.

Council on Foreign Relations. "Innovation and National Security: Keeping Our Edge." Independent Task Force Report No. 77, September 2019.

———. "U.S.-Taiwan Relations in a New Era: Responding to a More Assertive China." Independent Task Force Report No. 81, June 2023.

Danzig, Richard. "Driving in the Dark: Ten Propositions About Prediction and National Security." *Center for New American Studies*, October 26, 2011.

———. "Surviving on a Diet of Poisoned Fruit: Reducing the National Security Risks of America's Cyber Dependencies." *Center for New American Studies*, July 2014.

———. "Technology Roulette: Managing Loss of Control as Many Militaries Pursue Technological Superiority." *Center for New American Studies*, May 30, 2018.

Dixon, Norman. *On the Psychology of Military Incompetence*. Basic Books, 1976.

Dower, John. *Cultures of War: Pearl Harbor, Hiroshima, 9-11, Iraq*. W. W. Norton, 2010.

Duffel Blog. "B-21 Nukes DoD Budget," December 9, 2022, https://www.duffelblog.com/p/pentagon-debuts-new-stealth-budget.

Dugan, Regina E., and Kaigham J. Gabriel. "'Special Forces' Innovation: How DARPA Attacks Problems." *Harvard Business Review* (October 2013).

Eisenhower, Dwight D. "Farewell Address." Speech, January 17, 1961. https://www.archives.gov/milestone-documents/president-dwight-d-eisenhowers-farewell-address.

———. "Notes for Address to the Industrial Associations, Chicago," 1947. Eisenhower Presidential Library, https://www.eisenhower.archives.gov/all_about_ike/speeches.html.

———. "Scientific and Technological Resources as Military Assets." Memorandum for Directors and Chiefs of War Department General and Special Staff Divisions and Bureaus and the Commanding Generals of the Major Commands. Office of the Chief of Staff, War Department, Washington, D.C., April 30, 1946.

Fox, J. Ronald. *Defense Acquisition Reform, 1960–2009: An Elusive Goal*. U.S. Army Center of Military History, 2011.

Herman, Arthur. *Freedom's Forge: How American Business Produced Victory in World War II*. Random House, 2012.

Hoen, Andrew, and Thom Shanker. *Age of Danger: Keeping America Safe in an Era of New Superpowers, New Weapons, and New Threats*. Hachette, 2023.

Horowitz, Michael C. "The Algorithms of August: The AI Arms Race Won't Be Like Previous Competitions, and Both the United States and China Could Be Left in the Dust." *Foreign Policy*, September 12, 2018.

———. *The Diffusion of Military Power: Causes and Consequences for International Politics*. Princeton University Press, 2010.

Isaacson, Walter. *Elon Musk*. Simon & Schuster, 2023.

Jasanoff, Sheila. "Democracy in an Unknowable World." 2022 Holberg Prize Lecture, June 2022, https://holbergprize.org/en/news/holberg-prize/2022-holberg-lecture-sheila-jasanoff.

———. *The Ethics of Invention: Technology and the Human Future.* W. W. Norton, 2016.

———. "Technologies of Humility: Citizen Participation in Governing Science." *Minerva* 41, no. 3, Special Issue: Reflections on the New Production of Knowledge (2003): 223-244.

Karp, Alex. "Our Oppenheimer Moment: The Creation of A.I. Weapons." *New York Times*, July 20, 2023.

Kempner, Jesse, and Brooke Storkes. "Funding of Emerging-Technology Areas Pursued by Nontraditional Companies." McKinsey & Company, September 23, 2022.

Kirchhoff, Christopher. "Ebola Should Have Immunized the United States to the Coronavirus: What Washington Failed to Learn from the National Security Council's Ebola Report." *Foreign Affairs*, March 28, 2020.

———. "An Even Flatter World: How Technology Is Remaking the World Order." *The World Turned Upside Down: Maintaining American Leadership in a Dangerous Age.* Proceedings of the Aspen Strategy Group, 2017, pp. 93-99.

———. "Fixing the National Security State: Commissions and the Politics of Disaster and Reform." Ph.D. Dissertation. University of Cambridge, September 19, 2010.

———. "A Requiem for Defense Innovation?: Ukraine, the Pentagon's Innovator's Dilemma, and Why the United States Risks Strategic Surprise." In *Defense Budgeting for a Safer World: The Experts Speak*, ed. Michael J. Boskin, John N. Rader, and Kiran Sridhar. Stanford, CA: Hoover Institution Press, 2023, pp. 219-48.

———. "Reshaping National Security Institutions for Emerging Technology." *Reshaping National Security.* Proceedings of the Aspen Strategy Group, 2016, pp. 86-96.

———. "The Rise in Unconventional Military Power: Implications for Joint Force 2020." Memorandum for Chairman of the Joint Chiefs Martin Dempsey, unclassified, November 8, 2011.

———. "Why Silicon Valley Must Go to War." Op-ed, *New York Times*, May 2, 2018.

Kosar, Kevin R. "The Quasi Government: Hybrid Organizations with Both Government and Private Sector Legal Characteristics." *Congressional Research Service*, June 22, 2011.

Krepinevich, Andrew, and Barry Watts. *The Last Warrior: Andrew Marshall and the Shaping of Modern American Defense Strategy.* Basic Books, 2015.

Lerner, Josh, Kevin Book, Felda Hardymon, and Ann Leamon. "In-Q-Tel." *Harvard Business School Case 9-804-146*, May 2003.

Lynn, William. "Defending a New Domain: The Pentagon's Cyber Strategy." *Foreign Affairs*, March/April 2010.

———. "Remarks at the Global Security Forum, CSIS," June 8, 2011.

Mahnken, Thomas. *Technology and the American Way of War since 1945.* Columbia University Press, 2008.

Mallaby, Sebastian. *The Power Law: Venture Capital and the Making of the New Future.* Penguin Press, 2022.

Markoff, John. "Pentagon Turns to Silicon Valley for Edge in Artificial Intelligence," *New York Times*, May 11, 2016.

———. *What the Dormouse Said: How the Sixties Counterculture Shaped the Personal Computer Industry.* Viking, 2005.

Mazzucato, Mariana. *The Entrepreneurial State: Debunking Public vs. Private Sector Myths.* Anthem Press, 2013.

McMaster, H. R. *Battlegrounds: The Fight to Defend the Free World.* Harper Collins, 2021.

———. *At War with Ourselves: Overcoming Chaos in the Trump White House.* HarperCollins, 2024.

Metz, Cade. *Genius Makers: The Mavericks Who Brought AI to Google, Facebook, and the World.* Dutton, 2021.

Miller, Chris. *Chip War: The Fight for the World's Most Critical Technology.* Scribner, 2022.

National Security Commission on Artificial Intelligence. "Final Report." March 2023, https://www.nscai.gov/wp-content/uploads/2021/03/Full-Report-Digital-1.pdf.

O'Mara, Margaret. *The Code: Silicon Valley and the Remaking of America*. Penguin Books, 2020.

———. "Silicon Valley Can't Escape the Business of War: Many in the tech industry don't want to be part of the military-industrial complex. But defense work is already part of Silicon Valley's DNA." Op-ed, *New York Times*, October 26, 2018, https://www.nytimes.com/2018/10/26/opinion/amazon-bezos-pentagon-hq2.html.

Osama, Athar. "Washington Goes to Sand Hill Road: The Federal Government's Forays into the Venture Capital Industry." Research brief. Woodrow Wilson Center for Scholars. January 2008.

Pahlka, Jennifer. *Recoding America: Why Government Is Failing in the Digital Age and How We Can Do Better*. Metropolitan Books, 2023.

Petraeus, David, and Andrew Roberts. *Conflict: The Evolution of Warfare from 1945 to Ukraine*. HarperCollins, 2023.

Psalm 23. "A Psalm of David." *King James Bible*.

Reiber, Jonathan. "The Lessons Ash Carter Taught Me." Blog post. *Attack IQ*, October 31, 2022.

Rich, Ben R., and Leo Janos. *Skunk Works: A Personal Memoir of My Years at Lockheed*. Little, Brown, 1996.

Rosen, Steven. *Winning the Next War: Innovation and the Modern Military*. Cornell University Press, 1994.

Sanders, Gregory, Nicholas Velazquez, Emily Hardesty, and Audrey Aldisert. "Defense Acquisition Trends 2023: A Preliminary Look." Center for Strategic and International Studies, December 7, 2023.

Sanger, David E. *The Perfect Weapon: War, Sabotage, and Fear in the Cyber Age*. Penguin Random House, 2019.

———. *The Perfect Weapon*, documentary. HBO, 2020, https://www.hbo.com/movies/the-perfect-weapon.

Sapolsky, Harvey, Eugene Gholz, and Caitlin Talmadge. *US Defense Politics: The Origins of Security Policy*, 4th ed. Routledge, December 2020.

Schmidt, Eric. "Innovation Power: Why Technology Will Define the Future of Geopolitics." *Foreign Affairs*, March/April 2023.

———. "Remembering Ash Carter: The Innovative Secretary of Defense Who Changed the Pentagon, Silicon Valley, and the Trajectory of Our Nation." Special Competitive Studies Project, January 26, 2023.

———. "Trip Report from Ukraine." Special Competitive Studies Project, September 2022.

Schneider, Jacquelyn. "Investing in Emerging Technology: Lessons from Unmanned Systems." In Boskin, Michael J., John N. Rader, and Kiran Sridhar, eds. *Defense Budgeting for a Safer World: The Experts Speak*. Stanford, CA: Hoover Institution Press, 2023, pp. 185–200.

Shah, Raj M. "Testimony before the National Commission to Explore the Civil-Military Divide and Military Service Policy Options During Hearings." May 16, 2019.

———. "Testimony of Mr. Raj M. Shah, Future of Defense Task Force, House Armed Services Committee U.S. House of Representatives." Hearing Titled: "Supercharging the Innovation Base." February 5, 2020.

Singer, Peter W., and August Cole. *Ghost Fleet: A Novel of the Next World War*. Eamon Dolan/Houghton Mifflin Harcourt, 2015.

———. *Wired for War: The Robotics Revolution and Conflict in The 21st Century*. Penguin Random House, 2009.

Spence, Matt. "Ash Carter's Lasting Legacy: The Former Defense Secretary Leaves Behind a Much Stronger Pentagon-Silicon Valley Relationship." *Defense One*, October 26, 2022.

Weinberger, Sharon. *Imaginary Weapons: A Journey Through the Pentagon's Scientific Underworld*. Nation Books, 2007.

———. *The Imagineers of War: The Untold Story of DARPA, The Pentagon Agency That Changed the World*. Penguin Random House, 2018.

Wilson, Mark B. "U.S. Defense Budget Reform: Historical Perspectives (1940s–2020s)." In *Defense Budgeting for a Safer World: The Experts Speak*, ed. Michael J. Boskin, John N. Rader, and Kiran Sridhar. Stanford, CA: Hoover Institution Press, 2023, pp. 393–428.

Wittes, Benjamin, and Gabriella Blum. *The Future of Violence: Robots and Germs, Hackers and Drones—Confronting a New Age of Threat*. Basic Books, 2015.

Zegart, Amy. *Spies, Lies, and Algorithms: The History and Future of American Intelligence*. Princeton University Press, 2022.

Zelikow, Philip. "Defense Entropy and Future Readiness, Fast and Slow." In *The Future of American Defense, Proceedings of the Aspen Strategy Group*, Nicholas Burns, Jonathon Price, eds., pp. 49–74, https://www.aspeninstitute.org/wp-content/uploads/2014/02/FutureAmericanDefense.pdf.

Zenko, Micah. *Red Team: How to Succeed by Thinking Like the Enemy*. Basic Books, 2015.

NOTES

INTRODUCTION: SLOW BURN

4 *hobby drones sold on Amazon:* Thomas Gibbons-Neff, "ISIS Drones Are Attacking U.S. Troops and Disrupting Airstrikes in Raqqa, Officials Say," *Washington Post*, June 14, 2017, https://www.washingtonpost.com/news/checkpoint/wp/2017/06/14/isis-drones-are-attacking-u-s-troops-and-disrupting-airstrikes-in-raqqa-officials-say/; Emil Archambault and Yannick Veilleux-Lepage, "Drone Imagery in Islamic State Propaganda: Flying Like a State," *International Affairs* 96, no. 4 (July 2020): 955–73, https://academic.oup.com/ia/article/96/4/955/5813533.

4 *sunk in the opening minutes of a battle:* Stephen Chen, "Chinese Scientists War-Game Hypersonic Strike on US Carrier Group in South China Sea," *South China Morning Post*, May 23, 2023, https://www.scmp.com/news/china/science/article/3221495/chinese-scientists-war-game-hypersonic-strike-us-carrier-group-south-china-sea#; Jon Harper, "Incoming: Can Aircraft Carriers Survive Hypersonic Weapons?," *National Defense*, March 22, 2019, https://www.nationaldefensemagazine.org/articles/2019/3/22/incoming-can-aircraft-carriers-survive-hypersonic-weapons.

4 *advantage began to erode:* See Richard Danzig, "Technology Roulette: Managing Loss of Control as Many Militaries Pursue Technological Superiority," *Center for New American Studies*, May 30, 2018, https://www.cnas.org/publications/reports/technology-roulette.

4 *"China's Sputnik Moment":* See "China's Hypersonic Weapon Test Close to 'Sputnik Moment,' Says Top US General," *Financial Times*, October 27, 2021, https://www.ft.com/content/4a317b8c-d433-4f74-91d9-0be47fc0f04a and David E. Sanger and William Broad, "China's Weapon Tests Close to a 'Sput-

nik Moment,' U.S. General Says," *New York Times*, October 27, 2021, https://www.nytimes.com/2021/10/27/us/politics/china-hypersonic-missile.html.

5 *each bigger by market capitalization:* "Largest Companies by Market Cap," CompaniesMarketcap.com, December 2023, https://companiesmarketcap.com.

6 *Pentagon's "Valley of Death":* "Valley of Death" is a reference from Psalm 23, A Psalm of David. "Though I walk through the valley of the shadow of death, I will fear no evil: for thou art with me; thy rod and thy staff they comfort me . . ." The Holy Bible, King James Version.

6 *refuse to sign contracts with the military:* For an exploration of this cultural tension, see Council on Foreign Relations, "National Security and Silicon Valley," a conversation with David E. Sanger, Eleonore Pauwels, Mary Wareham, and Christopher Kirchhoff, January 15, 2019, https://www.cfr.org/event/national-security-and-silicon-valley-0.

7 *saw the slow-motion car crash:* Notably, Deputy Secretary of Defense William Lynn visited Silicon Valley in 2009 and 2010 while formulating the Pentagon's cyber strategy, including visits at Google and Facebook. See William Lynn, "Defending a New Domain: The Pentagon's Cyber Strategy," *Foreign Affairs*, March/April 2010, https://www.foreignaffairs.com/articles/united-states/2010-09-01/defending-new-domain, and William Lynn, "Remarks at the Global Security Forum, CSIS," June 8, 2011, https://go.gale.com/ps/i.do?id=GALE%7CA258415558&sid=sitemap&v=2.1&it=r&p=AONE&sw=w&userGroupName=anon%7E8b6bb609&aty=open-web-entry. Chairman of the Joint Chiefs of Staff Martin Dempsey also visited Silicon Valley shortly after being sworn in, visiting Google, Facebook, and the venture capital firm Kleiner Perkins. He went on to make innovation a centerpiece of his tenure as chairman. See for example "Security Paradox—A Public Address by General Martin E. Dempsey, Chairman of the Joint Chiefs of Staff," Harvard Institute of Politics, April 12, 2012, https://iop.harvard.edu/events/security-paradox-public-address-general-martin-e-dempsey-chairman-joint-chiefs-staff, and "Martin Dempsey Remarks Before the Joint Warfighting Conference," May 16, 2012, https://www.jcs.mil/Portals/36/Final%20-%20Selected%20Works%20Dempsey_1.pdf.

7 *In a prophetic 2001 paper:* Ashton B. Carter, Marcel Lettre, and Shane Smith, "Keeping the Technological Edge," in *Keeping the Edge: Managing Defense for the Future*, ed. Ashton B. Carter and John P. White (MIT Press, 2001), 129–164, https://www.belfercenter.org/sites/default/files/legacy/files/kte_ch6.pdf.

7 *There he spoke:* "Secretary of Defense Ashton Carter Unveils Cyber Strat-

egy, Calls for Renewed Partnership with Silicon Valley," *Stanford Center for International Security and Cooperation*, April 23, 2015, https://cisac.fsi.stanford.edu/news/secretary-defense-ashton-carter-unveils-cyber-strategy-calls-renewed-partnership-silicon-valley.

8 *building their products on research funded by the government:* Steve Blank, "Hidden in Plain Sight: The Secret History of Silicon Valley," lecture, November 2008, and slide deck, https://steveblank.com/secret-history/. See also Margaret O'Mara, *The Code: Silicon Valley and the Remaking of America* (Penguin Books, 2020).

8 *Google got its start:* Mariana Mazzucato, *The Entrepreneurial State: Debunking Public vs. Private Sector Myths* (Anthem Press, 2013).

8 *"We need to drill holes":* Secretary of Defense Ash Carter, "Remarks Announcing DIUx 2.0," U.S. Department of Defense, May 11, 2016, Mountain View, CA, https://www.defense.gov/News/Speeches/Speech/Article/757539/remarks-announcing-diux-20/. See also: Dan Lamothe, "Pentagon Chief Overhauls Silicon Valley Office," *Washington Post*, May 11, 2016, https://www.washingtonpost.com/news/checkpoint/wp/2016/05/11/pentagon-chief-overhauls-silicon-valley-office-will-open-similar-unit-in-boston/, and John Markoff, "Pentagon Turns to Silicon Valley for Edge in Artificial Intelligence," *New York Times*, May 11, 2016, https://www.nytimes.com/2016/05/12/technology/artificial-intelligence-as-the-pentagons-latest-weapon.html.

9 *Admiral Moffett—the station's namesake:* Lieutenant Philip D. Mayer, "Leading Technological Change: Lessons from Rear Admiral Moffett," *Proceedings of the U.S. Naval Institute* 146, no. 3 (March 2020): 1,405, https://www.usni.org/magazines/proceedings/2020/march/leading-technological-change-lessons-rear-admiral-moffett; William F. Trimble, *Admiral William A. Moffett: Architect of Naval Aviation* (Naval Institute Press, 2014).

9 *harness the power of venture capital firms:* For a history of venture capital, see Sebastian Mallaby, *The Power Law: Venture Capital and the Making of the New Future* (Penguin Press, 2022).

CHAPTER ONE: UNIT X

11 *was already sixth months old:* Deputy Secretary of Defense Robert Work, Memorandum to the Department of Defense, "Creation of New 'Point of Presence' Defense Innovation Unit Experimental," July 2, 2015.

11 *overseen by Bob Work:* Work launched a second incarnation in the Pentagon of an initiative called the Advanced Capability and Deterrence Panel (ACDP), first instantiated during the Cold War, to study how the U.S.

could achieve technological superiority over its adversaries. The newly reconstituted panel convened a series of meetings charting how technology from Silicon Valley could empower army, navy, and air force efforts to defeat projected adversaries. The group was briefed by Christopher Kirchhoff and enthusiastically embraced the idea to create DIUx. It also chartered what became the Maven Project and the Special Mission Missile Defeat Task Force, which gave rise to DIUx's involvement with Capella. For an early history of this important initiative, see Gian Gentile et al., "A History of the Third Offset, 2014–2018" (RAND Corporation, 2021), https://www.rand.org/pubs/research_reports/RRA454-1.html.

12 *wrote in his memoir:* Ash Carter, *Inside the Five-Sided Box: Lessons from a Lifetime of Leadership in the Pentagon* (Penguin Random House, 2020), p. 327.

13 *director of strategic planning:* For a general primer on strategic planning and future scenario development, see Micah Zenko, *Red Team: How to Succeed by Thinking Like the Enemy* (Basic Books, 2015), and Richard Danzig, "Driving in the Dark: Ten Propositions About Prediction and National Security," *Center for New American Studies,* October 26, 2011, https://www.cnas.org/publications/reports/driving-in-the-dark-ten-propositions-about-prediction-and-national-security%C2%A0.

14 *asked Chris to chair the Pentagon working group:* U.S. Department of Defense, "Point of Partnership—Silicon Valley Whitepaper," v. 2.0, April 9, 2015. This working group was empaneled by Bob Work at the urging of Ylli Bajraktari and Chris Kirchhoff. Work had taken multiple trips to Silicon Valley along with vice chairman of the Joint Chiefs Sandy Winnefeld and consulted with many leaders there, including Doug Beck, about how to launch a Pentagon unit. Work approved the group's concept and ordered us to move out on its creation on April 10, 2015. See Christopher Kirchhoff, email to Chairman of the Joint Chiefs of Staff Martin Dempsey and Vice Chairman of the Joint Chiefs of Staff James Winnefeld, "DSD Decision on DoD Silicon Valley Presence" (unclassified), April 10, 2015, at 3:57:28 PM EDT. See also: Doug Beck, email to James Winnefeld et al., "Reserve Idea Followup," March 28, 2015, at 21:41:07 CST, and Doug Beck to James Winnefeld et al., January 26, 2015, "Cyber article, V4 track changes + clean."

16 *4,018 nuclear warheads:* "Fact Sheet: Transparency in the U.S. Nuclear Weapons Stockpile," U.S. Department of State, October 5, 2021, https://www.state.gov/wp-content/uploads/2021/10/Fact-Sheet_Unclass_2021_final-v2-002.pdf; "Status Of World Nuclear Forces," Federation of American Scientists, March 31, 2023, https://fas.org/initiative/status-world-nuclear-forces/.

16 *lent his signature:* Defense Innovation Unit Experimental ORGANIZATIONAL PROCEDURES, May 16, 2016, signed by Eric Rosenbach and Raj M. Shah.

17 *put this in writing, in a directive-type memorandum:* Secretary of Defense Ash Carter, Memorandum to the Department of Defense, "Expansion of Defense Innovation Unit Experimental," July 5, 2016. These authorities were ratified in DIUx's official charter, "DOD DIRECTIVE 5105.85 DEFENSE INNOVATION UNIT EXPERIMENTAL (DIUX)," Office of the Deputy Chief Management Officer of the Department of Defense, July 5, 2016, https://www.esd.whs.mil/Portals/54/Documents/DD/issuances/dodd/510585p.pdf?ver=2018-11-23-075056-577.

17 *we'd end up failing, just like our predecessors:* For an oral history of the beginning of DIUx 2.0, see "Chris Kirchhoff, Laying the Foundation for DIUx," *The DIU-ex Podcast*, July 16, 2020, https://www.youtube.com/watch?v=7aI2lJ-ztu8.

22 *weekly updates the inaugural director sent back to the Pentagon:* In the DIUx Archives, see "George Duchek Weekly Reports" sent from Duchek to the Office of the Secretary of Defense for Acquisition, Technology, and Sustainment.

CHAPTER TWO: ZEROIZED

36 *it didn't have to be this way:* DIUx, for the first time, used its waiver authority to overcome objections in the Office of the Chief Information Officer. Secretary of Defense Ash Carter agreed with DIUx, and the next day we had working Gmail. See Raj M. Shah, Memorandum for Department of Defense Senior Information Security Officer re Commercial Service Provider Policy Waiver for Defense Innovation Unit Experimental (DIUx)," July 2016.

37 *twenty-page white paper:* Lauren Schmidt (nee Schmidt, now Dailey), "Ideas on Acquisition," internal DIUx working paper, May 2016.

41 *Defense Acquisition Reform, 1960–2009:* J. Ronald Fox, *Defense Acquisition Reform, 1960–2009: An Elusive Goal* (U.S. Army Center of Military History, 2011), https://history.defense.gov/Portals/70/Documents/acquisition_pub/CMH_Pub_51-3-1.pdf.

41 *in section 815:* United States Congress, Sec. 815, "Amendments to Other Transaction Authority," 2016 National Defense Authorization Act, Public law 114–92, passed November. 25, 2015, https://www.congress.gov/114/plaws/publ92/PLAW-114publ92.pdf. The key provision in section (f) reads, "FOLLOW-ON PRODUCTION CONTRACTS OR

TRANSACTIONS.— (1) A transaction entered into under this section for a prototype project may provide for the award of a follow-on production contract or transaction to the participants in the transaction. (2) A follow-on production contract or transaction provided for in a transaction under paragraph (1) may be awarded to the participants in the transaction without the use of competitive procedures, notwithstanding the requirements of section 2304 of this title, if (A) competitive procedures were used for the selection of parties for participation in the transaction; and (B) the participants in the transaction successfully completed the prototype project provided for in the transaction. (3) Contracts and transactions entered into pursuant to this subsection may be awarded using the authority in subsection (a), under the authority of chapter 137 of this title, or under such procedures, terms, and conditions as the Secretary of Defense may establish by regulation."

41 *The passage gave the Department permission:* For an explainer, see "Section 815 of Fiscal Year 2016 National Defense Authorization Act," C5 Consortium for Command, Control, and Communications in Space, https://cmgcorp.org/wp-content/uploads/2016/07/Section_815_MEMO.pdf.

41 *Greenwalt hoped:* Fred Kaplan, "The Pentagon's Innovation Experiment," *MIT Tech Review*, December 19, 2016, https://www.technologyreview.com/2016/12/19/155246/the-pentagons-innovation-experiment/.

43 *we posted the white paper:* "DIUx Commercial Solutions Opening How-to Guide," Defense Innovation Unit, November 30, 2016, https://apps.dtic.mil/sti/pdfs/AD1022451.pdf.

43 *first update to the Department's guidance on OTAs since 2004:* Department of Defense, "Other Transactions Guide for Prototype Projects," January 2017, https://www.acqnotes.com/wp-content/uploads/2014/09/Tab-5-OSD-OTA_Guide-17-Jan-2017-DPAP-signature-FINAL-002.pdf.

43 *Lauren had dubbed the Commercial Solutions Opening (CSO):* Victor Deal first coined the term CSO in 2015 while proposing a novel expansion of Broad Agency Announcement (BAA) authority. In collaboration with others, he then sought the Department's concurrence to propose to Congress that this new authority be codified in the NDAA and used, including in conjunction with the FAR. See "Reducing Acquisition Timelines to Attract Non-traditional Technology Providers" (USA006100-15), DoD memorandum from Undersecretary of Defense Frank Kendall to Secretary Ash Carter, November 13, 2015. See also "The Office of the Secretary of Defense's Other Transactions Agreements Workshop (for Prototype Projects)," November 2–3, 2016.

43 *army civilians based at Picatinny Arsenal:* Carolyn Wong, "Enhancing ACC

Collaboration with DIUx," RAND Working Report, https://www.rand.org/content/dam/rand/pubs/working_papers/WR1100/WR1177/RAND_WR1177.pdf.

44 *use Lauren's hack to buy $70 billion worth of technology:* "Department of Defense OTA spent, 2016–2023," Data from GovWinIQ, which amalgamates federal procurement data, current as of December 2023, https://iq.govwin.com/neo/home. For a breakdown of this spend, see Gregory Sanders et al., "Defense Acquisition Trends 2023: A Preliminary Look," Center for Strategic and International Studies, December 7, 2023, https://www.csis.org/analysis/defense-acquisition-trends-2023-preliminary-look, and Jesse Kempner and Brooke Storkes, "Funding of Emerging-Technology Areas Pursued by Nontraditional Companies," McKinsey & Company, September 23, 2022, https://www.mckinsey.com/industries/aerospace-and-defense/our-insights/funding-of-emerging-technology-areas-pursued-by-non traditional-companies.

CHAPTER THREE: THE GONKULATOR

45 *Combined Air Operations Center (CAOC):* "Combined Air Operations Center (CAOC)," U.S. Air Forces Central, https://www.afcent.af.mil/About/Fact-Sheets/Display/Article/217803/combined-air-operations-center-caoc/.

46 *The DIB's members:* "Secretary Carter Names Additional Members of Defense Innovation Advisory Board," Department of Defense press release, July 26, 2016, https://www.defense.gov/News/Releases/Release/Article/857710/secretary-carter-names-additional-members-of-defense-innovation-advisory-board/#:~:text=The%20new%20additions%20include%20Amazon,and%20author%20Neil%20deGrasse%20Tyson.

51 *"They were using fourteen apps":* Jeffrey Harrigian, interview with authors, March 6, 2023.

51 *twenty-six thousand strike aircraft sorties:* "Combined Joint Task Force Operation Inherent Resolve," U.S. Department of Defense, https://dod.defense.gov/OIR/; Becca Wasser et al., "The Role of U.S. Airpower in Defeating ISIS," RAND Corporation, 2021, https://www.rand.org/pubs/research_briefs/RBA388-1.html.

52 *212,000 pounds of fuel:* See "KC-46A Pegasus: The World's Most Advanced Multi-Mission Aerial Refueling Aircraft," Boeing, https://www.boeing.com/defense/kc-46a-pegasus-tanker/.

55 *"I'm on it," Enrique replied:* See Raj M. Shah and Enrique Oti, "A Story of Change," presentation, Code for America Annual Conference, May 2018, https://www.youtube.com/watch?v=XU8b3jX2JYk&t=3s.

55 *"a lot of people who can code in the air force":* Wayne Starr, interview with authors, January 26, 2023.

59 *Saving 25 million gallons of jet fuel per year:* "Optimizing Aerial Refueling Operations with Jigsaw," Planning Tools: Developing at the Speed of Relevance, Office of the Deputy Assistant Secretary of the Air Force for Operational Energy, https://www.safie.hq.af.mil/Portals/78/documents/IEN/21st%20Century%20Tools%20Leave-Behind.pdf?ver=nYyKQ9Awy55LcBEfgBVmnA%3D%3D.

61 *"Stolen emails released by WikiLeaks":* "Stolen Email Offers Unvarnished View of Military Leaders," *Associated Press*, October 30, 2016, https://apnews.com/united-states-presidential-election-events-304acd84f0c4443fb12b7ad8f5e7f11b. See also Thomas E. Ricks, "Pentagon official takes fire for giving his honest assessments of some generals: What's worse than civilians asking hard questions about top military officers? Not asking them," *Foreign Policy*, November 1, 2017, https://foreignpolicy.com/2016/11/01N/poetnEtaSgon-official-takes-fire-for-giving-his-honest-assessments-of-some-generals/.

67 *McCain and Senator Jack Reed issued a statement:* "SASC Statement on Air Force's Decision to Cancel AOC 10.2 Modernization Contract," Senate Armed Services Committee, July 13, 2017, https://www.armed-services.senate.gov/press-releases/sasc-statement-on-air-forces-decision-to-cancel-aoc-102-modernization-contract.

67 *Chris's golden retriever roamed the halls:* Chris's Golden Retriever, Ruku, became DIU's first dog under its first of a kind dog friendly policy. "DIUx Dog Friendly Policy," Defense Innovation Unit, August 31, 2016. This policy was contested immediately by National Guard personnel in charge of managing the office space where DIU was located. Luckily, DIU prevailed in maintaining the policy after some crafty maneuvering.

68 *create an air force "software factory":* The Defense Innovation Board showed the way on how to modernize DoD software practices in its report, "Software Is Never Done: Refactoring the Acquisition Code for Competitive Advantage," May 3, 2019, https://media.defense.gov/2019/May/01/2002126689/-1/-1/0/SWAP%20COMPLETE%20REPORT.PDF.

69 *"I plan to build a life for my son and his siblings in America":* Rob Schmitz, "The U.S. Air Base at the Heart of America's Biggest Airlift," National Public Radio, September 2, 2021, https://www.npr.org/2021/09/02/1030307280/afghan-refugees-airlift-ramstein-air-base-germany.

69 *a software app called Slapshot:* Damany Coleman, "Kessel Run's SlapShot Saves Lives," U.S. Air Force, September 28, 2021, https://www.aflcmc.af.mil/NEWS/Article-Display/Article/2791602/kessel-runs-slapshot-saves-lives/.

72 *He agreed to support us:* Ash Carter also wrote Thornberry urging him to support DIUx's budget request. See Secretary of Defense Ash Carter, "Memorandum to Chair of the House Armed Services Committee Rep. Mac Thornberry re: DIUx Budget," October 19, 2016.

CHAPTER FOUR: A NEW KILL CHAIN FOR NORTH KOREA

73 *"The President himself is pushing for this":* Reuben Sorensen, interview with authors, January 27, 2023. See also: "National Intelligence Estimate, North Korea: Scenarios for Leveraging Nuclear Weapons Through 2030," declassified on June 15, 2023," https://www.dni.gov/files/ODNI/documents/assessments/NIC-Declassified-NIE-North-Korea-Scenarios-For-Leveraging-Nuclear-Weapons-June2023.pdf.

73 *"The problem is North Korea":* Ryan Farris, interview with authors, February 2, 2023. See also: "North Korea Rocket Launch: Why Did Kim Fire a Missile Now? | BBC, February 7, 2016, https://www.bbc.com/news/world-asia-35516199.

74 *part of a special task force:* The task force, which was chartered by the Advanced Capabilities and Deterrence Panel, was officially named "Special Mission Missile Defeat."

74 *It wasn't like a James Bond movie:* David E. Sanger and William J. Broad, "Tiny Satellites from Silicon Valley May Help Track North Korea Missiles," *New York Times*, July 6, 2017, https://www.nytimes.com/2017/07/06/world/asia/pentagon-spy-satellites-north-korea-missiles.html.

75 *the intelligence community believed:* "North Korea's Military Capabilities," Backgrounder, Council on Foreign Relations, June 28, 2022, https://www.cfr.org/backgrounder/north-korea-nuclear-weapons-missile-tests-military-capabilities; Defense Intelligence Agency, "North Korean Military Power: A Growing Regional and Global Threat," September 2021, p. 21, https://www.dia.mil/Military-Power-Publications/.

75 *study published in the journal* Science: "The Rise, Collapse, and Compaction of Mt. Mantap from the 3 September 2017 North Korean Nuclear Test," *Science* 361, no. 6398 (May 10, 2018), https://www.science.org/doi/10.1126/science.aar7230.

75 *nuke the West Coast:* "Report of the Congressional Commission on the Strategic Posture of the United States," U.S. House Armed Services Committee, October 2023, https://armedservices.house.gov/sites/republicans.armedservices.house.gov/files/Strategic-Posture-Committee-Report-Final.pdf. See also: Alexander Ward, "North Korea Displays Enough Icbms to Overwhelm U.S. Defense System Against Them," *Politico*, February 8, 2023,

https://www.politico.com/news/2023/02/08/north-korea-missile-capability-icbms-00081993; Ankit Panda, *Kim Jong Un and the Bomb* (Hurst: June 2020).

77 *The first U.S. reconnaissance satellite, the KH-1 Corona:* "Cold War in Space: Top Secret Reconnaissance Satellites Revealed," National Museum of the United States Air Force, https://www.nationalmuseum.af.mil/Visit/Museum-Exhibits/Fact-Sheets/Display/Article/195923/cold-war-in-space-top-secret-reconnaissance-satellites-revealed/.

78 *high percentage of successful intercepts:* "The Missile Defense System," Missile Defense Agency, U.S. Department of Defense, https://www.mda.mil/system/system.html.

78 *"left of launch" solution:* Theresa Hitchens, "Beyond 'Bullet on Bullet': NORTHCOM's New Defense Plan Looks to Kill Missiles Before They Launch," *Breaking Defense*, August 9, 2023, https://breakingdefense.com/2023/08/beyond-bullet-on-bullet-northcoms-new-defense-plan-looks-to-kill-missiles-before-they-launch/.

79 *"We had a good 'right of launch' solution":* Admiral Sandy Winnefeld (ret.), correspondence with authors, February 20, 2023.

79 *Winnefeld's staff had created a graph:* Admiral Sandy Winnefeld, correspondence with authors, July 18, 2023; Ryan Farris, interview with authors, February 2, 2023.

79 *sufficient KN-08 missiles to overwhelm our defenses:* Ryan Farris, interview with authors, February 2, 2023.

79 *sour on the Nike anti-ballistic missile system:* Robert McNamara, "Memorandum from Secretary of Defense McNamara to President Johnson, SUBJECT Production and Deployment of the Nike-X," January 1967, https://history.state.gov/historicaldocuments/frus1964-68v11/d173.

79 *Winnefeld believed our only recourse:* Admiral Sandy Winnefeld (ret.), correspondence with authors, February 20, 2023.

79 *having a high "revisit rate":* Admiral Sandy Winnefeld (ret.), correspondence with authors, February 20, 2023.

80 *payloads into space cheaper than NASA:* Matthew Weinzierl and Mehak Sarang, "The Commercial Space Age Is Here," *Harvard Business Review*, February 12, 2021, https://hbr.org/2021/02/the-commercial-space-age-is-here.

80 *Now that Datahub was up and running:* The success of the Datahub pilot was disclosed publicly by Deputy Secretary Robert Work in 2016. See "Remarks by the Deputy Secretary of Defense at the In-Q-Tel CEO Summit," San Jose, CA, February 25, 2016. See also "Deputy Secretary

NOTES

Work Visits Planet Labs," February 25, 2016, https://www.defense.gov/Multimedia/Photos/igphoto/2001459490/.

81 *Lockheed deployed a SAR sensor on its SR-71 Blackbird:* "Synthetic Aperture Radar: 'Round the Clock Reconnaissance,'" Lockheed Martin, October 1, 2020, https://www.lockheedmartin.com/en-us/news/features/history/sar.html.

82 *"But he hasn't even built a prototype":* Major General Steve "Bucky" Butow, interview with authors, January 16 and April 4, 2023. Payam Banazadeh, interview with authors, January 20 and 25, 2023.

83 *as I pulled that thread:* Steve Blank, "Why the Lean Start-Up Changes Everything," *Harvard Business Review*, May 2013, https://hbr.org/2013/05/why-the-lean-start-up-changes-everything. See also: https://steveblank.com/about/.

84 *The Secret History of Silicon Valley:* Steve Blank, "Hidden in Plain Sight: The Secret History of Silicon Valley," lecture, November 2008, and slide deck, https://steveblank.com/secret-history/.

85 Four Steps to the Epiphany: Steve Blank, *Four Steps to the Epiphany* (K&S Ranch, 2nd edition, July 2013).

90 *"we could get into a very fast escalation cycle":* Remarks by General Vincent Brooks to Defense Innovation Board (unclassified), Seoul, South Korea, September 8, 2017.

91 *"We have a more virulent form of Kim":* Remarks by General Vincent Brooks to Defense Innovation Board (unclassified), Seoul, South Korea, September 8, 2017.

91 *Fire sixteen thousand rounds an hour at Seoul alone:* Jeongmin Kim, "Seoul Officials Suggest North Korea Capable of 'Hamas Tactics' to Attack South," *NK News*, October 11, 2023, https://www.nknews.org/2023/10/seoul-officials-suggest-north-korea-capable-of-hamas-tactics-to-attack-south/.

91 *"The cost to life is extraordinarily high":* Remarks by General Vincent Brooks to Defense Innovation Board (unclassified), Seoul, South Korea, September 8, 2017.

93 *David E. Sanger reported:* David E. Sanger and William J. Broad, "Tiny Satellites from Silicon Valley May Help Track North Korea Missiles," *New York Times*, July 6, 2017, https://www.nytimes.com/2017/07/06/world/asia/pentagon-spy-satellites-north-korea-missiles.html.

98 *Capella finally won more DoD business:* "Capella Space Awarded Commercial Radar Contract by National Reconnaissance Office," Capella Space, January 21, 2022, https://www.capellaspace.com/press-releases/capella-space-awarded-commercial-radar-contract-by-national-reconnaissance-office/.

CHAPTER FIVE: UNIT X LOSES THE X

99 *contracts for 48 projects:* DIU Annual Report 2017 and DIU Annual Report 2018.

99 *we moved two projects from pilot stage into production:* "Tanium Gets $750 Million DoD Contract for Cybersecurity," Meritalk, November 2, 2017, https://www.meritalk.com/articles/tanium-gets-750-million-dod-contract-for-cybersecurity/.

100 *recognized Mayhem's potential:* For a history of modern cyberwarfare, see David E. Sanger, *The Perfect Weapon: War, Sabotage, and Fear in the Cyber Age* (Penguin Random House, 2019). See also: the documentary by the same name, HBO, 2020, https://www.hbo.com/movies/the-perfect-weapon, and Richard Danzig, "Surviving on a Diet of Poisoned Fruit: Reducing the National Security Risks of America's Cyber Dependencies," *Center for New American Studies,* July 2014, https://s3.us-east-1.amazonaws.com/files.cnas.org/documents/CNAS_PoisonedFruit_Danzig.pdf.

100 *contract worth $45 million:* "What Is Mayhem?," *Mayhem Security,* https://www.mayhem.security/about.

101 *"first autonomous robot of its kind used in combat":* Elliot Ackerman, "A Navy SEAL, a Quadcopter, and a Quest to Save Lives in Combat," *Wired,* October 30, 2020, https://www.wired.com/story/shield-ai-quadcopter-military-drone/; Christopher Mims and Michael Bucher, "100 Years of Robots," *Wall Street Journal,* January 23, 2021, https://www.wsj.com/story/100-years-of-robots-d44df980?mod=e2twd.

104 *drones could convey back to Chinese servers:* Haye Kesteloo, "Department of Defense Bans the Purchase of Commercial-Over-the-Shelf UAS, Including DJI Drones Effective Immediately," Drone DJ, June 7, 2018, https://dronedj.com/2018/06/07/department-of-defense-bans-the-purchase-of-commercial-over-the-shelf-uas-including-dji-drones/.

104 *army had issued an edict:* Lily Hay Newman, "The Army Grounds Its DJI Drones Over Security Concerns," *Wired,* August 7, 2017, https://www.wired.com/story/army-dji-drone-ban/.

104 *drone team called Rogue Squadron:* See Mark Jacobsen, "DIU and Rogue Squadron," markdjacobsen.com, https://markdjacobsen.com/portfolio/rogue-squadron/. See also Mark Jacobsen, "Why the Flying IED Threat Has Barely Started," *War on the Rocks,* October 19, 2016, https://warontherocks.com/2016/10/why-the-flying-ied-threat-has-barely-started/.

105 *Rogue Squadron published the hack:* DoD and U.S. Special Operations Command has publicly acknowledged this software fix to safe DJI drones for

U.S. military use—"software has been developed (specific to this model) and implemented to eliminate the cyber security concerns that are inherent to the DJI Mavic Pro." https://www.voanews.com/a/usa_us-military-still-buying-chinese-made-drones-despite-spying-concerns/6175967.html. The DoD comptroller has also released an unclassified summary of the program, called RIZER, and its budget, here: https://comptroller.defense.gov/Portals/45/Documents/defbudget/fy2022/budget_justification/pdfs/03_RDT_and_E/WHS_PB2022.pdf. Ryan Beall, interview with authors, May 1, 2023.

105 *"we can't go get the drone operator":* Ryan Beall, interview with authors, May 1, 2023.

106 *no way to recover in real time:* Mark Jacobsen, correspondence with authors, July 2023.

106 *Beall finished the Android app:* For a description of the app see Mark Jacobsen, web post, https://markdjacobsen.com/portfolio/wicker/.

106 *"I just taught myself that tool":* Ryan Beall, interview with authors, May 1, 2023.

106 *forty drone incursions in a single day:* Marc Jacobsen, interview with authors, April 27, 2023.

107 *he was just a fellow hacker:* Ryan Beall, interview with authors, May 1, 2023.

108 *Skydio, became the primary supplier:* "Skydio, Inc.—Short Range Reconnaissance," Defense Innovation Unit, 2021, https://www.diu.mil/solutions/portfolio/catalog/a0Tt0000009En3rEAC-a0ht000000AYgy9AAD.

108 *a larger program called Blue UAS:* "Cleared List: A Quick Reference Guide of All Blue UAS," Defense Innovation Unit X, https://www.diu.mil/blue-uas-cleared-list.

109 *"I enthusiastically embrace it":* "Media Availability with Secretary Mattis at DIUx," US. Department of Defense, August 10, 2017, https://www.defense.gov/News/Transcripts/Transcript/Article/1275373/media-availability-with-secretary-mattis-at-diux/. See also: Tajha Chappllet-Lanier, "Secretary Mattis Ready to 'Enthusiastically Embrace' DIUx," *FedScoop*, August 11, 2017, https://fedscoop.com/secretary-mattis-ready-enthusiastically-embrace-diux; Tom Simonite, "Defense Secretary James Mattis Envies Silicon Valley's AI Ascent," *Wired*, August 10, 2017, https://www.wired.com/story/james-mattis-artificial-intelligence-diux/.

109 *removed the "x" from our name:* Deputy Secretary of Defense Patrick Shanahan, "Redesignation of the Defense Innovation Unit," Memorandum, *FedScoop*, August 3, 2018, https://www.fedscoop.com/wp-content/uploads

/sites/5/2018/08/REDESIGNATION-OF-THE-DEFENSE-INNOVATION-UNIT-OSD009277-18-RES-FINAL.pdf.

109 *Rogue Squadron eventually moved out:* "Rogue Squadron Transitions from Defense Innovation Unit to Defense Digital Service," Defense Digital Service, February 12, 2020, https://www.dds.mil/media/2020-05-rogue-squadron-transitions-from-defense-innovation-unit-to-defense-digital-service.

111 *"I didn't even know who the defense secretary was":* Richard Jenkins, interview with authors, June 16, 2023.

112 *Iran's navy seized a pair of Saildrone vessels:* Andrew Jeong, "Iran Releases Saildrones Seized in Red Sea after U.S. Navy," *Washington Post*, September 2, 2022, https://www.washingtonpost.com/world/2022/09/02/iran-us-navy-drone-capture/.

114 *a "fleet in being":* Marc Santora, "How Ukraine, with No Warships, Is Thwarting Russia's Navy," *New York Times*, November 12, 2023, https://www.nytimes.com/2023/11/12/world/europe/ukraine-navy-admiral-black-sea.html.

115 *test its prototypes at Fort Hunter Liggett:* "Joby and the US Government Kickstart the Air Mobility Revolution," Joby Aviation, February 8, 2922, https://www.jobyaviation.com/blog/joby-us-government-kickstart-air-mobility-revolution/.

115 *"We took an old remote site":* JoeBen Bevirt, interview with authors, June 28, 2023.

116 *$131 million contract to provide eVTOL aircraft:* "Joby Delivers First eVTOL Aircraft to Edwards Air Force Base Ahead of Schedule," Joby Aviation, September 25, 2023, https://www.jobyaviation.com/news/joby-delivers-first-evtol-edwards/. To see how bureaucratized technology development by the primes has become when compared with historical benchmarks, including the development of the SR-71 and F-117 in months and years rather than decades, see Ben R. Rich and Leo Janos, *Skunk Works: A Personal Memoir of My Years at Lockheed* (Little, Brown, 1996).

116 *Algorithmic Warfare Cross-Functional Team:* Deputy Secretary of Defense Robert Work, "Establishment of an Algorithmic Warfare Cross-Functional Team (Project Maven)," April 26, 2017, https://www.govexec.com/media/gbc/docs/pdfs_edit/establishment_of_the_awcft_project_maven.pdf.

117 *"Maven is designed to be that pilot project":* Lieutenant General John "Jack" Shanahan (ret.), interview with authors, April 17, 2023.

118 *"a clarion call for progress in AI":* Brendan McCord, interview with authors, May 3, 2023.

119 *make sense of only 5 percent of this data:* "Gorgon Stare Wide-Area Mo-

tion Imagery (WAMI)," SNC, Inc., https://www.sncorp.com/capabilities/wide-area-motion-imagery/. See also: "Gorgon Stare," Wikipedia, https://en.wikipedia.org/wiki/Gorgon_Stare.

119 *able to track bad actors:* Lt. Gen. John N. T. "Jack" Shanahan, "Software-Defined Warfare: Architecting the DOD's Transition to the Digital Age," Center for Strategic & International Studies, September 7, 2022.

120 *"Google Is Helping the Pentagon Build AI for Drones":* Kate Conger and Dell Cameron, "Google Is Helping the Pentagon Build AI for Drones," Gizmodo, March 6, 2018, https://gizmodo.com/google-is-helping-the-pentagon-build-ai-for-drones-1823464533#:~:text=Google%20has%20partnered%20with%20the,they%20learned%20of%20Google's%20involvement.

120 *"Google should not be in the business of war":* For a comprehensive account of the Maven controversy, see Cade Metz, *Genius Makers: The Mavericks Who Brought AI to Google, Facebook, and the World* (Dutton: 2021).

120 *helping to defend the United States:* For a history of how protest movements shaped technology and Silicon Valley culture, see John Markoff, *What the Dormouse Said: How the Sixties Counterculture Shaped the Personal Computer Industry* (Viking Adult, 2005).

120 *"Why Silicon Valley Must Go to War":* Christopher Kirchhoff, "Why Silicon Valley Must Go to War," op-ed, *New York Times*, May 2, 2018, https://www.nytimes.com/2018/05/02/opinion/silicon-valley-pentagon.html. For a deeper exploration of technology and ethics, see Sheila Jasanoff, *The Ethics of Invention: Technology and the Human Future* (W. W. Norton, 2016), "Technologies of Humility: Citizen Participation in Governing Science," *Minerva* 41, no. 3, Special Issue: Reflections on the New Production of Knowledge (2003): 223–44, and "Democracy in an Unknowable World," 2022 Holberg Prize Lecture, June 2022, https://holbergprize.org/en/news/holberg-prize/2022-holberg-lecture-sheila-jasanoff. Of course, as one considers how to apply technology in warfare, it is essential to also be cognizant of the long and difficult history of misapplying technology in warfare. See John Dower, *Cultures of War: Pearl Harbor, Hiroshima, 9-11, Iraq* (W. W. Norton, 2010); Andrew Cockburn, *Kill Chain: The Rise of the High-Tech Assassins* (Henry Holt, 2015); and Sharon Weinberger, *The Imagineers of War: The Untold Story of DARPA, The Pentagon Agency That Changed the World* (Vintage Books, 2018).

121 *"There is a lot of misunderstanding":* Troy Wolverton, "Vint Cerf Defended Google's Project Maven," *Business Insider*, December 13, 2018, https://www.businessinsider.com/vint-cerf-defended-googles-project-maven-defense-pilot-program-2018-12.

122 *Defense Innovation Board devised a set of principles:* Defense Innovation

Board, "AI Principles: Recommendations of the Ethical Use of Artificial Intelligence by the Department of Defense," U.S. Department of Defense, October 31, 2019, https://media.defense.gov/2019/Oct/31/2002204458/-1/-1/0/DIB_AL_PRINCIPLES_PRIMARY_DOCUMENT.PDF.

124 *no service secretary likes to be embarrassed:* See Eric Lofgren, "Is it an embarrassment how the US Air Force treated SpaceX?," January 30, 2020, https://acquisitiontalk.com/2020/01/did-spacexs-experience-doing-business-with-the-us-air-force-embarrass-the-service/, and "A Conversation with General John Hyten, Vice Chairman of the Joint Chiefs of Staff," Center for Strategic and International Studies, January 17, 2020, https://www.csis.org/events/conversation-general-john-hyten-vice-chairman-joint-chiefs-staff.

125 *"Instead, it was a joke":* Trae Stephens, interview with authors, June 20, 2023.

125 *trying to win business:* In-Q-Tel, the intelligence community's venture capital fund, is the longest standing government-affiliated office to engage Silicon Valley. Its unique status as a government-funded venture capital program has been widely studied, as have other government entities with a venture mission. See Athar Osama, "Washington Goes to Sand Hill Road: The Federal Government's Forays into the Venture Capital Industry," research brief, Woodrow Wilson Center for Scholars, January 2008, https://www.wilsoncenter.org/article/washington-goes-to-sand-hill-road; three HBS case studies, Josh Lerner, Kevin Book, Felda Hardymon, and Ann Leamon, "In-Q-Tel," Harvard Business School Case 9-804-146, May 2003, and Kevin R. Kosar, "The Quasi Government: Hybrid Organizations with Both Government and Private Sector Legal Characteristics," Congressional Research Service, June 22, 2011, https://sgp.fas.org/crs/misc/RL30533.pdf.

126 *"tech's most controversial startup":* Joshua Brustein, Tech's Most Controversial Startup Now Makes Attack Drones," Bloomberg, October 3, 2019, https://www.bloomberg.com/news/features/2019-10-03/tech-s-most-controversial-startup-now-makes-attack-drones.

126 *set of combat drones, including one called Anvil:* See "Autonomous Kinetic Defeat: Anvil Seeks and Destroys Enemy Drones," Anduril, https://www.anduril.com/hardware/anvil/.

126 *stealth drone called Ghost:* See "Autonomous Flight: Future-Proof UAS Platform," Anduril, https://www.anduril.com/hardware/ghost-autonomous-suas/.

126 *AI software program called Lattice:* See "Anduril's Lattice: A Trusted Dual-Use—Commercial and Military—Platform for Public Safety, Security, and Defense," *Anduril Blog,* https://blog.anduril.com/andurils-lattice-a

-trusted-dual-use-commercial-and-military-platform-for-public-safety-770b83c082e9.

126 *arrived at the White House to meet with the President:* Toluser Olorunnipa, "Trump Meets with Tech Executives on Drones, Internet of Things," Bloomberg, June 21, 2017, https://www.bloomberg.com/news/articles/2017-06-22/trump-to-meet-with-tech-executives-on-drones-internet-of-things?leadSource=uverify%20wall.

CHAPTER SIX: WASHINGTON AND THE RISE OF THE MACHINES

133 *"AI could create infinitely stable dictatorships":* Noor Al-Sibai, "Open AI Chief Says Advanced AI May Already Be Conscious," *The Byte*, February 13, 2022, https://futurism.com/the-byte/openai-already-sentient.

133 *"Technology & National Security: Maintaining America's Edge":* Aspen Institute, January 31, 2019, https://www.amazon.com/Technology-National-Security-Maintaining-Americas/dp/0578427958.

135 *"And by 2025 you're done":* Danzig ran across the analogy in a *Mother Jones* magazine article. Kevin Drum, "Welcome, Robot Overlords. Please Don't Fire Us?," *Mother Jones*, May/June 2023, https://www.motherjones.com/media/2013/05/robots-artificial-intelligence-jobs-automation/.

136 *stationed Chinese police forces in Chinese embassies:* Megha Rajagopalan and William K. Rashbaum, "With F.B.I. Search, U.S. Escalates Global Fight Over Chinese Police Outposts: Beijing says the outposts aren't doing police work, but Chinese state media reports say they 'collect intelligence' and solve crimes far outside their jurisdiction," *New York Times*, January 12, 2023, https://www.nytimes.com/2023/01/12/world/europe/china-outpost-new-york.html.

136 *Xi was also amassing military power:* China's explosive growth in military capability has been well highlighted elsewhere. See for example U.S. Department of Defense, "Military and Security Developments Involving the People's Republic of China, 2022"; U.S. Department of Defense, "Annual Threat Assessment of the U.S. Intelligence Community 2022," Director of National Intelligence, February 2022; "2022 Report to Congress," U.S.-China Economic and Security Review Commission, November 2022.

137 *"The China Reckoning":* Kurt Campbell and Ely Rattner, "The China Reckoning: How Beijing Defied American Expectations," *Foreign Affairs*, February 13, 2018, https://www.foreignaffairs.com/articles/china/2018-02-13/china-reckoning.

137 *The U.S. had no plan at all:* Christian Brose, *The Kill Chain Defending America in the Future of High-Tech Warfare* (Hachette, 2020).

137 *China was in fact spending 88 percent:* "Innovation and National Security: Keeping Our Edge," Independent Task Force Report No. 77, Council on Foreign Relations, September 2019, pp. 36–37, https://www.cfr.org/report/keeping-our-edge/pdf/TFR_Innovation_Strategy.pdf.

138 *Algorithms that detect signals can defeat stealth:* The German sensor manufacturer Hensoldt contends that its passive radar detected and tracked two F-35s from a pony farm just outside the Berlin Airshow in 2018. See Sebastian Sprenger, "A German Radar Maker Says It Tracked the F-35 Stealth Fighter in 2018 from a Pony Farm," *Business Insider*, September 30, 2019, https://www.businessinsider.com/german-radar-maker-hensoldt-says-it-tracked-f35-in-2018-2019-9.

138 *Xi called it "civil-military fusion":* Emily Weinstein, "Don't Underestimate China's Military-Civil Fusion Efforts," *Foreign Policy*, February 5, 2021, https://foreignpolicy.com/2021/02/05/dont-underestimate-chinas-military-civil-fusion-efforts/.

139 *"An Even Flatter World":* Christopher Kirchhoff, "An Even Flatter World: How Technology Is Remaking the World Order," *The World Turned Upside Down: Maintaining American Leadership in a Dangerous Age*, Proceedings of the Aspen Strategy Group, 2017, pp. 93–99, https://www.aspeninstitute.org/wp-content/uploads/2017/11/FINAL-ASG-World-Upside-Down-FINAL.REV_.pdf. See also: Christopher Kirchhoff, "Reshaping National Security Institutions for Emerging Technology," *Reshaping National Security*, Proceedings of the Aspen Strategy Group, 2016, pp. 86–96.

143 *"Trump White House has been slow":* "Innovation and National Security: Keeping Our Edge," Independent Task Force Report No. 77, Council on Foreign Relations, September 2019, pp. 46–48, https://www.cfr.org/report/keeping-our-edge/pdf/TFR_Innovation_Strategy.pdf.

144 *"wrote my Ph.D. dissertation on national security commissions":* Christopher Kirchhoff, "Fixing the National Security State: Commissions and the Politics of Disaster and Reform," Ph.D. Dissertation, University of Cambridge, September 19, 2010, https://www.repository.cam.ac.uk/items/1a2e1953-6494-440c-bcd1-80659b1ec334.

144 *based on a study of all fifty-five national security commissions:* Jordan Tama, *Terrorism and National Security Reform: How Commissions Can Drive Change During Crises* (Cambridge University Press, 2011).

145 *Ylli went into the Trump White House:* "Feds at Work: Right-hand men to the Pentagon's top officials," *Partnership for Public Service*," July 11, 2016, https://medium.com/@RPublicService/feds-at-work-right-hand-men-to-the-pentagons-top-officials-ca99b6c93fbf.

146 *borrowed conference room for their first meeting:* "National Security Com-

mission on Artificial Intelligence Holds Inaugural Meeting," National Security Commission on Artificial Intelligence, March 12, 2019, https://www.nscai.gov/2019/03/12/national-security-commission-on-artificial-intelligence-holds-inaugural-meeting/.

146 *Chris spoke to the group:* Jordan Tama and Christopher Kirchhoff, "What Makes Commissions Successful—Lessons from the Political Science Literature on Past Commissions," memorandum to the National Security Commission on Artificial Intelligence, January 11, 2019, https://static1.squarespace.com/static/5a644faef14aa1dadc5db4f1/t/65866c0489358d3cadd85873/1703308293046/Tama-Kirchhoff+Memo+for+National+Security+Commission+on+AI.pdf.

146 *It hadn't yet proved to be a Terminator:* Sebastien Roblin, "Russia's Uran-9 Robot Tank Went to War in Syria (It Didn't Go Very Well)," *National Interest*, January 6, 2019, https://nationalinterest.org/blog/buzz/russias-uran-9-robot-tank-went-war-syria-it-didnt-go-very-well-40677.

149 *"China's Technology Transfer Strategy":* Michael Brown and Pavneet Singh, "China's Technology Transfer Strategy: How Chinese Investments in Emerging Technology Enable a Strategic Competitor to Access the Crown Jewels of U.S. Innovation," *Defense Innovation Unit Experimental*, January 2018, https://nationalsecurity.gmu.edu/wp-content/uploads/2020/02/DIUX-China-Tech-Transfer-Study-Selected-Readings.pdf.

150 *"China Bets on Sensitive U.S. Start-Ups":* Paul Mozur and Jane Perlez, "China Bets on Sensitive U.S. Start-Ups, Worrying the Pentagon," *New York Times*, April 7, 2017, https://www.nytimes.com/2017/04/07/business/china-defense-start-ups-pentagon-technology.html.

150 *Foreign Investment Risk Review Modernization Act:* "Summary of the Foreign Investment Risk Review Modernization Act of 2018," U.S. Department of the Treasury, https://home.treasury.gov/system/files/206/Summary-of-FIRRMA.pdf.

151 *prototyping two modular underwater vehicles:* "Defense Innovation Unit and PMS-408 Partner to Bring Advanced Mine Detection Capability to the Fleet Two Years Ahead of Schedule," Defense Innovation Unit, April 2022, https://www.diu.mil/latest/defense-innovation-unit-and-pms-408-partner-to-bring-advanced-mine-detection.

151 *infinitely more advanced in the way they used AI:* Stew Magnuson, "Navy Minesweepers Look to AI to Boost Speed, Reduce Risk, *National Defense*, February 9, 2022, https://www.nationaldefensemagazine.org/articles/2022/2/9/navy-minesweepers-look-to-ai-to-boost-speed-reduce-risk.

152 *implement a "full life cycle" approach:* Jared Dunnmon, interview with authors, April 18 and 23, 2023.

153 *"selecting projects that would have broader impacts":* Michael Brown, interview with authors, July 7, 2023.

154 *"to whom should DIU report?":* Ben FitzGerald, correspondence with authors, January 26, 2023.

155 *Brown continued to put points on the board:* Mark Sullivan, "Silicon Valley Wants to Power the U.S. War Machine: Amid rising tensions with China, a cadre of defense insiders and tech players want to remake the Pentagon in Silicon Valley's image," *Fast Company,* November 1, 2021.

158 *The interim report:* "Interim Report," National Security Commission on Artificial Intelligence, November 2019, https://www.nscai.gov/wp-content/uploads/2021/01/NSCAI-Interim-Report-for-Congress_201911.pdf.

158 *publicly pledging to work with the Department of Defense:* Microsoft CEO Satya Nadella was a forceful advocate on the front, saying publicly, "We made a principled decision that we're not going to withhold technology from institutions that we have elected in democracies to protect the freedoms we enjoy." See Charles Riley and Samuel Burke, "Microsoft CEO defends US military contract that some employees say crosses a line," *CNN Business,* February 25, 2019, https://www.cnn.com/2019/02/25/tech/augmented-reality-microsoft-us-military/index.html. Jeff Bezos similarly said, "If big tech companies are going to turn their back on the U.S. Department of Defense, this country is going to be in trouble. . . . This is a great country and it does need to be defended." See Heather Kelly, "Jeff Bezos: Amazon will keep working with the DoD," *CNN Business,* October 15, 2018, https://www.cnn.com/2018/10/15/tech/jeff-bezos-wired/index.html. See also: Margaret O'Mara, "Silicon Valley Can't Escape the Business of War: Many in the tech industry don't want to be part of the military-industrial complex. But defense work is already part of Silicon Valley's DNA," op-ed, *New York Times,* October 26, 2018, https://www.nytimes.com/2018/10/26/opinion/amazon-bezos-pentagon-hq2.html.

158 *"The fact that it happened when it did":* "NSCAI Conference—Lunch Keynote: AI, National Security and the Public-Private Partnership," National Security Commission on Artificial Intelligence, November 15, 2019, https://www.youtube.com/watch?v=3O]iUl1Tzj3c.

159 *executive order and national strategy:* Office of Science & Technology Policy, The White House, "Artificial Intelligence for the American People," 2019, https://trumpwhitehouse.archives.gov/ai/executive-order-ai/.

160 *high-tech fabs moved to Asia:* Chris Miller, *Chip War: The Fight for the World's Most Critical Technology* (Scribner, 2022).

163 *Chris, who had served on the White House Ebola Task Force:* Christopher Kirchhoff, "Ebola Should Have Immunized the United States to the Coronavirus:

What Washington Failed to Learn from the National Security Council's Ebola Report," *Foreign Affairs*, March 28, 2020, https://www.foreignaffairs.com/united-states/ebola-should-have-immunized-united-states-coronavirus.

165 *"attempted to discuss AI two years ago":* "Townhall on Artificial Intelligence," Munich Security Forum, February 2, 2020, https://securityconference.org/en/medialibrary/asset/townhall-on-artificial-intelligence-20200215-1600/.

168 *paper on restructuring the National Security Council:* "Looking Back to Go Forward: Strategic Mismanagement of Platform Technologies and the Race for the Future," German Marshall Fund, Alliance for Securing Democracy Papers for the Presidential Transition, July 22, 2020, https://securingdemocracy.gmfus.org/looking-back-to-go-forward-strategic-mismanagement-of-platform-technologies-and-the-race-for-the-future/.

169 *a thirty-four-page report:* Eric Schmidt et al., "Asymmetric Competition: A Strategy for China & Technology," October 2020, http://industrialpolicy.us/resources/SpecificIndustries/IT/final-memo-china-strategy-group-axios-1.pdf.

170 *Pentagon created a Chief Digital:* Chief Digital and Artificial Intelligence Office (CDAO), "Secretary of Defense Establishes Office of Strategic Capital," press release, U.S. Department of Defense, December 1, 2022.

170 *Office of Strategic Capital:* U.S. Department of Defense Office of Strategic Capital, https://www.cto.mil/osc/.

172 *leaked to the press a whistleblower complaint:* Jason Barnett, "DIU's Mike Brown Pushed 'Unethical' Contracting and Hiring, Former CFO Alleges," FedScoop, April 29, 2021, https://fedscoop.com/mike-brown-diu-ig-investiation-unethical-contracting-former-cfo-says/.

172 *leading Brown's nomination to collapse:* Joe Gould, "Biden's Nominee for Pentagon Weapons Chief Withdraws," *Defense News*, July 14, 2021, https://www.defensenews.com/congress/2021/07/14/bidens-nominee-for-top-dod-weapons-chief-withdraws/.

172 *IG fully exonerated Brown:* Courtney Albon, "Inspector General Clears Former DIU Chief of Ethics Allegations," *Defense News*, September 13, 2022, https://www.defensenews.com/pentagon/2022/09/13/inspector-general-clears-former-diu-chief-of-ethics-allegations//.

173 *praising the approach Brown took:* "Report of Investigation: Mr. Michael A. Brown Former Director Defense Innovation," DoD Inspector General, September 9, 2022, https://media.defense.gov/2023/Jan/05/2003140631/-1/-'20201102-067934-CASE-01.PDF.

174 *commission's final report, at 746 pages: Final Report, National Security*

Commission on Artificial Intelligence, March 2023, https://www.nscai.gov/wp-content/uploads/2021/03/Full-Report-Digital-1.pdf.

174 *Senator Schumer, minority leader Kevin McCarthy:* "Global Emerging Technology Summit," National Security Commission on Artificial Intelligence, July 13, 2021, https://www.nscai.gov/all-events/summit/.

176 *one analyst called "technological asphyxiation":* See Chris Miller, *Chip War: The Fight for the World's Most Critical Technology* (Scribner, 2022).

CHAPTER SEVEN: VENTURE CAPITAL GOES TO WAR

182 *"please come talk to me":* David Merrill, interview with authors, May 1, 2023.

183 *secured agreements to provide five hundred units:* "Elroy Air Unveils Its Chaparral, a First-of-Its-kind, Autonomous, Hybrid-Electric VTOL Cargo Aircraft," Elroy Air, January 26, 2022, https://elroyair.com/company/news/press-releases/chaparral-autonomous-vtol-unveil/.

187 *Raj and Philip recognized that technology:* Raj M. Shah, "Testimony of Mr. Raj M. Shah, Future of Defense Task Force, House Armed Services Committee U.S. House of Representatives," Hearing Titled: "Supercharging the Innovation Base," February 5, 2020, https://www.congress.gov/116/meeting/house/110475/witnesses/HMTG-116-AS00-Wstate-ShahR-20200205.pdf.

187 *U.S. aerospace and defense industry had consolidated:* Department of Defense, "State of Competition within the Defense Industrial Base," Office of the Under Secretary of Defense for Acquisition and Sustainment, February 2022, p. 25, https://media.defense.gov/2022/Feb/15/2002939087/-1/-1/1/STATE-OF-COMPETITION-WITHIN-THE-DEFENSE-INDUSTRIAL-BASE.PDF.

190 *closed its first fund in the fall of 2021:* "Shield Capital Closes $186 Million Inaugural Venture Capital Fund," Shield Capital, October 16, 2023, https://shieldcap.com/announcements/shield-capital-closes-186-million-inaugural-venture-capital-fund#:~:text=Shield%20Capital%20announced%20the%20final,of%20institutional%20and%20private%20investors.

191 *VCs pumped $33 billion:* Marina Temkin, "Sizing Up the Boom in Defense Tech," November 3, 2023, PitchBook, https://pitchbook.com/news/articles/defense-tech-boom-ukraine-china-Israel. See also: Krystal Hu, "VCs Invest $33b in Defense Tech in 2022," Reuters, June 16, 2023.

195 *55 percent were founded or cofounded by immigrants:* Peter Vandor, "Research: Why Immigrants Are More Likely to Become Entrepreneurs,"

Harvard Business Review, August 04, 2021, https://hbr.org/2021/08/research-why-immigrants-are-more-likely-to-become-entrepreneurs.

197 *More senior officials from the Pentagon helping startups:* Eric Lipton, "New Spin on a Revolving Door: Pentagon Officials Turned Venture Capitalists: Retired officers and departing defense officials are flocking to investment firms that are pushing the government to provide more money to defense-technology startups," *New York Times*, December 20, 2023, https://www.nytimes.com/2023/12/30/us/politics/pentagon-venture-capitalists.html?smid=nytcore-ios-share&referringSource=articleShare; Eric Lipton, "The Pentagon Road to Venture Capital: Here is a list of people who have jumped from the Pentagon and other government posts into jobs with venture capitalists that are backing defense technology startups," *New York Times*, December 20, 2023, https://www.nytimes.com/2023/12/30/us/politics/the-pentagon-road-to-venture-capital.html?action=click&module=RelatedLinks&pgtype=Article.

CHAPTER EIGHT: UKRAINE AND THE BATTLEFIELD OF THE FUTURE

200 *Capella satellites saw it happening in real time:* See capellaspace.com and https://www.capellaspace.com/press-releases/capella-space-awarded-commercial-radar-contract-by-national-reconnaissance-office/.

200 *"Putin kept saying, 'I'm not going to invade'":* Michael Brown, interview with authors, July 7, 2023.

200 *Pentagon released a Capella image to CNN:* "February 24, 2022 Russia-Ukraine news," CNN International, February 25, 2022, https://edition.cnn.com/europe/live-news/ukraine-russia-news-02-24-22-intl/index.html.

200 *"first unclassified, open-source satellite imagery":* Payam Banazadeh, interview with authors, January 20 and 25, 2023.

201 *"Welcome to hell":* Stephen Witt, "Weapons of Influence: A New Drone Has Changed the Nature of Warfare and Enabled Turkey's Rise," *New Yorker*, May 16, 2022, https://www.newyorker.com/magazine/2022/05/16/the-turkish-drone-that-changed-the-nature-of-warfare.

202 *82 percent of Iranian drones' components:* Natasha Bertrand, "Biden task force investigating how US tech ends up in Iranian attack drones used against Ukraine," CNN, December 21, 2022, https://www.cnn.com/2022/12/21/politics/iranian-drones-russia-biden-task-force-us-tech-ukraine/index.html.

202 *HawkEye 360:* Marina Temkin, PitchBook, October 26, 2022, data through October 13, 2022.

202 *Skydio:* Heather Somerville, "Ukraine Sounds Alarm on Chinese Drones, Opening Skies to U.S. Startups," *Wall Street Journal*, April 22, 2022, https://www.wsj.com/articles/ukraine-sounds-alarm-on-chinese-drones-opening-skies-to-u-s-startups-11650619800.

202 *BlueHalo:* "Ukraine will receive Titan counter-UAV systems from the USA," press release, Ukrainian Ministry of Defense, https://mil.in.ua/en/news/ukraine-will-receive-titan-counter-uav-systems-from-the-usa/.

202 *Palantir:* David Ignatius, "How the Algorithm Tipped the Balance in Ukraine," *Washington Post*, December 19, 2022, https://www.washingtonpost.com/opinions/2022/12/19/palantir-algorithm-data-ukraine-war/.

202 *Somewear Labs:* Mark Sullivan, "Silicon Valley Wants to Power the U.S. War Machine," *Fast Company*, November 1, 2021.

202 *"entire government on a Snowball":* Russ Mitchell, "How Amazon Put Ukraine's 'Government in a Box'—and Saved Its Economy from Russia," *Los Angeles Times*, December 15, 2022, https://www.latimes.com/business/story/2022-12-15/amazon-ukraine-war-cloud-data/.

202 *Microsoft's rapid response team:* Brad Smith, "Defending Ukraine: Early Lessons from the Cyber War," *Microsoft Blog*, June 22, 2022, https://blogs.microsoft.com/on-the-issues/2022/06/22/defending-ukraine-early-lessons-from-the-cyber-war/; Lauren Naniche, Jafer Ahmad, and Joe Wang, "Lessons Learned from Ukraine: Protecting Nations' Digital Freedom from External Aggression," Special Competitive Studies Project, December 16, 2022, https://scsp222.substack.com/p/lessons-learned-from-ukraine-protecting.

204 *There was no ready mechanism:* Jared Dunnmon, interview with authors, April 18 and 23, 2023.

204 *"Our team couldn't share the data":* Jared Dunnmon, interview with authors, April 18 and 23, 2023.

205 *"The amount of effort":* Jared Dunnmon, interview with authors, April 18 and 23, 2023.

207 *"Ukraine was learning what happens":* Special Competitive Studies Project, "Ukraine War Tech Lessons," June 28, 2023, https://scsp222.substack.com/p/ukraine-war-tech-lessons.

208 *"I promise I will never die":* Palmer Luckey, interview with authors, July 26, 2023.

209 *having its fire directed by drones:* "Game-Changers: Implications of the Russo-Ukraine War for the Future of Ground Warfare," Atlantic Council, April 2023, https://www.atlanticcouncil.org/wp-content/uploads/2023/04/Game-Changers-or-Little-Change-Lessons-for-Land-War-in-Ukraine-.pdf. See also: Special Competitive Studies Project, "Ukraine War Tech

Lessons," June 28, 2023, https://scsp222.substack.com/p/ukraine-war-tech-lessons.

210 *Eric Schmidt marveled at the small kamikaze drones:* Eric Schmidt, "Trip Report from Ukraine," Special Competitive Studies Project, September 2022, https://scsp222.substack.com/p/the-first-networked-war-eric-schmidts.

210 *"nearly impossible to shoot down":* Eric Schmidt, op-ed, "The Future of War Has Come in Ukraine: Drone Swarms," *Wall Street Journal,* July 7, 2023, https://www.wsj.com/articles/the-future-of-war-has-come-in-ukraine-drone-swarms-kamikaze-kyiv-31dd19d7.

211 *Ukraine was losing five thousand drones a month:* Jack Watling and Nick Reynolds, "Meatgrinder: Russian Tactics in the Second Year of Its Invasion of Ukraine," Royal United Services Institute for Defense and Security Studies, May 19, 2023, https://static.rusi.org/403-SR-Russian-Tactics-web-final.pdf.

211 *Tobol works by blending:* Alex Horton, "Russia Tests Secretive Weapon to Target Spacex's Starlink in Ukraine," *Washington Post,* April 18, 2023, https://www.washingtonpost.com/national-security/2023/04/18/discord-leaks-starlink-ukraine/.

212 *"the war answers a central question":* Eric Schmidt, "Trip Report from Ukraine," Special Competitive Studies Project, September 2022, https://scsp222.substack.com/p/the-first-networked-war-eric-schmidts.

213 *"If you go into battle with old school technology":* Eric Lipton, "Start-Ups Bring Silicon Valley Ethos to a Lumbering Military-Industrial Complex," *New York Times,* May 21, 2023, https://www.nytimes.com/2023/05/21/us/politics/start-ups-weapons-pentagon-procurement.html.

213 *there was strong continuity with the past:* The analyst Stephen Biddle has made a fascinating and important comparison between the historical continuities of classic land warfare attrition in the twentieth century and what's happening in Ukraine. Stephen Biddle, "Back in the Trenches: Why New Technology Hasn't Revolutionized Warfare in Ukraine," *Foreign Affairs,* September/October 2023, https://www.foreignaffairs.com/ukraine/back-trenches-technology-warfare.

213 *"We're not fighting in Ukraine with Silicon Valley right now":* Valerie Insinna, "LaPlante Pokes Silicon Valley 'Tech Bros,' Calls for Increased Munitions Production for Ukraine," *Breaking Defense,* November 8, 2022. Full remarks by LaPlante available at *Acquisition Talk* podcast, "Getting Weapons into Production with USD A&S Bill LaPlante," November 10, 2022, https://acquisitiontalk.com/2022/11/podcast-getting-weapons-into-production-with-usd-as-bill-laplante/.

214 *misses the wider view:* Former U.S. CTO Nick Siani penned a forceful

rebuttal to LaPlante, stating: "Commercial technology matters in the current conflict. More so than in any recent combat operation.... I'd humbly suggest to Dr. LaPlante that if commercial technology isn't scaling fast enough inside the DoD, it is precisely because the DoD isn't focused on scaling commercial technology. And that falls squarely in his inbox as DoD's chief acquisition executive." Nick Siani, "Forging the Defense Industrial Base for the Digital Age," op-ed, *Defense Scoop*, December 1, 2022, https://defensescoop.com/2022/12/01/forging-the-defense-industrial-base-for-the-digital-age/.

214 *miss the beguiling hybridity and asymmetry:* Analysis of Ukraine and of the history of Pentagon innovation, as well as several passages of text in Chapter 8 and 9, are drawn from Christopher Kirchhoff, "A Requiem for Defense Innovation?: Ukraine, the Pentagon's Innovator's Dilemma, and Why the United States Risks Strategic Surprise," in *Defense Budgeting for a Safer World: The Experts Speak*, edited by Michael J. Boskin, John N. Rader, and Kiran Sridhar (Hoover Institution Press, Sanford, CA, 2023), pp. 219–48.

214 *"one of the most significant lessons emerging":* Christopher Kirchhoff, "A Requiem for Defense Innovation?: Ukraine, the Pentagon's Innovator's Dilemma, and Why the United States Risks Strategic Surprise," in *Defense Budgeting for a Safer World: The Experts Speak*, ed. Michael J. Boskin, John N. Rader, and Kiran Sridhar (Stanford, CA: Hoover Institution Press, 2023), pp. 219–48, https://static1.squarespace.com/static/5a644faef14aa1dadc5db4f1/t/65788b081dd2036095820802/1702398730938/Requiem_for_Defense_Innovation.pdf.

215 *$70 billion in purchases to date:* "Department of Defense OTA spent, 2016–2023," data from GovWinIQ, which amalgamates federal procurement data, current as of December 2023, https://iq.govwin.com/neo/home. See also: Jon Harper, "2021 Brought Another Banner Year for OTAs," Special Report, *National Defense*, February 3, 2021, https://www.nationaldefensemagazine.org/articles/2022/2/3/2021-brought-another-banner-year-for-otas.

216 *Marine Corps retiring tanks:* See 38th Commandant of the Marine Corps, "Commandant's Planning Guidance," July 16, 2019; US Department of the Navy, "Force Design 2030," US Marine Corps, March 2020.

216 *reported unit cost of $692 million:* W. J. Hennigan, "Exclusive: The Making of the US Military's New Stealth Bomber," *Time*, December 3, 2022, https://time.com/6238168/b-21-raider-bomber-us-military-exclusive/.

216 *their cost compared with other approaches:* The high unit cost of the B-21 led the *Duffel Blog*, a satirical publication focusing on the military, to publish an article titled "B-21 Nukes DoD Budget." Its key faux quote came in

the third graph. "When we talk about low observability, it is incredibly low observability," said Kathy Warden, chief executive of Northrop Grumman. "You'll hear it, but you really won't see it eat into the defense budget until it's too late." "B-21 Nukes DoD Budget," *Duffel Blog*, December 9, 2022, https://www.duffelblog.com/p/pentagon-debuts-new-stealth-budget.

217 *"China is close to this":* Chris Buckley, "China Draws Lessons from Russia's Losses in Ukraine, and Its Gains: With an eye on a possible conflict over Taiwan, analysts have scrutinized the war for insights ranging from the importance of supply lines to the power of nuclear threats," *New York Times*, April 1, 2023, https://www.nytimes.com/2023/04/01/world/asia/china-russia-ukraine-war.html.

217 *The war's opening moves:* For a primer on Taiwan's economic and security vulnerabilities, see Council on Foreign Relations, "U.S.-Taiwan Relations in a New Era: Responding to a More Assertive China," Independent Task Force Report No. 81, June 2023, https://live-tfr-cdn.cfr.org/sites/default/files/2023-06/TFR81_U.S.-TaiwanRelationsNewEra_Single Pages_2023-06-05_Online.pdf.

218 *turn itself into a "porcupine":* Meeting with former Taiwanese National Security Advisor Linwu Guo and former member of Parliament Jason Hsu, Residence of Taipei's Mayor, December 31, 2023, Taipei, Taiwan.

CHAPTER NINE: FROM STEEL TO SILICON

221 *"I have some idea how hard this is":* "Memorial Service for Former Defense Secretary Ashton Carter," C-SPAN, January 12, 2023, https://www.c-span.org/video/?525318-1/memorial-service-defense-secretary-ashton-carter.

221 *"Over the course of four decades":* Two of Carter's former staffers as well as Eric Schmidt wrote eloquent tributes in the days after his death that capture well the force and depth of his personality. See Matt Spence, "Ash Carter's Lasting Legacy: The Former Defense Secretary Leaves Behind a Much Stronger Pentagon-Silicon Valley relationship," Defense One, October 26, 2022, https://www.defenseone.com/ideas/2022/10/ash-carters-lasting-legacy/378954/; Jonathan Reiber, "The Lessons Ash Carter Taught Me," blog post, *Attack IQ*, October 31, 2022, https://www.attackiq.com/2022/10/31/the-lessons-ash-carter-taught-me/; and Eric Schmidt, "Remembering Ash Carter: The Innovative Secretary of Defense Who Changed the Pentagon, Silicon Valley, and the Trajectory of Our Nation," Special Competitive Studies Project, January 26, 2023, https://scsp222.substack.com/p/remembering-ash-carter.

222 *"bear the imprint of Ash Carter":* Remarks by President Biden at Ash Carter Memorial, The White House, January 12, 2023, https://www.whitehouse.gov/briefing-room/speeches-remarks/2023/01/12/remarks-by-president-biden-at-a-memorial-service-for-secretary-ash-carter/?stream=top.

222 *"A Requiem for Defense Innovation?":* Christopher Kirchhoff, "A Requiem for Defense Innovation?: Ukraine, the Pentagon's Innovator's Dilemma, and Why the United States Risks Strategic Surprise," in *Defense Budgeting for a Safer World: The Experts Speak*, ed. Michael J. Boskin, John N. Rader, and Kiran Sridhar (Stanford, CA: Hoover Institution Press, 2023), pp. 219–248, https://static1.squarespace.com/static/5a644faef14aa1dadc5db4f1/t/65788b081dd2036095820802/1702398730938/Requiem_for_Defense_Innovation.pdf.

223 *out of ten contracts that Shyu announced:* See "Critical Technologies," Office of the DoD CTO; "Technology Vision for an Era of Competition," memorandum by Heidi Chu, February 1, 2022; and "DoD Announces First Set of Projects to Receive Funding from the Pilot Program to Accelerate the Procurement and Fielding of Innovative Technologies (APFIT)," DoD Press Release, July 19, 2022.

223 *"For where your treasure is":* Mac Thornberry, "Can We Buy Like We Talk," in *Defense Budgeting for a Safer World: The Experts Speak*, edited by Michael J. Boskin, John N. Rader, and Kiran Sridhar (Hoover Institution Press, Stanford, CA, 2023), pp. 471–86. Note that Thornberry dropped from the final published version of his paper the *Jerry Maguire* quote that he had included in the working draft presented at Stanford.

223 *nuclear-capable hypersonic weapon:* Sara Sorcher and Karoun Demirjian, "Top U.S. General Calls China's Hypersonic Weapon Test Very Close to a 'Sputnik Moment,'" *Washington Post*, October 27, 2021, https://www.washingtonpost.com/nation/2021/10/27/mark-milley-china-hypersonic-weapon-sputnik/.

224 *"the ship is slowly sinking":* Caleb Laron, "'Sinking Slowly': Admiral Warns Deterrence Weakening Against China," *National Interest*, November 7, 2022, https://nationalinterest.org/blog/buzz/'sinking-slowly'-admiral-warns-deterrence-weakening-against-china-205759.

224 *The balloon itself:* Nancy Youssel, "Chinese Balloon Used American Tech to Spy on Americans," *Wall Street Journal*, July 29, 2023, https://www.wsj.com/articles/chinese-balloon-used-american-tech-to-spy-on-americans-2e3f5039. See also: Chris Buckley, "China's Top Airship Scientist Promoted Program to Watch the World from Above," *New York Times*, February 13, 2023, https://www.nytimes.com/2023/02/13/world/asia/china-spy-balloon.html.

224 *Elon Musk now had more control:* Adam Satariano et al., "Elon Musk's Unmatched Power in the Stars: The tech billionaire has become the dominant power in satellite internet technology. The ways he is wielding that influence are raising global alarms," *New York Times,* June 28, 2023, https://www.nytimes.com/interactive/2023/07/28/business/starlink.html.

224 *Refused to extend Starlink's capabilities:* Victoria Kim, "Elon Musk Acknowledges Withholding Satellite Service to Thwart Ukrainian Attack: The Starlink satellite internet service, which is operated by Mr. Musk's rocket company SpaceX, has been a digital lifeline for soldiers and civilians in Ukraine," *New York Times,* September 8, 2023, https://www.nytimes.com/2023/09/08/world/europe/elon-musk-starlink-ukraine.html.

225 *Would Elon decide to sell his services to Taiwan:* Cade Metz, Adam Satariano, and Chang Che, "How Elon Musk Became a Geopolitical Chaos Agent," *New York Times,* October 26, 2022, https://www.nytimes.com/2022/10/26/technology/elon-musk-geopolitics-china-ukraine.html. See also Walter Isaacson, *Elon Musk* (Simon & Schuster, 2023).

225 *hair-raising new weapons:* William J. Broad and Ainara Tiefenthäler, "Putin Flaunted Five Powerful Weapons. Are They a Threat?," *New York Times,* March 2, 2018, https://www.nytimes.com/2018/03/02/world/europe/putin-weapons-video-analysis.html.

225 *space-based neutron bomb:* David E. Sanger, "U.S. Warns Allies Russia Could Put a Nuclear Weapon in Orbit This Year," *New York Times,* February 21, 2024, https://www.nytimes.com/2024/02/21/world/europe/us-russia-nuclear-weapon-space.html.

225 *Then there was quantum technology:* "Science & Tech Spotlight: Quantum Technologies," U.S. Government Accountability Office, May 28, 2020, https://www.gao.gov/products/gao-20-527sp.

225 *Lloyd Austin . . . named Doug Beck:* See "Secretary of Defense Lloyd J. Austin III Announces New Director of the Defense Innovation Unit," press release, Department of Defense, April 4, 2023, https://www.defense.gov/News/Releases/Release/Article/3351281/secretary-of-defense-lloyd-j-austin-iii-announces-new-director-of-the-defense-i/; Deputy Secretary of Defense, "Memorandum for Senior Pentagon Leadership," April 4, 2023, https://media.defense.gov/2023/Apr/04/2003192904/-1/-1/1/REALIGNMENT-AND-MANAGEMENT-OF-THE-DEFENSE-INNOVATION-UNIT.PDF.

226 *more than fifty separate organizations:* "Innovation Organizations," U.S. Department of Defense, https://www.ctoinnovation.mil/innovation-organizations.

228 *two thousand supersonic drones:* Secretary of the Air Force Frank Kendall

Address at the Ash Carter Exchange, June 30, 2023, https://www.buzzsprout.com/2212972/13138615-the-honorable-frank-kendall.

229 *the drones would carry out:* Eric Lipton, "A.I. Brings the Robot Wingman to Aerial Combat," *New York Times*, August 27, 2023, https://www.nytimes.com/2023/08/27/us/politics/ai-air-force.html.

229 *"In the next fifteen years":* Remarks by Chairman of the Joint Chiefs General Mark A. Milley, the Ash Carter Exchange, June 30, 2023, https://www.buzzsprout.com/2212972/13138567-general-mark-a-milley.

230 *"communicate views . . . directly to the Secretary":* United States Congress, Sec. 913, "Codification of The Defense Innovation Unit," 2024 National Defense Authorization Act, H.R. 2670, pp. 230–233, passed December 14, 2023, https://www.congress.gov/118/bills/hr2670/BILLS-118hr2670enr.pdf.

232 *Ukrainian drone operators:* Carlotta Gall, "Both Sides Pay a Bloody Price for Coveted Ukrainian City," *New York Times*, October 30, 2023, https://www.nytimes.com/2023/10/30/world/europe/ukraine-avdiivka.html.

234 *meetings in Warsaw:* "DIU Hosts Ukraine and the Future of Unmanned Aerial Systems Forum in Warsaw," Defense Innovation Unit, October 30, 2023, https://www.diu.mil/latest/diu-hosts-ukraine-and-the-future-of-unmanned-aerial-systems-forum-in-warsaw; "Brave 1 Linkedin Post," https://www.linkedin.com/posts/brave1ukraine_brave1-defensetech-ugcPost-7125146625102032896-jr7x?utm_source=share&utm_medium=member_desktop.

238 *"A typhoon of steel":* Chris Miller, *Chip War: The Fight for the World's Most Critical Technology* (Scribner, 2022), p. 3.

238 *Google collaboration suites:* Colin Demarest and Davis Winkie, "US Army Rolls Out Google Collaboration Suite to 180,000-Plus Personnel," C4ISNET, https://www.c4isrnet.com/battlefield-tech/it-networks/2023/01/13/us-army-rolls-out-google-collaboration-suite-to-180000-plus-personnel/.

239 *The Department also expanded:* Federal Register, "Defense Federal Acquisition Regulation Supplement: Modification of Authority of the Department of Defense to Carry Out Certain Prototype Projects," DFARS Case 2023-D006, May 25, 2023, https://www.federalregister.gov/documents/2023/05/25/2023-11140/defense-federal-acquisition-regulation-supplement-modification-of-authority-of-the-department-of.

239 *generative AI revolution:* For a historically informed characterization of this important moment, see Alex Karp, "Our Oppenheimer Moment: The Creation of A.I. Weapons," *New York Times*, July 20, 2023, https://www

.nytimes.com/2023/07/25/opinion/karp-palantir-artificial-intelligence.html.

239 *"Task Force Lima":* "DOD Announces Establishment of Generative AI Task Force," U.S. Department of Defense, August 10, 2023, https://www.defense.gov/News/Releases/Release/Article/3489803/dod-announces-establishment-of-generative-ai-task-force/; "Welcome to Task Force Lima," U.S. Department of Defense, https://www.dds.mil/taskforcelima.

239 *establishing AI battle labs:* "DOD to Establish AI Battle Labs in EUCOM, INDOPACOM," U.S. Department of Defense, September 27, 2023, https://www.defense.gov/News/Releases/Release/Article/3540283/dod-to-establish-ai-battle-labs-in-eucom-indopacom/.

239 *"Replicator Initiative":* "Deputy Secretary of Defense Kathleen Hicks Keynote Address: 'The Urgency to Innovate' (As Delivered)," U.S. Department of Defense, August 28, 2923, https://www.defense.gov/News/Speeches/Speech/Article/3507156/deputy-secretary-of-defense-kathleen-hicks-keynote-address-the-urgency-to-innov/.

240 *Ukraine was shaping how those in the E-ring:* Eric Lipton, "Pentagon Vows to Move Quickly to Buy More Drones, Citing China Threat," *New York Times*, August 28, 2023, https://www.nytimes.com/2023/08/28/us/politics/pentagon-drones-china.html.

240 *Austin visited DIU:* "SecDef Visits Defense Innovation Unit X and Hosts AUKUS Ministers," Secretary of Defense photo stream, December 1, 2023, https://www.flickr.com/photos/secdef/albums/72177720313099274/; "Readout of Deputy Secretary of Defense Kathleen Hicks' Visit to Silicon Valley, California," press release, December 12, 2023, https://www.defense.gov/News/Releases/Release/Article/3615717/readout-of-deputy-secretary-of-defense-kathleen-hicks-visit-to-silicon-valley-c/.

240 *AUKUS at DIU:* Lolita Baldor, "Pentagon Forges New High-Tech Agreement with Australia, United Kingdom, Aimed at Countering China, Associated Press, December 1, 2023, https://www.whec.com/national-world/pentagon-forges-new-high-tech-agreement-with-australia-united-kingdom-aimed-at-countering-china/; "Readout of Secretary of Defense Lloyd J. Austin III Meeting with Australian Deputy Prime Minister and Minister for Defense Richard Marles," press release, Department of Defense, December 1, 2023, https://www.defense.gov/News/Releases/Release/Article/3604612/readout-of-secretary-of-defense-lloyd-j-austin-iii-meeting-with-australian-depu/.

240 *left some primes grumbling:* Matt Berg, "'Disorganized and Confusing': Lawmakers, Industry Rip Pentagon Plans for Drones: Critics Say They

Want More Specifics on DOD's Replicator Program—Including How They Plan to Pay for It," *Politico*, December 17, 2023, https://www.politico.com/news/2023/12/17/pentagon-drones-replicator-program-funding-00132092.

240 *posted on LinkedIn:* Christian Brose, LinkedIn post, December 18, 2023, https://www.linkedin.com/posts/christian-brose-50b026ab_disorganized-and-confusing-lawmakers-activity-7142570681048735744-kXfw/.

240 *six thousand advanced kamikaze:* Julian Barnes and Christoph Koettl, "A Drone Factory That Iran Is Helping Russia Build Could Be Operational Next Year, the U.S. Says," *New York Times*, June 9, 2023, https://www.nytimes.com/2023/06/09/world/europe/iran-russia-drone-factory.html.

240 *Russian strategists saw:* Dalton Bennett and Mary Ilyushina, "Inside the Russian Effort to Build 6,000 Attack Drones with Iran's Help," *Washington Post*, August 17, 2023, https://www.washingtonpost.com/investigations/2023/08/17/russia-iran-drone-shahed-alabuga/.

241 *Fourteen hundred fighters:* Aric Toler, "How Hamas Attacked Israel's Communications Towers," *New York Times*, October 10, 2023, https://www.nytimes.com/2023/10/10/world/middleeast/hamas-israel-attack-gaza.html?smid=url-share.

241 *injured over twenty:* Courtney Kube and Mosheh Gains, "Drone Attacks on American Bases Injured Two Dozen U.S. Military Personnel," NBC News, October 24, 2023, https://www.nbcnews.com/politics/national-security/drone-attacks-american-bases-injured-two-dozen-us-military-personnel-rcna121961.

241 *executed multiple airstrikes:* Eric Schmitt and Helene Cooper, "U.S. Strikes Iran-Linked Facility in Syria in Round of Retaliation," *New York Times*, November 8, 2023, https://www.nytimes.com/2023/11/08/us/politics/us-iran-airstrikes.html?smid=url-share; Eric Schmitt, "U.S. Carries Out Another Round of Airstrikes on Targets Tied to Iran," *New York Times*, November 12, 2023, https://www.nytimes.com/2023/11/12/us/politics/us-airstrikes-syria.html.

241 *over one hundred by the end of 2023:* Meghan Myers, "US Troops in Iraq and Syria Have Faced Over 100 Attacks since October," *Military Times*, December 21, 2023, https://www.militarytimes.com/news/your-military/2023/12/21/us-troops-in-iraq-and-syria-have-faced-over-100-attacks-since-october/#.

241 *$2 million missiles:* Helene Cooper, "U.S. Navy Destroyer Shoots Down Three Drones in Red Sea: Pentagon says a Pentagon official said the U.S.S. Carney shot down the drones as several commercial ships nearby came

under fire on Sunday, in attacks that U.S. Central Command said came from Iran-backed Yemeni Houthis," *New York Times*, December 3, 2023, https://www.nytimes.com/2023/12/03/world/middleeast/navy-red-sea-attack-pentagon.html; Laura Seligman and Matt Berg, "A $2M Missile vs. a $2,000 Drone: Pentagon Worried over Cost of Houthi Attacks," *Politico*, December 19, 2023, https://www.politico.com/news/2023/12/19/missile-drone-pentagon-houthi-attacks-iran-00132480; Benoir Faucon, Doc Lieber, and Gordon Luboud, "Iranian Spy Ship Helps Houthis Direct Attacks on Red Sea Vessels: Assistance raises pressure on Israel and the U.S. to take action against the Yemen-based rebels," *Wall Street Journal*, December 22, 2023, https://www.wsj.com/world/middle-east/iranian-spy-ship-helps-houthis-direct-attacks-on-red-sea-vessels-d6f7fd40.

241 *Oil prices rose overnight:* Shariq Khan, "Oil Rises 1% as Red Sea Shipping Concerns Unnerve Traders," Reuters, December 19, 2023, https://www.reuters.com/markets/commodities/oil-prices-extend-gains-red-sea-attacks-disrupt-supply-chains-2023-12-19/.

241 *18,000 unmanned Saildrones:* Ben Watson, "Mapped: America's Collective Defense Agreements," Defense One, February 3, 2017, https://www.defenseone.com/ideas/2017/02/mapped-americas-collective-defense-agreements/135114/.

242 *Pentagon will not win a future war:* See Eric Schmidt, "Innovation Power: Why Technology Will Define the Future of Geopolitics," *Foreign Affairs*, March April 2023, https://www.foreignaffairs.com/united-states/eric-schmidt-innovation-power-technology-geopolitics.

244 *2024 New Year's address:* "China's Xi Says 'Reunification' with Taiwan Is Inevitable," Reuters, January 1, 2024, https://www.reuters.com/world/asia-pacific/china-calls-taiwan-president-frontrunner-destroyer-peace-2023-12-31/.

244 *purged senior military leadership:* Chris Buckley, "China Appoints Naval Commander as Defense Minister: The promotion of Adm. Dong Jun may calm uncertainty after the unexplained disappearance of the previous minister, Gen. Li Shangfu," *New York Times*, December 29, 2023, https://www.nytimes.com/2023/12/29/world/asia/china-defense-minister.html.

244 *death spiral in China's economy:* Evan Osnos, "China's Age of Malaise: Party officials are vanishing, young workers are 'lying flat,' and entrepreneurs are fleeing the country. What does China's inner turmoil mean for the world?," *New Yorker*, October 23, 2023, https://www.newyorker.com/magazine/2023/10/30/chinas-age-of-malaise.

245 *Commission on Planning:* See "About Us," Commission on Planning, Programming, Budgeting, and Execution Reform, https://ppbereform.senate

.gov. For a historical overview of defense budgeting since the Second World War, see Mark B. Wilson, "U.S. Defense Budget Reform: Historical Perspectives (1940s–2020s), in *Defense Budgeting for a Safer World: The Experts Speak*, ed. Michael J. Boskin, John N. Rader, and Kiran Sridhar (Stanford, CA: Hoover Institution Press, 2023), pp. 393–428.

246 *three thousand line items:* See Michael Brown, "Chris Buckley, of Defense Budgeting: The Unrecognized National Security Threat," in *Defense Budgeting for a Safer World: The Experts Speak*, ed. Michael J. Boskin, John N. Rader, and Kiran Sridhar (Stanford, CA: Hoover Institution Press, 2023), pp. 249–64.

246 *The literature on this point:* Harvey M. Sapolsky, Eugene Gholz, and Caitlin Talmadge, *US Defense Politics: The Origins of Security Policy*, 4th edition (Routledge, December 2020). See also: Michael C. Horowitz, *The Diffusion of Military Power: Causes and Consequences for International Politics* (Princeton University Press, 2010); Steven Rosen, *Winning the Next War: Innovation and the Modern Military* (Cornell University Press, 1994).

246 *"remotely piloted vehicles":* For a fascinating exploration of the tensions between the culture of military services and the advance of technology that threatens fundamental identities, see Jacquelyn Schneider, "Investing in Emerging Technology: Lessons from Unmanned Systems," in *Defense Budgeting for a Safer World: The Experts Speak*, ed. Michael J. Boskin, John N. Rader, and Kiran Sridhar (Stanford, CA: Hoover Institution Press, 2023), pp. 185–200.

PHOTO CREDITS

1. Courtesy of the authors
2. The White House
3. Win McNamee/Getty Images
4. Department of Defense
5. Department of Defense
6. Capella Space
7. Shield AI
8. Courtesy of Mark Jacobsen
9. Drone Shield
10. Joby Aviation
11. Department of Defense
12. Saildrone
13. *San Francisco Chronicle*/Hearst Newspapers via Getty
14. Courtesy of *The New York Times*
15. The White House
16. Department of Defense
17. Hoover Institution
18. Pew Research Center
19. Lauren Dailey
20. Courtesy of the authors
21. Courtesy of the authors
22. Office of the President, Ukraine
23. Courtesy of the authors

INDEX

Afghanistan, 45, 51, 81, 105, 129, 153, 190
   AI software used in, 119
   Kabul evacuation and Slapshot app, 68–69
AFWERX technology accelerator, 102, 132
AI (artificial intelligence), ix, 36, 99, 195
   Albright and, 142–43
   Anduril software, 126–27, 209
   Aspen Security Group and, 139–40, 163
   C3.ai software, 100
   ChatGPT, 103, 239
   China and, 133, 138, 141–42, 148, 162–68
   conflict escalation risk, 146–47
   Datahub AI system, 80, 81, 86, 98
   de-mining vehicles, 151–52
   DIU and, x, 100, 119, 150–52, 203, 239
   DoD and, 5, 100, 116–22, 133, 148, 152, 212, 239
   Evolv Technology and, 117–18
   exponential progress and, 138
   global cooperation and, 166
   Google DeepMind and, 140
   JAIC and, 121–22, 132, 158, 212
   Munich Security Conference, 162–68
   national security and, 138–40, 143, 146–48, 152
   natural language processing, 181
   Nexla software "pipes," 181
   NSCAI and, ix, xi, 143–48, 155–59, 162–68
   NSC and, 130, 140
   Palantir data analytics, 101, 123, 202
   privacy and, 165–66
   Project Maven and, 100, 116–22, 212
   Russian tanks and, 146
   Trump administration and, 143, 159
   Ukraine War and, 202, 206–7, 209, 210, 212, 213
   U.S. policy and, 158–59
   war at sea and, 114
   wide-area motion imagery/Gorgon Stare, 119
   See also drones; JAIC; NSCAI
Albedo, 190
Albright, Madeleine, ix, 133, 134, 142, 145–46, 174–75, 220
Alibaba, 137
Allen, John, 167
Altman, Sam, 103, 174
Amazon, 5, 144, 158
   Project Maven and, 100, 116, 132
   Snowball drive, 202
Andreessen, Marc, 103

Andreessen Horowitz, 103, 108
Anduril, 101, 109, 123, 124–28, 132, 180, 191, 202, 240
   AI software program, 126–27, 209
   border sensors and, 126, 209
   DoD acquisition methods and, 124
   drones, 126, 132, 202, 209, 211, 216
   Ghost drone, 209
   Ukraine War and, 208–12, 217
Apple, ix, 5, 8, 21, 118, 179, 203
Ardern, Jacinda, 174
Armenia-Azerbaijan, 214
Army Futures Command, 102
Aspen Strategy Group, 133, 138
   Kirchhoff paper, "An Even Flatter World" and, 139–41
   Munich meeting on AI, 163
   U.S. technology strategy and, 133–35, 139
AUKUS (Australia, UK, U.S. coalition), 239, 240, 245
Austin, Lloyd, 223, 225–27, 230, 240
autonomous craft (non-aerial), x, 99, 182
   ocean drones, 3, 110–14
   Saildrone, 110–13, 131, 241
   UUVs (demining vehicles), 151–52
   See also drones

Bajraktari, Ylber, 145
Bajraktari, Ylli, ix, 145–46, 219, 220, 238
   as NSCAI director, 145–46, 157–59, 163, 168
ballistic missile defenses, 77
   "Brilliant Pebbles," 78
   Datahub AI system, 80, 81, 86, 98
   "left-of-launch" solution, 78, 79, 91
   Nike air defense system, 77, 79
   Strategic Defense Initiative (Star Wars), 77–78
Banazadeh, Payam, ix, 82, 83, 84, 151
   Butow and, 82, 84, 85–86
   Capella Space and, 81, 82, 85, 199
   DoD funding for, 87–88, 96–97, 199

   Lunar Flashlight project, 83–84
   vision for small satellite SAR, 83
Beachkofski, Brian, 70
Beacon AI, 239
Beall, Ryan, 104–10
   app to find drone operators, 106, 131
   drone startup of, 109
Beck, Doug, ix, 18, 21, 134, 179, 220, 225–26
   Ash Carter Exchange meeting, 228
   DIU 3.0 and, 225–30
   Warsaw DIU-led meeting, 234–36
Bevirt, JoeBen, ix, 114–16
Biden, Joe, 141, 200, 229–30
   China threat and, 239
   death of Ash Carter and, 219–22
   Kirchhoff and, 168–69
   Ukraine War funding and, 203, 205
   U.S. investment in China and, 245
   weaponized IG and, 172–73
Bilden, Philip, ix, 179, 180, 185–89, 191
bin Laden, Osama, 95
Bio, Ernie, 44, 243
Blank, Steve, 54, 84–85, 179
BlueHalo, 202
Blue Origin, 79
Boeing, 80, 103, 123
Bolton, John, 142
Brin, Sergey, 49, 162, 186
Britain's Controller's Cabin, World War II, 46–47, 49–50
Brooks, Vincent, 89–92, 93, 98
Brose, Christian, v, 64, 65, 240
Brown, Charles, 230
Brown, Mike, ix–x, 130, 148–50, 227
   advisors for, 172
   "China's Technology Transfer Strategy," 149, 170
   DIU directorship, ix–x, 130, 148–55, 171–73, 223
   Mattis and, 152–53
   Shield Capital and, 173, 190
   Tech Track 2 and, 178
   Ukraine War and, 200

INDEX

Brumley, David, 100
Bush, George W., 14
Bush, Vannevar, 181
Butow, Steve "Bucky," x, 76, 81–88, 92–94, 98, 155, 230

C3.ai company, 100
Campbell, Kurt, 137
    "The China Reckoning," 137
CAOC (Combined Air Operations Center) at Al Udeid, x, 2, 45–54
    cost of an inefficient system, 52, 58
    DIUx's apps for, 59
    DIUx's tanker refueling project, 54–59, 65, 68, 102
    Hanscom/Grumman tech overhaul and, 53, 59–60, 63, 66–68
    obsolete technology at, 46, 47, 50–54, 57
    Shah and DIB group visits, 45–46, 49
    Slapshot app, 69
Capella Space, ix, 81, 82, 92–98, 151, 180
    DIUx/DoD funding and venture capital for, 85–88, 91–98, 129
    growth and revenue, 215
    Kirchhoff in South Korea and, 89, 91
    left-of-launch solution enabled by, 91
    opponents of, 87–88
    Ukraine War and, 199, 200, 231–32
    use of, versus defense contractor, 88
Carter, Ash, x, 7, 21, 32, 65, 66, 77, 111, 145, 172, 179, 185, 190, 221
    appoints Kirchhoff and Shah to DIUx, 11, 13, 14, 16
    approves Dailey's CSO idea, 42, 43
    at Aspen Strategy Group (2018), 134
    death and funeral, 219–21
    Defense Digital Service, 231
    on defense innovations, 7, 111
    DIB created by, 47
    DIUx and, 10, 11–13, 17–18, 20, 23, 26, 28, 42, 48, 109, 155, 223, 242

Mattis replaces, 102, 109, 153
    overtures to Silicon Valley, 7–9
    Shield Capital and, 189
    vision of, 9, 99, 132, 216, 228, 229
Cerf, Vint, 35, 120–21
ChatGPT, 103, 239
China, 188
    aggression under Xi Jinping, 136
    AI and, 133, 138, 141–42, 148, 162–68
    American investment in, 245
    Belt and Road initiative, 244
    Biden's policies and, 169–70
    "China's Sputnik Moment," 4
    CHIPS Act and, 176
    civil-military fusion, 138, 177, 196, 214, 244, 245
    Clinton visit (summer 1998), 136
    COVID-19 and, 163, 168
    Cuba and, 244
    displaced as biggest U.S. trading partner, 245
    economic problems, 244
    global ambitions, 137
    "Guo Wang" satellites, 225
    as investors in U.S. startups, 149
    manufacturing and industrial production, 137
    military budget, 217
    "national champion" companies, 137
    need for technological containment of, 141–42, 156
    nuclear-capable hypersonic weapon launched, 4, 223–24
    plans to win the technology race, 137
    R&D and, 137, 138
    Schmidt meets with top AI diplomat, Fu Ying, 162–68
    spy balloon over the U.S. (2023), 224
    as threat to Taiwan, 216–18, 224, 244
    technological superiority, 3, 4, 55, 136–38
Tencent, 177
Trump's policies and, 139–41

China (cont.)
  U.S. companies outperforming Chinese companies, 178
  U.S. policy turnaround, x, 176, 177
  U.S. technology sold to, x, 15
  as threat to U.S., 130–31, 136–37, 141, 149, 217, 223–24, 239, 244
"China's Technology Transfer Strategy" (Brown), 149, 170
CHIPS Act, 130, 161–62, 176, 238
Clark, James "Snake," 95
Clinton, Bill, ix, 136
Clinton, Hillary, 61, 62
cloud services, v, 5, 120, 148, 202, 239
CNAS (Center for a New American Security), 154
computer chips, 80, 159–62
  national security vulnerability, 161
  See also CHIPS Act
Cook, Tim, 21
Cope, Clint, 182
Council on Foreign Relations, 14, 143, 220
COVID-19, 163, 168, 169, 189
CSO (Commercial Solutions Opening), DIUx's Dailey's acquisition process, x, 24, 37–38, 40–43
Cukor, Drew, 119
cyberattacks
  defense for, 202
  Russia attacks on Estonia and the Ukraine, 164–65, 200, 207
cybersecurity, 9, 132, 158, 194, 195, 211
  Cybersecurity Commission, 156–57
  DIUx and ForAllSecure's Mayhem, 100
  Shah's startups, 2, 14, 15, 21, 184, 190, 197
  Symantec, 149
  Tanium company, 99, 132

Dailey, Lauren, x, 24, 37–38, 40–43
Danzig, Richard, 134–35
DARPA, 8, 24, 35, 40, 71, 155
  Grand Challenge awards, 8, 100
  Kirchhoff and, 14, 35
  Mayhem software and, 100
Datahub AI system, 80, 81, 86, 98
DCGS-A (Distributed Common Ground System—Army), 123
Deal, Victor, 42
defense contractors, the "primes," 5, 53, 59–60, 67, 76, 88, 98, 123, 127, 173, 189, 196, 240
  building a new prime, 208
  Defense Industry Association conference, 239–40
  ousting, by a disrupter, 242
  repackaging aging technology, 242
  Replicator Initiative and, 240
  Ukraine War and, 215
  working with startups, 243
Dereliction of Duty (McMaster), 139
DIB (Defense Innovation Board), xi, 46, 47, 154, 155
  AI principles and, 122
  Kirchhoff in South Korea with, 89–92
  recommendations sent to DIU, 49
  Schmidt heads, 46, 47, 48–49, 155
  tour of CAOC at Al Udeid, 46, 49
  Ukraine War and, 212
Disbrow, Lisa, 67
DIU (Defense Innovation Unit, formerly DIUx or Unit X), 2, 202
  accomplishments, 71, 99–122, 128, 131–32, 155, 178, 242
  adversaries, 26–31, 75, 77, 87–88, 93–98, 129, 153
  AI and, x, 100, 150–52, 119, 203, 239
  Albright visits, 142–43
  allies launching their own DIUs, 245
  alumni joining Shield Capital, 190
  Ash Carter Exchange meeting, 228–30
  Austin and, 223, 225–28, 240

INDEX

Beck and DIU 3.0, ix, 179, 225–30
Biden administration and, 223
Brown as director, ix–x, 130, 148–55, 171–73
CAOC tanker refueling project, 54–59, 60, 65, 68
Capella and secret North Korea project, 73–98, 129
Carter's vision, to use Silicon Valley methodology for defense, 9–10, 88
challenges for Shah and Kirchhoff, 35
commercial IT solutions and, 238
contracts awarded in 2017, 99
Dailey's CSO idea, x, 24, 37–38, 40–43
defense contractors' antagonism, 59–60
directives for, 22–23
early failure and reboot, 11–13, 20, 32
entrepreneur funding, defense investing, and, 9, 17, 85, 87, 92, 96–99, 101, 103, 107–8, 112, 127, 184, 202
first all-hands meeting, 19, 21–24
flat structure for, 20
formula for a tech-forward DoD, 242–43
"frozen middle" problem, 70
funding and funding problems, 9, 25–44, 71–72, 86–87, 93–99, 108, 110, 154–55, 230
future of warfare and, 129, 199–218, 228, 240, 241–42, 243–44
Griffin and, 130, 154
Hacking for Defense course and, 84
Hanscom/Northrop Grumman software overhaul and, 66–68
hiring directive and O-7 billet, 23
importance of, 92, 102
Kessel Run team, 67–70, 102
Kirchhoff leaves, 129–30
Kirchhoff's leaked memo, 61–63
"lean" methodology of, 54

Mattis and, 102–4, 108–9, 153–55, 242
mission of, 3, 15, 21–22, 56, 88, 172, 228
office, Moffett Field, Mountain View, 8–9, 10, 12, 17, 35–36, 38, 44, 54–55, 58, 67–68, 92, 101, 104
offices opened, 30–31, 71, 101, 118
OTA contracting system, 40–41, 99, 112, 213, 239
personnel: full-time, reservists, and guardsmen, 32, 101, 243
"Points of Presence," 30
portfolio areas and companies, 36, 99–128, 131, 132
Project Maven and, 116–22
racing to sign deals, 36–44
removal of the "x," 109
Replicator Initiative and, 240
reporting and authorities for, 16–17, 22–24, 242
Reserve Unit, ix, 18, 21, 225, 226
Rogue Squadron, 104–10, 210, 211
role in changes to key Operational Plans (O-Plans), focus on war planning, 227–28
Shah and Kirchhoff heading, 2, 11, 15–17, 24
Shah leaves, 130
Slapshot app, 69
Space Portfolio, x, 76, 81, 155
speed of deal-making, 99, 101
supporters, 10, 23, 26, 28, 67–68, 89, 93, 102–3, 108–9, 129, 153–54, 189, 242, 245
team members, 19–21, 23, 37, 44, 55
Ukraine War and, 203–5, 215, 223
U.S. policy shift on foreign investment and, 149
venture capital model for, 20, 36
Warsaw conference on Ukraine technology scaling, 234–36
zeroized crisis, 25–36, 72, 97
See also Kirchhoff, Christopher; Shah, Raj M.; *specific projects*

INDEX

DJI (Chinese drone company), 103, 104, 107, 137, 209, 211
   Rogue Squadron's hacking and reverse engineering, 106–7
Donovan, Matt, 63–64
drones (UAS, unmanned aircraft system), 114, 237
   Afghanistan War and, 105
   AI-empowered, 210, 228–29
   Air Force purchase of, 228–29
   attacks on U.S. service members in the Mideast by, 241
   Beall's Android app to locate enemy operators, 106
   Blue UAS program, 108, 131, 235
   changing fighter aviation, 114, 237–38, 241
   cost of, versus conventional craft, 241
   "counter-UAS" solutions (drone-killers), 9, 106, 126, 202, 210, 237, 238, 241
   DIU funding of U.S. makers, 107–8
   DIU Rogue Squadron, 104–10, 210, 211
   DJI Chinese drones, 104–7, 137, 201
   in DoD inventory, 103
   DoD's Replicator Initiative, 239–40
   Gorgon Stare sensors on, 119
   Iranian-made drones, 201–2, 209, 240
   kamikaze drones, 201, 210, 232, 235, 237, 240, 241
   North Korean use of, 214
   quadcopters, 3, 4, 107, 201, 202, 209, 232, 240
   Russia and, 240
   Shield AI, 100–101, 131
   Skydio, 202
   terrorists' using, 240–41
   Turkish Bayraktar TB2s, 209
   Ukraine War and, 201, 204, 208–12, 232–35, 237
   used by ISIS and insurgents, 3–4, 103
   used to surveil U.S. military bases and ports, 106
   U.S. military vulnerability, 238
   weaponizing of hobby drones, 3–4, 103, 106
Duchak, George, 20
Dunford, Joseph, 62, 63, 119
Dunnmon, Jared, x, 150–51
   DIU AI technical director, 151, 203
   partnership with PMS-408, 152
   Ukraine War and, 203, 204–5

Edgesource, 210
Elroy Air, 181–84
End of History and the Last Man, The (Fukuyama), 218, 237
ESL company, 84, 85
Esper, Mark, 154
EUCOM, 205
Evolv Technology, 117–18
eVTOL (electric-powered vertical takeoff and landing aircraft), ix, 3, 114–16, 181–84
   aerial cargo options, 182–83
   air taxi, 115
   "dual-use" product, 115
   Elroy Air's Chaparral, 181–84
   Joby Aviation and, 116
   military use, 182, 183

F-16 Viper, 1, 4, 14, 34, 237–38
Facebook, 123, 124
FAR (Federal Acquisition Regulations), 38, 39, 40, 43
   defense supplement (DFAR), 38
Farris, Ryan, 73, 74, 76–77, 78, 87
   Banazadeh and SAR satellites, 86
   Capella funding and, 95
   Datahub project and, 81
   J-39 SWAT team and, 74, 80
   Orbital Effects founded, 97
FedEx, 182
Felter, Joe, 179
FitzGerald, Ben, 154
5G telecommunications, 4
Flake, Jeff, 195

Fog of War (film), 147
ForAllSecure, 100, 132
Fort Hunter Liggett, California, 115
Founders Fund, 122, 123, 124
Four Steps to the Epiphany (Blank), 85
Fukuyama, Francis, 218
Fu Ying (Chinese AI diplomat), 162–68

Gallagher, Mike, 156–57, 161, 244
Garg, Avichal, 169
General Dynamics, 1
Giannandrea, John, 118
Ginkgo Bioworks, 174
Giustina, Marissa, 169
Goldfein, David, x, 59–60, 63, 68, 178, 179, 189
Google, xi, 5, 48, 162, 169, 195, 203
   AI research, 48, 118
   Cloud AI, 239
   government grants to, 8
   Project Maven and, 100, 116, 119–21, 127–28
   rebuffs Secretary of Defense Carter, 7
   resumes working with the DoD, 158
   Schmidt as CEO, 48, 49, 186
   self-driving car project, 20, 48
   Taylor recruited from, 20–21, 114
   U.S. Army using collaboration suites, 238
Google Brain, 119, 121
Google DeepMind, 140
Google Earth, 190
Google Glass, 20
Google Translate, 48
Google X, 20, 114
Grady, Claire, 42
Granberg, Brett, 181
Greene, Diane, 120
Greenwalt, Bill, 41, 42
Griffin, Mike, 121–22, 130, 154, 223

Haines, Avril, 184
Hanscom Air Force Base, Massachusetts, 53, 59, 63

HarbourVest Partners, ix, 180
Hariprasad, Vishaal "V8," 21, 131, 184, 243
Harrigian, Jeffrey "Cobra," x, 51, 54, 56, 57–58, 60, 63, 65
HawkEye 360, 181, 189, 202, 232
HealthCare.gov, 13, 48
Hicks, Kathleen, 222, 226, 239–40
   Innovation Steering Group, 226
   "Replicator Initiative" and, 240
Hill, Lisa, 190
Hobbes, Thomas, 218
Hoffman, Reid, 123, 143
Holland, Dan, 190
Holmes, Elizabeth, 103
Horvitz, Eric, 144
Hsu, Jason, 218
Huawei, 137, 163–64
human systems, 36, 100
   earbuds for high-noise, 100
   wearables to monitor soldiers, 100
Huntington Ingalls Industries, 187
Hyten, John, 123–24

IARPA (Intelligence Advanced Research Projects Activity), 134
Ierardi, Tony, 94
In-Q-Tel, 117, 125, 127, 181
Interstellar (Nolan), 225
Iran
   capture of Saildrones, 112–13
   drones used by terrorists, 241
   drones used in Ukraine, 201–2, 209
   Houthi attacks on Red Sea shipping and, 241
   Russian contract for drones with, 240
Iraq, 45, 51, 119, 129, 154, 237
ISIS, 45, 52
   AI to track, 100
   use of hobby drones, 3–4
Israel
   Hamas drone attacks on, 240–41
   war in Gaza, 241

IT (information technology), 5, 35, 36, 54, 100, 238
Iyer, Akhil, 190

Jacobsen, Mark, 104–10, 210, 216
JAIC (Joint Artificial Intelligence Center), 121–22, 132, 158, 212
Japan, 160, 197, 238, 239, 245
Jassey, Andrew, 144
Jenkins, Richard, x, 110–13
    DIU contact and venture capital, 112
    Greenbird "land yacht," 110–11
    Iranian capture of Saildrones, 112–13
    NOAA partnership, 111
    Saildrone, 110–11
Jobs, Steve, v
Joby Aviation, ix, 115–16, 131, 182, 239
Johnson, Lyndon B., 139, 147
Joint Chiefs of Staff
    Brown as Chairman, 230
    Dunford as Chairman, 62, 63, 119
    Hyten as Vice Chairman, 124
    Kirchhoff and, 145
    North Korea threat and, 75, 79, 80
    Selva as Vice Chairman, 75, 78, 93
    Winnefeld as Vice Chairman, xi, 78, 80, 114, 138
Joint Futures, 238
Joint Staff J-8, 94
Joint Staff J-39, 74
    Banazadeh and SAR satellites, 85–86
    Datahub project, 80, 81, 86, 98
    DIU and, 74
    North Korean nuclear missile surveillance, xi, 74–86, 98
    SWAT team, 80

Kaljulaid, Kersti, 164–65, 167
Karp, Alex, 213
Katz, Safra, 144
Kendall, Frank, 111, 228–29
Kennedy, John F., 246
Kernan, Joseph, 122
Kespry company, 128–29
Kessel Run, 69–70, 132
    Beachkofski as commander, 70
    CAOC software overhaul and, 67–68
    Slapshot app, 69
    vision of, 70
Killian, James, v
Kim Il-sung, 91
Kim Jong-il, 90–91
Kim Jong-un, 7, 73, 75, 91, 98
King, Angus, 156–57
Kirchhoff, Christopher, 150
    advice for Shah, 185
    Albright and, 143
    at Aspen Strategy Group (2018), 134
    background, 13–14, 33, 62, 145
    briefs Congressional Cybersecurity Commission, 156–57
    Capella Space project and, 89, 94–95
    Carter's death and, 219, 220
    China's aggressive AI plan and, 138
    China's threat and, 130–31
    COVID-19 and, 163
    Dailey's CSO idea and, 24, 42–43
    declines joining Biden administration, 169–71
    DIU-led Warsaw conference and, 234–36
    DIU 3.0 and, 226–27
    DIUx recruits him, with Shah, 2, 11, 15–17, 20–21
    Ebola Task Force and, 163, 170
    "An Even Flatter World: How Technology Is Remaking the World Order," 139, 202
    expertise on national security commissions, 144
    fight to restore DIUx budget, 28–36
    helps write Obama's technology strategy, 140–41
    as lead NSC strategist for technology, 2, 13, 62
    leaked email of, 61–62

leaves DIUx, 129–30
meetings with staffers "Evelyn and Ed," 29–31, 34
mission of, at DIUx, 2
at Moffett Field office, 67–68
Munich Security Conference and, 163, 167
New York Times op-ed, 120
NSCAI and, 144–45
relationship with McCord, 33
"A Requiem for Defense Innovation? Ukraine, the Pentagon's Innovator's Dilemma, and Why the U.S. Risks Strategic Surprise," 222
Schmidt Futures and, 130, 134
in South Korea, with the DIB, 89–92
Taiwan and, 218
as Ukraine advisor, 236
Ukraine War and, 201, 203, 204, 206, 214–15, 222–23, 230–34
Kissinger, Henry, 136, 141
Klain, Ron, 170
Kubasik, Chris, 188, 189
Kushnerska, Nataliia, 235

Langevin, Jim, 157
LaPlante, Bill, 213–14, 216
"lean" methodology, 54
  minimum viable product and, 54, 58
LinkedIn, 123
Linwu Guo, 218
Liscovich, Andrey, 205–6, 231
Lockheed Martin, 1, 5, 80, 215
  F-35 fighter jet, 116
  SAR R&D, 81
  ULA and, 123
Long, Letitia "Tish," 189
Lopes, Crane, 24
Lord, Ellen, 154
L3Harris Technologies, 188–89
Luckey, Palmer, 124, 127, 208–9, 211–12, 217
Lynn, Bill, 172

MacArthur, Douglas, 238
Marcuse, Josh, 49
Matheny, Jason, 134–35
Mattis, James "Jim," x, 102–3, 129, 179, 222
  DIU and, 102–4, 108–9, 153–55, 242
  as Trump's Secretary of Defense, x, 102, 110, 153–54
McCain, John, x, 63–68
McCarthy, Kevin, 174
McCord, Brendan, 117–19, 121–22
  AI use in warfare and, 118–19
  Evolv Technology and, 117
  JAIC and, 121–22
  Project Maven and, 118–19, 121–22
McCord, Michael, 32, 33–34, 36
McFaul, Mike, 179
McMaster, H. R., x, 139–41, 145, 157, 172, 185
  Aspen Strategy Group and, 139–41
  Dereliction of Duty, 139
  Shield Capital and, 189
  Tech Track 2 and, 178
  U.S. China policy and, 140
McNamara, Robert, 79, 147, 245
Merrill, David, 181–84
Mexico, 142, 245
Microsoft, 5, 55, 144
  Project Maven and, 100, 116, 132
  pledge to work with the DoD, 158
  Ukraine War and, 202
Milenkowic, Paul, 43
Milley, Mark, 102, 215, 228, 229, 238–39
Moffett, Admiral, 9, 19
Moore, Andrew, 239
Moorhead, Nini, 181
MOS (military occupational specialties), 55, 56
Mullen, Mike, 222
Musk, Elon, 101, 123, 201, 224–25

NASA, 40, 79, 80
  Ames Research Center, 81–82

INDEX

NASA (cont.)
   Jet Propulsion Laboratory, 82, 83
   Lunar Flashlight project, 83–84
National Geospatial Agency, 212
National Reconnaissance Office, 75, 98
NATO, 233, 236, 245
NDAA (National Defense Authorization Act), 33–34, 41, 143, 230, 245
NDI (National Democratic Institute), 133
NETCOM (Army Network Enterprise Technology Command), 99
New York Times
   "China Bets on Sensitive U.S. Start-Ups, Worrying the Pentagon," 150
   "Tiny Satellites from Silicon Valley May Help Track North Korean Missiles," 92
   "Why Silicon Valley Must Go to War," 120
Nexla, 181
Ng, Andrew, 121
Nixon, Richard, 136
NOAA (National Oceanic and Atmospheric Administration), 111
Nolan, Christopher, 225
North Korea, 73
   drones and, 98, 214
   KN-08 truck-mounted ICBM, 73–74, 76, 78, 79, 87, 98
   McCord and war-game analysis, 119
   new uranium enrichment facility, 90
   nuclear weapons and, 73, 75, 90–91
   threat to South Korea, 89–92, 98
   threat to the U.S., 75, 78–79
   U.S. need for surveillance of, 74, 79, 80, 81, 86, 98, 98
   U.S. surveillance, DIU and SAR sensor project, 74–98
Northrop Grumman, 5, 53
   B-21 strategic bomber, 216
   CAOC software overhaul and, 53, 63, 64, 66–67
   DIUx and Kessel Run, 67–70, 102
   effort to shut down DIUx, 59–60, 65
   Slapshot app, 69
   software and, 53
   Ukraine War and, 215
NSA (National Security Agency), 6, 7
NSC (National Security Council)
   Brown advises on China investing, 150
   Kirchhoff as lead strategist for technology, 2, 13, 62
   Kirchhoff's paper on technology and, 168–69
   Kirchhoff's recommendation, 170
   Korea's nuclear threat and, 75
   Pottinger and, 141
   technology strategy of 2016, 140
NSCAI (National Security Commission on Artificial Intelligence), ix, xi, 143–48, 155–59, 168, 206
   Bajraktari, executive director, 145–46
   final report and CHIPS Act, 173–76
   first executive session, 147–48
   first meeting, 146–47
   Global Emerging Technology Summit (2021), 173–75
   interim report, 157–59
   Kirchhoff and, 144–45
   national AI strategy by, 175–76
   Schmidt and, 143–45, 147–48, 155–57
   Schmidt-Fu Ying meeting, 162–68
   staff for, 157
   Trump meeting with, 159
   U.S.-China relations and, 177

Obama, Barack, 137
   Carter as Secretary of Defense, x, 7
   China policy, 141
   HealthCare.gov website crash, 13, 48
   Kirchhoff and, 14
   Korea's nuclear threat and, 75
   Podesta and, 61–62
   Schmidt and, 47
   technocratic optimism of, 47–48

technology strategy of 2016, 140–41
Todd as chief technology officer, x
OpenAI, 103, 119, 174
Oracle, 144
Orbital Effects, 97
O'Sullivan, Stephanie, 75–76, 94–95, 98
OTA (Other Transactions Authority) contracting system, 40, 41, 99, 112, 213, 239
Oti, Enrique, 54–55, 67–68

Packard, David, 171
Page, Larry, 49, 162, 186
Palantir, 101, 123–25, 127, 132, 202, 213
    Gotham Platform, 123
Palo Alto Networks, 15
Panetta, Leon, 222
Park, Todd, x, 13, 20, 21, 48, 220
PayPal, 123, 125
Pelosi, Nancy, 161–64, 224
Pentagon. *See* U. S. Department of Defense
Perry, William, 171
Petraeus, David, 134
Picatinny Arsenal, New Jersey, 43–44
Pivotal, 55, 56–58
Planet Labs, 79, 202
Podesta, John, 61–62
Pottinger, Matthew, 141
Pratt & Whitney, 215
Profiles in Courage (Kennedy), 246
Project Maven, 100, 116–22, 132, 203
    AI development in the DoD and, 121
    computer vision and, 118
    goal of, 117
    Google pulls out, 120–21, 127–28, 158
    image-tagging used in the Ukraine War, 212
    JAIC and, 121–22
    joint venture of DIU, Amazon, Google, and Microsoft, 100, 116, 119–21
    Shanahan and, 117, 121, 212
    wide-area motion imagery, 119

Work and, 116–17
Putin, Vladimir, 7, 179, 200, 225, 237
    Ukraine War and, 199–200, 218

Qatar, 2, 3, 45, 47, 52, 56, 69, 102, 124
quadcopters. *See* drones

Raps, Susan, 42–43
Rasmussen, Anders Fogh, 175
Raytheon, 5, 123, 215
Reagan, Ronald, 77
Resilience, 131, 184, 190
Rice, Condoleezza, 134, 178
Richardson, John, 224
Rieschel, Gary, 169
Rosenbach, Eric, 16, 26, 220
Ross, Wilbur, 129
ROTC (Reserve Officers' Training Corps), 191–92, 194
Rothzeid, David, 190
Russia (former Soviet Union)
    Black Sea Fleet, 114
    electronic warfare system (Tobol), 211
    Iranian drones and, 201, 209, 240
    jammers used by, 211
    military budget, 217
    new weapons, 225
    nuclear weapons and, 79
    SAM missiles, 84
    Ukraine War and, 98, 114, 190, 199–201, 210–11, 218
    as threat to U.S., 225

Saildrone, x, 110–13, 131
Sanger, David E., 92
SAR (synthetic aperture radar) technology, ix, 74, 80–81
    Banazadeh and, 82–83
    "Douser" system and, 81
    funding for, 87–88
    KN-08 surveillance problem and, 76
    microsatellites and Capella, 81–83, 91–93, 199, 215, 232
    traditional designs, 83

INDEX

Sasse, Ben, 157
satellites
   Albedo high resolution, 190
   Capella's microsatellites, 81–83, 86–88, 91–98, 199, 215, 232
   commercial companies, 83
   DIUx and SAR sensor North Korea project, 74–86
   for Google Earth, 190
   "Guo Wang" satellites, 225
   HawkEye 360, 181, 189, 202, 232
   KH-1 Corona, 77
   optical-based, limitations, 83
   Planet Labs, 202
   reconnaissance, 77, 79, 80, 83
   Starlink, 201, 204, 224–25
Scale AI, 169, 239
   Donovan platform, 239
Schadlow, Nadia, 139–40, 141
Schmidt, Eric, xi, 46, 47, 118, 130, 134, 220
   advice for Shah, 184, 186
   Biden administration and, 169–70
   CAOC misuse of IT and, 54
   career history, 48–49, 186
   heads the DIB, 46, 47, 48–49, 155
   Munich meeting with China's top AI diplomat, Fu Ying, 162–68
   NSCAI and, 143–45, 147–48, 155–57, 175
   Pelosi and, 162
   SCSP and, 206
   Trump and, 159
   Ukraine War and, 210, 212
Schmidt Futures, 130, 134, 143
Schumer, Chuck, 158, 161, 174
SCIF (sensitive compartmented information facility), 73
Scott, Denise, 43
SCSP (Special Competitive Studies Project), 206
Seidman, Ricki, 170–71
Selva, Paul, 75, 78, 88, 93–95
SenseTime, 137
Serafini, John, 181, 189
Shah, Raj M.
   angel investing and, 131, 180–84, 202
   Ash Carter Exchange meeting, 228
   background, 14, 187
   Banazadeh and SAR satellites, 85–86
   Brown and, 172
   "The Business of the UAS Industry," 235
   Capella and, 73–75, 86–88, 92–98
   Carter and, 219
   on Commission on Planning, Programming, Budgeting, and Execution Reform, 245–46
   cybersecurity startups, 2, 14, 15, 21, 184, 190, 197
   DIU 3.0 and, 226–27
   DIUx, personal investment in, 129
   DIUx all-hands meeting, 19, 21–23
   DIUx mission, 2, 21–22
   DIUx recruits him, with Kirchhoff, 2, 11, 15–17
   DIUx team members and, 19–21
   as "dual fluency" reservist, 21
   as F-16 pilot, 1, 44, 64, 65, 237
   fight to restore DIUx's budget, 28–36
   founding CEO, Resilience, 131
   as Hoover Institution fellow, 179
   leaves DIUx, 130
   Mattis and, 108
   meeting with McCain, 64–66
   meeting with Thornberry, 71–72
   NATO's Innovation Fund and, 233, 245
   need for national strategy on AI, 143
   North Korea surveillance project, 76–77, 78
   NSCAI and, 144
   number of trips to D.C., 28, 71
   policy changes to improve U.S. military readiness, 192–96
   Project Maven and, 117–18, 120–21
   Schmidt and, 155, 184, 186

Shield Capital and, 173, 177, 179, 184–91
Stanford class, 179
Stephens and Luckey meet, 125–26
Taiwan and, 218
tanker refueling project, 54–55
Tech Track 2 and, 178–80, 230
Trump meeting with, 128–29
Ukraine and, 215, 232–34
venture capitalists and, 103
visit to CAOC at Al Udeid, 45–46, 49
visit to Hanscom Air Force Base, 53
Warsaw conference on UAS scaling and, 234–36
Wert tries to shut down DIU, 59–60
Shanahan, John "Jack," xi, 117, 121
JAIC and, 121, 158, 212
NSCAI and, 158–59
Ukraine War and, 212–13
Shanahan, Patrick, 153
Shield AI, 100–101, 131, 191
Nova drones, 101
Shield Capital, ix, 173, 177, 179, 181, 184–91, 197, 239
Shyu, Heidi, 222–23
Silicon Valley, 97
acceptable attire in, 17–18
advantages of, 76
Carter's overtures to, 7–9
China's venture capital in, 149
deal-making in, 36–37, 38
defense investing in, 138, 143, 177–91
defense-oriented startups, 101, 103, 127, 131, 191, 215, 237
DIUx contracts and raising venture capital for startups, 9, 85, 96, 97, 98, 99, 101, 202
DIUx located in, 8–9, 12
DIUx's mission to link startups with the Pentagon, 2, 9–10, 89
DoD relations with, 5–6, 40, 97, 122–28, 178, 237 (see also Project Maven; *specific products*)
"fail fast" philosophy and, 13

global technology market and, 39
"lean" methodology, 54, 84
moral objections to weapons of war, 6, 120–21, 127–28, 183, 188
need for H-1B visas for critical engineers, 195
NSA spying and, 6, 7
Replicator Initiative and, 240
startups created by immigrants, 195–96
startups surpassing big defense contractors, 116
startups with transformational technology, 5
startups with warfare innovations, 3
Ukraine War and, 190, 202–3, 206, 207
way of, better to beg forgiveness, 66, 243
"Working backward from the customer," 46, 85
world's ten largest tech companies based in the U.S., 177
See also venture capital; *specific startups*
Skydio, 108, 202
Smith, Megan, 140
Snowden, Edward, 6, 7, 10
Somewear Labs, 202, 205
Sorensen, Reuben, xi, 73–74, 76, 78, 87, 92
Banazadeh and SAR satellites, 86
Capella funding and, 95
Datahub project and, 80, 81
J-39 SWAT team and, 74, 80
Orbital Effects founded, 97
SOUTHCOM, Saildrone project, 111
South Korea, 89–92
Brooks as U.S.-Korea forces commander, 89–92, 98
China threat and, 239
Demilitarized Zone (DMZ), 90
as a democracy, 91
joint technology projects with allies, 239

South Korea (*cont.*)
  left-of-launch solution for, 91
  North Korean acts of aggression, 90
  Pusan Air Base, 90
  Seoul threatened by North Korea, 89–92, 98
space technology, 36, 79–80, 100
  See also satellites; SpaceX
SpaceX, 79, 80, 101, 123, 127, 195
  lawsuit against the Air Force, 123, 127
Starlink, 201, 204, 211, 224–25, 231
Stackley, Sean, 189
Stanford University
  Hacking for Defense course, 84, 85, 151, 179
  SAR research group at, 82
  Space Rendezvous Lab, 82
  "Technology, Innovation, and Great Power Competition" class, 179
Starr, Wayne, 55–56, 57, 58
Stavridis, James "Jim", 185, 189
Stefanik, Elise, 174
Stephens, Trae, 124–28, 208
Stephenson, Randall, 128–29
Stepka, Matthew, 203
Suleyman, Mustafa, 140
Sullenberger, Chesley "Sully," 184
Symantec, ix, 130, 149
Syria, 45, 51, 52, 153
  drone factories in, 241

Taiwan, 216–18, 224, 244
Tanium cybersecurity, 99, 132
Taylor, Isaac, 20–21, 114, 243
Tech Track 2, 178–80, 230
  Stanford conference, 178–79
Theranos, 102–3
Thiel, Peter, 122–23
Thornberry, Mac, 71–72, 143, 161, 222, 223
Thucydides, 218
TikTok, 137
Toyota AI Ventures, 115, 116

transformational technology
  China and, 136–38
  Edison's lightbulb, 135
  exponential shifts and, 135
  "the in-between times," 135
  startups with, 5
  Western democracies, advantage over autocracies, 196–97
Trump, Donald, 44, 111, 187
  AI and, 143
  Bolton as National Security Advisor, 142
  China policy change, 139–41
  COVID-19 and, 168
  expenditures on DIU, 154–55
  Mattis as Secretary of Defense x, 102, 110, 153–54
  McMaster as National Security Advisor, x, 139–40, 145
  NSCAI interim report and, 159
  Schadlow writing national security strategy, 139–40
  Shah meeting with, 128–29
  Syria withdrawal, 153
  U.S. policy shift on foreign investment and, 150
Tseng, Brandon, and Ryan Tseng, 100–101
TSMC (Taiwan Semiconductor Manufacturing Co.), 160, 161, 177

Uber, 115
Uber Elevate, 116
Uber Works, 205–6
Ukraine, 223
  AI and, 202, 206–7, 209, 210, 212, 213
  battlefield of the future and, 199–218, 240
  Capella satellites and, 98, 199, 200, 232
  commercial technology used by, 201, 203, 214, 231–32
  crowd-sourced intelligence in, 4, 207

cyberattack on, 200
DIU-led Warsaw conference on scaling tech companies, 234–36
DIU technologies used in, 203–5, 215, 223
drone war, 4, 201, 204, 206, 208–12, 231–32, 233, 234, 235, 237, 240
High Mobility Artillery Rocket Systems (HIMARS), 209
Kirchhoff and, 230–34, 236
"last-mile gap," 206
lessons for the DoD from, 212–16
ocean drones and, 114
robotics manufacturers in, 233
Russian invasion of, 98, 114, 190, 199–218, 223, 230–37
Shah visits, 232–34
Silicon Valley and, 190, 202–3, 206, 207
sinking of the cruiser *Moskva*, 114
Starlink, 201, 204, 206, 211, 231
techno-guerrillas, 205–8, 223, 231, 233
technological infrastructure of, 207–8
"Uber for Artillery," 207
U.S. funding, 203, 205
ULA (United Launch Alliance), 80, 123
Unit X. *See* DIU
U.S. Air Force
AFWERX technology accelerator, 102, 132
antiquated technology and, 1, 2
"Collaborative Combat Aircraft" program, 228–29
contract with Elroy Air, 183
counter-UAS systems lacking, 238
defense contractors and, 59–60
DIUx's tanker refueling project, 54–59, 60
eVTOL aircraft, 116
Goldfein as chief of staff, x, 59–60
innovation and, 242
Kessel Run team, with Northrop Grumman, 67–70, 102, 132

Office of Operational Energy, 58
reconnaissance satellites, 77
resistance to change, 60
SpaceX's lawsuit against, 123
Special Operations Command, 183
stereotype of pilots, 65
talent swap with Apple, 179
See also CAOC
U.S. Army
Army Futures Command technology incubator, 102, 132
DCGS-A, 123
Google collaboration suites for, 238
innovation and, 242
modernization of, 102
outdated technology used by, 118–19
Palantir Gotham Platform, 123–24
Palantir's lawsuit, 123–24, 125
Supercomputer Center, Aberdeen Proving Ground, 118–19
U.S. Congress
Anti-Deficiency Act, 95–96
Brown advises on China investing, 150
CHIPS Act, 130, 161–62, 176, 238
Commission on Planning, Programming, Budgeting, and Execution Reform, 245
Cybersecurity Commission, 156–57
disconnect from the military by, 192
DIU 3.0 funded, 230
DIUx budget cut, staffers behind zeroizing of, 27–31, 94, 97, 110
DIUx difficulties with the Appropriations Committee, 26–31
Foreign Investment Risk Review Modernization Act of 2018, 150
House Appropriations Subcommittee on Defense (HAC-D), 27, 94, 109–10
House Armed Services Committee, 71, 215
military innovation and, 243
National Defense Authorization Act, 33–34, 41, 143, 230, 246

INDEX

U.S. Congress (*cont.*)
  power of the purse and, 27, 34
  Select Committee on the Chinese Communist Party, 245
  Senate Armed Services Committee, 63–64, 66–67, 215
  Shah's policy changes to improve U.S. military readiness, 192–96
  STAPLE Act, 195
  Ukraine War funding, 203, 205
U.S. Cyber Command, 202
U.S. Department of Defense (DoD, the Pentagon), 102, 131
  acquisitions, processes, and contracting practices of, x, 37, 38, 39–40, 87, 123–244, 196, 204–5, 214, 215, 239, 246
  Advanced Capabilities and Deterrence Panel, 11
  AI and, 5, 100, 116–22, 133, 147–48, 152, 212, 239
  antiquated technology and military vulnerability, 1–4, 7, 35–36, 53–54, 124–25, 131–33, 148, 204
  "bespoke" solutions, 76, 87, 238
  biggest obstacle to innovation, 246
  bridging the cultural divide, recommendations, 191–96
  Brown's nomination and, 171–73
  budget battle in 2016, 71
  budgeting system, 245–46
  bureaucracy as an impediment to innovations, 109–10, 129
  Capella Space and, 87–88, 96–97, 199, 200
  Carter's message to Silicon Valley about, 8
  Carter's vision of public-private cooperation, 9, 99, 132
  Chief Digital and Artificial Intelligence Office, 170
  "civil-military fusion" and, 191, 196
  commercial technology companies and, 76, 131, 132, 196, 197, 238
  congressional budget control, 26–28
  counter-UAS systems lacking, 238
  cyber strategy for, 14
  defense contractors, the "primes" and, 5, 53, 59–60, 67, 76, 88, 98, 123, 127, 173, 189, 196, 215, 223, 240, 242
  defense venture fellowship program, 239
  directive-type memorandum, 17
  DIU's formula for a tech-forward military, 242–43
  DIU's impact on, 242
  DIU 3.0 and, 226–27
  DIUx companies and modernizing of, 131–32
  DIUx mission to bring fast-moving ethos of Silicon Valley to, 56–57, 102
  drone program, Blue UAS, 108, 131, 235
  drones, ScanEagles and Predators, 103–4
  Early Bird news clips, 138
  email system, 35
  Founders Fund's lawsuits, 123–24
  "frozen middle" problem, 70
  "Future Years Defense Program," 228
  innovation as deterrence, 246–47
  JAIC, xi, 121–22, 132, 158
  joint technology projects with allies, 239, 240, 245
  military bases closed by, 193–94
  mind-set, versus Silicon Valley's, 39, 53, 56–57, 196
  MOS positions, 55
  national security and technology, 237–47
  negative cultural trends and, 191–93
  OTA contracting system, 239
  outdated systems engineering approach, 53–54
  Presidential Drawdown Authority (PDA), 204

quick fixes proving impossible, 53
Replicator Initiative, 239–40
resistance to change, 10, 60, 88, 213–14, 223, 242
Rogue Squadron and, 109–10
Senate Armed Services Committee and budget, 63–64, 66–67
size of, number of employees, 10
spending by, 4, 8, 53, 60, 67, 87
spending on technology, 131–32
"Task Force Lima," 239
Ukraine War and, 203–5
Ukraine War lessons for, 212–16
"Valley of Death" of, 6, 10, 42, 242
war of the future, 199–218, 240–42
U.S. Department of Homeland Security, 126, 127
U.S. Marine Corps, 216
U.S. Navy
carrier-launched aircraft and, 9
future of war at sea, x, 114
global supply chains and, 128
largest shipbuilder for, 187
naval mines, 151
PMS-408 (unmanned maritime systems, UUVs), 151–52
role of ocean drones, 114
stereotype of pilots, 65
U.S. Special Operations Command, 127

Vannevar Labs, 181
venture capital (VC)
American, in China, 245
angel investing, 131, 180–84, 202
defense investing, 101, 138, 143, 177–97, 237
defense unicorns, 190–91

DIUx helping entrepreneurs raise funds, 9, 17, 85, 87, 92, 96, 97, 98, 99, 101, 103, 112, 127, 184, 202
DIUx set up like a fund, 36
how they raise money, 185
NATO starts fund, 233, 245
the Pentagon as a customer and, 196
risk and reward of, 185–86
Shah and, 131, 180–84, 202
See also Founders Fund; In-Q-Tel; Shield Capital; *specific firms*
Vietnam War, 139
Gulf of Tonkin incident, 147
virtual reality goggles, x, 2, 20, 124

Walker, Ken, 158
Wang, Alex, 239
Wang, Alexandr, 169
Warsaw, Poland, 236–37
DIU-led conference in, 234–36
Washington Headquarters Service, 35
Wert, Steven, 53, 59–60, 64, 67, 68
WikiLeaks, 61–62
Winnefeld, Sandy, xi, 78, 80, 114, 138
Wireshark, 105
Work, Bob, xi, 11, 88, 93–95, 97, 116–17, 144, 156
World Food Programme, 182–83

Xi Jinping, 7, 136, 141, 218, 244

Y Combinator, 103
Yoon Suk Yeol, 98

Zakaria, Fareed, 174
Zegart, Amy, 178
Zelensky, Volodymyr, 200, 206, 209, 211